Rob,

HERE'S WISHING YOU ALL
LIFE HAS TO OFFER

K Gff

From Ken's Desk

From Ken's Desk

Ken Griffith

Library of Congress Control Number:		2012923536
ISBN:	Hardcover	978-1-4797-6624-6
	Softcover	978-1-4797-6623-9
	Ebook	978-1-4797-6625-3

To order additional copies of this book, contact:
Xlibris Corporation
1-888-795-4274
www.Xlibris.com
Orders@Xlibris.com
124763

Preface

This book is designed for three groups of people: (1) for the sales manager of any corporation that has staff meetings, right down to the single car dealership, (2) for any salesperson who wishes to soar to the top of his/her field, and (3) for anyone who simply wishes to grow both personally and professionally. The sales manager can use a topic plus sales tip to inspire his/her team to become the best, the salesperson can read and apply the principles to outshine the rest, and the individual will grow to be the person they wish to become. It is a collection of wisdom gained through the hundreds of books read and thousands of seminars attended. I took great notes from each, applied them to myself, and created miniseminars through my practical experiences. I started reading and attending seminars while my own business was in shambles, leaving me not enough money to pay my bills. All that time, I knew the answers were within me, and my only hope was to invest in myself if I stood any chance to make it. I took on delivering pizzas at night to cover the costs of seminars, which ranged from $60 to $2,000. Eventually, I went from not being able to heat my house to building a formidable sales team of thirty, with revenues of $25 million per year, and from there I began speaking at corporate and political events with seminars that went from thirty minutes to two hours. About a year ago, I decided that each day I would send out two e-mails—one on personal and professional development and one sales tip of the day—to my own sales team. From there, I believe it spawned this book, a collection of those e-mails so that your sales staff could become the best. I recognized that the recession created a scenario where cutbacks seemed to be the key to survival for so many, and that blinded them to the fact that good investments are not invested in corporations that had executives who lost the will to sell. Selling is not just some function of a corporation but is something done by every one every day. People across this continent have become far too focused in their own cutbacks and less focused on their ability to earn and gain more. As mentioned, I built this book for those looking to excel in sales and in life. It is the ideal sales trainer/manager guide to set sales meeting by. Read one personal and professional segment and one sales tip segment, and your meetings will be of great content and motivation. As for the salesperson, this book will put that person in the top ten of any sales organization and will become the first in line when promotions are available. Most importantly, this book will improve your life. It is a collection of wisdom passed down through the ages—simplified—and I have seen it as my duty to hand them to you. I was very fortunate in my life to have had great mentors take me on—for some reason—and it is my turn to give back. Again, the key to digesting this book is reading one page at a time. Digest each title before moving on. Become able to teach the title within a three-day period, and you'll be well under your way to sales and life mastery.

With special thanks to:
Don McNabb
Dr. Robert Anthony
Casey Comden
Dr. Joe Rubino
Preston Manning
David Cameron
Blair Singer
Randy Taylor
If you get a chance to attend any of their seminars, do it!

Today I am in a battle with lung cancer, and even with that, I know I will win because all I have learned taught me to focus in the right areas of life and not in my limitations.

If you wish to have me speak at your corporate event, please refer to the contact information at the back of this book. Enjoy!

Wishing you all life has to offer.

"Each personal and professional development topic is to be read one per day. The same goes for the today's sales tip, but they are to be repeated until the first section is done . . . perhaps repeated on and on till mastered."

Table of Contents

Personal and Professional Development

Today's Sales Tip

Introduction

A Life Lived

What is a life lived? A life lived is to live a life where the future is bigger than the past . . . where we are mentally, emotionally, spiritually, and physically running at peak performance without breaking a sweat. Yes, it has the big homes, the fancy cars, the boats, and the travel; but it also carries the responsibilities of leadership, of charity, and of challenges. It is a life void of the trivia and which is rich with the relevant. It is a life where all the pieces of health, wealth, business, and relationships come together in perfect harmony. OK, perfect may be a stretch, but you know what I mean—progress. It's when others look to you in awe . . . not for what you have but for what you have accomplished and who you have become. It's a life taken to the next level . . . a daring adventure, a chance to find your real potential. It's a chance to lead teams, to be the example, to live in abundance, and to self-actualize. It's a life living your dreams so that others can live their dreams, or at least begin to dream. It's about doing something big! I have been on a quest to find at least a half-dozen people who want to lead teams down a path less traveled . . . Better yet, to create a new path. These people haven't stopped thinking, "Wouldn't it be great if . . ." They haven't stopped dreaming. In fact, they probably daydream at work more than their bosses would like. They think about traveling the world, about driving exotic cars, and about the lifestyle they want to create, as opposed to existing till death. These people—and perhaps it is you—envision a life where men conquer their challenges and bring home the spoils of victory . . . and where women still have the soul of a child and will not let it be taken from them. A life lived is a life for that person who simply wants their freedom back! If you want this life, then it is time to take off your old, worn-out running shoes and strap on a pair of jet shoes and get this newly born you into action. Now, go forth and multiply.

From Ken's desk

Personal and Professional Development

Three Beliefs That Will Make You an Instant Success

The way you think about yourself and your goals can determine your success and failure in your career and life. Make sure that you have the right attitude. If you want to be successful, incorporate the following beliefs into your daily way of thinking:

1. **"I am confident."** If you believe in yourself, you tend to see problems and challenges as speed bumps rather than roadblocks and have certainty that you'll eventually succeed.
2. **"I am committed."** If in your heart of hearts, you are absolutely determined to succeed, you'll find that motivation emerges naturally from that commitment.
3. **"I am in control."** If you view yourself as the captain of your destiny rather than a pawn of fate, you'll have the motivation to continue moving forward, even when the going gets a bit rough.

How to Create Failure?

On the other hand, if you want to be a failure, incorporate these three very different beliefs into your daily way of thinking:

1. **"Nobody believes in me."** Some people define themselves based upon how they suspect their boss, their coworkers, their relatives, and friends see them. Convinced that people think poorly of them, such people suffer from low self-esteem and lack of confidence. If you had a big project that needed handling, would you trust someone who didn't even trust himself?
2. **"I am probably going to fail."** Some people believe that failure is so unpleasant that it must be avoided at all costs. Because of this, they avoid all situations where failure is a risk. But any meaningful endeavor entails risk, so such people seldom (if ever) accomplish anything significant.
3. **"Fate controls destiny, so why try?"** Some people believe that their status in life and potential as a human being is determined at birth or by the circumstances of their lives. Believing this allows them to deflect the blame for failures onto things over which they have no control, thereby lessening the pain.

I AM confident. I AM committed. I AM in control. Repeat these many times and notice the "I AM."

Success is yours, baby.

Wishing you all life has to offer.

From Ken's desk

Three Principles for Using the Law of Attraction (LOA)

I want to share with you the basics of the LOA and how you can use it to help you make more money, have a better relationship with your family, be healthier, be more energetic, and be happier in every area of your life.

The most successful people I know are making the most of the LOA, whether they know it or not.

In fact, we're learning that science backs up what LOA students have always known, but that is another article all of its own.

You see, when you follow the ideas of the LOA and take a positive and empowering mind-set, the universe steps in and three things happen:

1. You recognize more opportunities and take advantage of them.
2. People respond to you more positively and offer you the assistance you're looking for.
3. You find yourself coming up with the most incredible ideas to reach your goals, and you wonder why you never thought of these before!

You know what the best part is about the LOA? You don't even need to believe it to make it work for you! All you need to do is apply the basic principles, and you will be astounded at the results.

Now, I'm going to give you a few core strategies to get the LOA to work for you. Over the years, I've seen that these strategies work for anyone who simply applies them. They worked in favor for me, once I knowingly practiced them.

That's how I know they will work for you too, no matter where you are financially or how much spare time you have.

Principle #1: Get really clear with what you actually want.

If I were to ask you what you want in life, what would you say?

For a lot of people, it's "Oh, come on, anything but this!" It's much easier to know what we don't want. Because of that, it's what we tend to constantly think about.

We don't like being stuck in traffic, we don't like disappointment, and we don't like mountains of debt.

The problem is that whatever you focus on tends to expand. Anytime you think strongly about something you hate, you put energy into whatever you're thinking about and attract more of the same.

Instead, switch it around to thinking about what you DO want. Maybe it's a thirty-hour workweek or the ability to spend more time with your loved ones.

If it's difficult to think about what you want, I have an exercise for you. Take a piece of paper and split it into three columns. In the first, write what you don't want. In the second, write the opposite of that, which is what you do want. In the third column, write briefly why you want it. This will help you get clear on your goals and motivate you to focus on them.

Principle #2: Feel good and visualize what you want, making sure to feel the emotions flooding through you.

To use the LOA to your advantage, you're going have to make some changes in how you think. You need to feel happy and confident, both about your goals coming true and about life in general.

This is the part where a lot of people have trouble with. You see, unless you can actually feel the emotions of having already achieved what it is you want, you won't get the best benefits from using the LOA.

Each day, you should close your eyes, and when focusing on your goals, see in your mind's eye that it has already come true. Also, make sure you FEEL the emotions of already having everything in existence right now. Basically, you should fully visualize yourself already living your dream life and experience those emotions of gratitude, accomplishment, joy, and peace.

Once you have nurtured this mind-set, it's typical to start having those things start physically appearing in your life, one way or another.

A great tool to help you stay focused is to create a list of positive affirmations in the present tense that represent what you want, such as "Every month, I pay my bills with plenty left over," or "I am so happy I can't stop smiling."

When you're visualizing, repeat this affirmations to yourself, almost like a personal mantra, to get yourself pumped up and really feeling the emotion. Get excited because you're starting to learn how great things will be when you have your goals.

Tell me . . . how much time do you set aside every day to think about problems and worry about silly things that will probably never happen? Could you set aside the same amount of time to find out what you do want? Sure you can.

The truth is that there are actually two types of time—internal time and external time—and they don't always line up.

Right now, you probably have dozens of thoughts a minute that you're conscious of and thousands of thoughts you're unconscious of. If you simply use your downtime to think positively—whether you're waiting in line, working out, or driving—you'll be amazed at how much the world will open up for you.

Principle #3: Take action when appropriate.

One of the hang-ups that a lot of people have with the LOA is the idea that good things can come to you without hard work.

Don't get me wrong; you can still work hard if you want to. However, the more you follow the principles I've outlined so far, the less struggle you have to go through when taking action.

You see, no matter what path you're on, there's probably an easier way you haven't thought of yet. Using the LOA is the surest way to cut down the effort needed for success. This was a very big lesson for me. I ran on the belief that it was all my hard work and self-sacrifice that made things work out. I was the proverbial hamster on the wheel—working so hard and getting nowhere.

But the truth is, you do need to take some action if you want to give the universe the best opportunities to provide you with what you want, but the most important point to remember is that you don't need to see the whole plan.

To take action, you just need to take a single step in the direction of your goal. Just keep focusing on the next step. That's all you need to do as far as action is concerned!

So when you see something in front of you that seems applicable to your goals in life, don't hesitate for a single second. Take whatever action step you see and just watch what happens.

You'll see that once you've finished each step, a new one on the invisible staircase will become apparent to you. As you start gaining momentum, the entire staircase begins to reveal itself, often showing you so much more than you ever expected or dreamed at the top.

If you follow the three principles I've outlined, you'll begin to start seeing incredible opportunity everywhere you look.

Someone you meet at a function might pass you a business card and reveal she's an insider in an industry you've wanted to open a business in.

You might take a wrong turn and find yourself in front of a hidden mall with incredible deals, and you'll always find that great parking spot.

You might run into someone who knows someone who is looking for you and your talents.

In my experience, if you're prepared to take action but open to the idea that it could be easy, things tend to just fall into place, so you slide through life a lot more smoothly.

Then people will call you "lucky," and that is your opportunity to teach them what you know.

Wishing you all life has to offer.

From Ken's desk

Three Most Important Values

Question: What are the three most important values to you?

I don't mean valuables. I mean your values. What are the three core values you have when considering a life decision? When choosing a mate, when choosing a career path, when deciding to take on responsibilities, or when choosing a lifestyle, the three values you hold most dear should guide you in all of these.

Without considering your values, you make decisions without being true to yourself, and later on you may not be happy with the decisions you make, not because of the outcome, but because you feel out of sync.

So take the time to consider what three values you hold closest to your being and examine where you are in life based on those values. Have you made good choices? Do you need to go in a different direction in some areas of your life to match up properly?

Do you truly value your values? Or have you allowed yourself to meander along the river of life, taking you where it wants to go instead?

Don't get me wrong. It is good to sometimes see where a situation will take you, but you'll know where to get off the river if you take charge of your desires—based on your values—and that is what will allow you to take the best of what that life-river offers.

So, again, please take the time to think of what your values are and prioritize the top three.

Remember, your DREAMS are made up of your visions, your values, and your purpose.

Last week, we touched on your purpose, so here's your homework for this week: what are your top three values?

Wishing you all life has to offer.

From Ken's desk

Four Best Practices to Grow Your Bank Account

There are specific guidelines one should follow when looking to save and grow wealth. Abide by these best practices, and you will be shocked by how much wealth you can build! Professional salespeople are commission based. Setting up your future is critical. No one else will do it for you.

1. Have an Automatic Plan. Experts claim that you must be very disciplined if you want to build wealth. However, I believe disciple is outrageously overrated. We don't have that much discipline! Just go to your local buffet and see how disciplined we are. For those who know me, they know that I can resist anything . . . except temptation . . . LOL. Discipline is a limited resource that we possess and should not be a primary tool in creating your wealth.

I'm not saying that you don't need discipline; you just don't want to depend on it on a daily basis. Instead, use your discipline to set up an automatic savings plan.

Your savings should be automatically deducted from your bank or automatically sent to your savings (and I'm not referring to the savings attached to your checking account). Your funds should be sent to an account where you cannot readily access the funds. Out of sight equals out of mind. If you never see the money, and if you can't access it, you won't depend on it.

Set up an automatic savings for your retirement and a separate savings for emergencies. Your retirement funds should be virtually inaccessible. The emergency funds should be more easily accessible.

You want to sit down with a financial advisor to discuss your saving options. An "automatic plan" is all about paying yourself first! You must pay yourself first.

2. Have a Budget. This is a very simple key, but one that I would be remiss not to include. You must have a budget! You must know the budget; you must understand the budget; you and your family must follow the budget. The budget should also include money for taxes, vacations, and unexpected expenditures.

The purpose of the budget is to ensure that you rarely need to access your emergency funds, affording you the ability to stay on track with your financial goals and even creating additional wealth from your emergency fund.

Your budget must include money for you to "blow" and enjoy yourself as well. Why work every day and never enjoy the money that you work for? Enjoying your money will make the saving process more enjoyable.

Set up a budget that allows you to have fun with your money every month. Maybe it's a night out on the town. Maybe it's going to the movies every weekend. Maybe it's getting a pedicure every month.

KEN GRIFFITH

So eliminate unnecessary expenses and attempt to lower bills in an effort to have money to "blow."

3. Use Cash. Unless you're starting a business, which you know is going to succeed, avoid using debt. Debt is a double-edged sword. It can be used to make you rich, but it can be used to bankrupt you. Save debt for business ventures where you have a significant advantage over the competition. Otherwise, just use cash; it will simplify your life.

4. Diversify Your Funds. It's probably not the best idea to keep all of your funds in a sock or even in your local bank's savings account. You want to diversify!

It's true that cash is king, but compounded interest is a greater king. You want to diversify your funds to ensure that you're getting the best rate of return on your funds and yet staying within your comfort level for risk. Once again, you want to talk to a financial advisor to see what options work best for you.

If you put $1,000 in the bank at a rate of 6 percent interest, it would turn into $44,000 after sixty-five years. If the interest rate was 9 percent, the $1,000 would have turned into $270,000. The more time, the higher the interest rate, and the more you can afford to save, the quicker you will build your wealth.

Time is a very critical component of building wealth; some may say it's the most important. The earlier you can start saving, the more time you have for compounded interest to take effect and make you a millionaire.

Other tips: Get married to someone who has money. Don't get divorced unless they are sucking you dry. Stay out of court or at least win. Keep your kids out of jail and out of trouble. Have sons—they will cost you bail money, whereas girls will cost you wedding money. Start saving as soon as possible. Stick to your budget. Get promoted on your job. Invest your passive income. Don't gamble (and yes, the lottery is gambling). Avoid risky investments (lost $55,000 a year ago). Get the lowest interest rate on your mortgage and cars (buy investment real estate, and if you need a mortgage for your car, I want a ride in it). Take care of your health. Don't go out. Don't stay in. Buy gifts without the batteries. Reuse toilet paper. Comb your hair before brushing it. And keep proper insurance, including life insurance. Oh, and use sunscreen. ☺

Wishing you all life has to offer,
From Ken's desk

Achieve Your Dreams

It's nice and right to have dreams, but at the end of the day, they are never going to come true unless you act on them. These four tips will help you clarify your dreams and work toward them in the most efficient way.

1. Write Them Down. A dream written down and attached to dated goals sounds oversimplistic, yet that simple act is the difference between a dreamer and a doer. The statistics are staggering. People who set written goals are much more successful than those that don't. Putting your goals where you can see them is really important.

2. Dream BIG Dreams. It's funny, but the amazing thing to me is the fact that it is easier to accomplish a BIG dream than a small one. Big dreams are exciting and keep us motivated. They get us up in the morning and keep us motivated through the day. They attract other people to get involved. Little dreams are easily forgotten and often abandoned.

3. Focus on One Dream at a Time. An old Chinese proverb states, "A man who chases two rabbits catches none." Focus is critical to achieving our goals. Steve Jobs commented that the single thing that made Apple successful was the thousand projects they didn't do. Focusing on one important goal at a time will help you stay on track.

4. Visit Your Dreams often. The most common mistake made is writing your goals down and even getting dream boards but then putting them in a place where you don't see them every day. An even bigger step missed is not going to see/touch that dream of yours. Go find it and visit every time things look tough out there.

Wishing you all life has to offer,
From Ken's desk

Five Steps to Eliminate Negative Thoughts

Did you know that although you walk around in a body, you actually live in your thoughts?

I don't mean that you have thoughts that you listen to all day. You actually "live" in your thoughts. It's these thoughts that create our self-beliefs. They can also create the mortal enemy of belief, which is self-doubt.

So it's time to become better acquainted with the tone and dynamic of your inner voice.

Focus on what you are really like as you talk to yourself throughout the day.

You might be shocked to find out your voice routinely tells you it's OK to be lazy. Eat that bag of M&M's even though dinner is in an hour. Ignore your partner after dinner even though you know you have important matters to discuss.

Few people realize that we are not our thoughts. Rather, we have the power to create and alter them. We can choose to turn our thoughts into positive forces to help produce the life we really want.

Learning to listen to your thoughts will give you the opportunity to change your life. The voices in your head reflect your self-beliefs and even create them. They are at the core of your limiting beliefs and self-doubts. We all have those little voices, so don't feel it is only you (some have committees, and some have conventions ☺).

Here Are Five Steps to Get You Started:

1. At least three times a day, sit down for a few minutes and write down the thoughts going through your head at that moment. It doesn't matter how trivial the thoughts are. Write them down.

2. Write your thoughts down in a variety of situations: while sitting in traffic, while standing at the stove watching your dinner simmer, while you're surfing the Internet, before going to bed, after work, etc.

Writing frequently in a journal in a variety of situations will help you better understand your personality by uncovering the patterns in your comments.

Make an effort to notice recurrent themes that shape your self-beliefs and doubts.

Some examples of common themes might include low self-esteem ("I just know I'm going to screw up"); anxiety about terrible things that could happen ("What if he gets mad and fires me?"); anger ("I'll leave him if he says that again!"); and fears of many kinds, including accidents, the unknown, death, sickness, and more.

3. Use a voice recorder (cell phones often have them), notebook, the computer, or even Post-it notes for your journal, whatever is easiest for you.

4. Don't edit! This is a common mistake, but you won't learn much unless you write down the exact words of your thoughts. Writing down the words that provoke, justify, or demand these behaviors provides insight into what is really in your head. So you can start to separate from them and take charge of your life.

5. Remember this above all: not all your thoughts are bad or boring! You'll learn good things about yourself too.

Once you finally know what your thoughts are, you can start using your voice of reason to silence the thoughts that hold you back! You'll learn when to acknowledge them yet and then ignore them.

Wishing you that life has to offer,
From Ken's desk

Five Tips to a More Efficient Day

Finding enough time in the day to get everything done tends to be an impossible task. Increasing one's efficiency is the best way to ensure that everything gets completed. Find out how you can become truly effective here!

1. Set Daily Goals. One of the best ways to ramp up your efficiency is to set daily goals. Each morning, before your work day begins, make a list of the top things that you want or need to accomplish during the work day. Rank them in order of importance. Depending upon how long each task will take you, your list may contain two items or ten. Once constructed, use the list as your guide to keep you focused throughout the day to work toward completing those goals. Keep the list readily accessible and in plain sight on your work space so that it will act as a constant reminder for those tasks that you want to complete in a given day. As you complete each of your predetermined objectives, check them off. If you do not complete a given goal, move it forward into the next day. This simple task of setting and monitoring daily goals is amazingly effective at increasing your productivity. We all know this. Now, practice it.

2. Delegate. If you are in a position to delegate, make sure to do so. Too often we are saddled with a belief that we are the only person that can do a specific task or do it well enough. I had been particularly afflicted with this mistaken belief. Learning to delegate is an acquired art form, one everyone should try to master. Believing that a task cannot be delegated is truly more about control issues and less about whether or not it truly can be assigned to someone else. Why spend two hours on a task yourself if, instead through crafting ten minutes of detailed instructions, you can delegate the project to another? Accordingly, if you have someone to whom you can delegate, learn how to delegate and learn how to do it well.

3. Let the Phone Ring. Let E-mails Go Unanswered. You're in the middle of solving an issue relating to one of your goals for the day. The phone rings. You answer. On the other end of the phone is someone who needs to speak with you about something that is important but not related to the task at hand. The conversation only lasts three minutes and then ends. However, when you go to pick up where you left off, you need to quickly review where you were, get your brain back on track, and then finally pick up and keep moving on the same.

Do not assume that picking up that quick call only cost you three minutes of being off task. It cost you your focus, the three minutes, and ultimately the review time of thinking about where you left off and the time it takes to reengage your brain on the specific project you were working on before you were interrupted. All in all, that three-minute call, depending upon the complexity of the issues being dealt with, may cost you six, seven, even ten minutes!

You would be amazed at how simply allowing callers to leave a voice mail and then responding later in the day, in bulk, to all of your messages can truly amplify your efficiency.

However, it doesn't have to end there. The same policy should be employed as regards e-mails. How many e-mails do you really get that need to be viewed or read almost instantaneously? So don't. Let them sit. They'll still be there when you complete the task at hand. Like your calls, just designate a time during the day, or two if you prefer, to answer all of your e-mails. Once again, by not allowing these constant interruptions, the efficiency with which you can accomplish the goals on your list will be increased exponentially.

4. Close the Door.

Why do I mention all of this? If you have the capability, sometimes you just need to close the door. If you work in an open work space, hang a sign. Open-door policies are great, but they can often lead to an erosion of efficiency that is disturbing. Don't be afraid to shut the door and politely let people know this is my efficient time. If they need to speak with you, they can come back later or, better yet, set up daily prescheduled times in which they will have your undivided attention. By moving away from constant interruptions, you will be able to stay on task and, consequently, move more efficiently through the goals you set every day.

5. Facebook, Twitter, and Instant Messaging. The secret time killers. Let's say you spend ten minutes on Facebook a day. Let's further say you use Twitter. Chalk up another ten minutes. By the way, did you IM any of your friends today while at work? Come on, you know you did. Maybe the wife or the hubby had a funny story to share with you, or Madonna just announced her latest concert dates and everyone had to BUZZ each other over it (you know where I am on that stuff). Another ten minutes. So how much did we spend? Ten minutes? Twenty? Thirty? Wrong. It was more like one hundred thirty hours. Over three forty-hour workweeks.

Huh? You might be asking yourself. What are you talkin' 'bout, Willis? ☺

It's simple. If you spend thirty minutes a day on social media and instant messaging, that adds up to two and a half hours per week. There are fifty-two weeks in a year. Fifty-two times two and a half is one hundred thirty hours. One hundred and thirty hours equates to over three forty-hour workweeks you are spending on social media and chatting online per year. It's like a whole other vacation.

Is this overly dramatic? Maybe a little. But recognize what spending time on these sites does to your productivity. Thirty minutes a day, on average, equates to a loss of up to three plus weeks of work per year. So if you are just spending ten minutes a day doing the same, that's like one entire lost week of work. Wow!

I'm not saying don't do it. I am just saying recognize how the numbers add up. Once you see how they do, if you want to ramp up your efficiency, limit the social chats to only designated times during the day when you are already taking a break. Trust me, that wicked awesome zinger you've been waiting to post on Facebook can wait.

Wishing you all life has to offer,
From Ken's desk

Five Ways to Build Confidence

Maintaining a confident attitude is key to doing well, earning money, and ultimately getting where you want to be. You may think that your personality makes it difficult for you to emit that assured demeanor, but this is not the case. You too can be confident. These five steps will build that confidence you've been looking for.

Make a List. Write down some of your most recent significant achievements along with an explanation of why they were important. Post that list in a very visible place. Reminding yourself about your previous challenges and accomplishments builds self- confidence and offers a quick, detailed reference as to exactly why you were successful.

Dress the Part. Reevaluate the way you dress. If you're strapped for cash, upgrade your footwear or get a new professional haircut or style. This is a way to manifest the change taking place internally.

Surround Yourself with Positives. "Don't hang out with malcontents, also-rans, or poor performers." By reading positive market and industry information and surrounding yourself with successful people, you will improve your knowledge base, your vision of the market, and boost your skill set.

Keep Your Thinking Upbeat. Make sure your internal dialogue about yourself and others is positive by assuming whatever you say in your mind is being heard out loud. "Never use self-deprecating comments that may get a laugh" (this is not to say humor in humility; self-deprecating is much stronger) as that ultimately diminishes you in the eyes of others.

Be Proactive. Find out what tasks are falling through the cracks at work and complete them.

Remember, the keys to success are master the skills, correct your thinking, and go to work. It is often taught that knowledge is power. Not true! Knowledge in action is power! Action creates knowledge, which creates more action, which creates confidence.

Wishing you all life has to offer,
From Ken's desk

Worry, Doubt, Fear, and Anxiety = EGO

We are not born with courage, but neither are we born with **fear**. Maybe some of our fears are brought on by your own experiences, by what someone has told you, and by what you've read in the papers or have seen on TV.

Some fears are valid, like walking alone in a bad part of town at two o'clock in the morning. But once you learn to avoid that situation, you won't need to live in fear of it. Fears, even the most basic ones, can totally destroy our ambitions. Fear can destroy fortunes. Fear can destroy relationships. Fear, if left unchecked, can destroy our lives. Fear is one of the many enemies lurking inside us. **Face it head-on**.

Let me tell you about five of the other enemies we face from within. The first enemy that you've got to destroy before it destroys you is **indifference**. What a tragic disease this is. "Ho-hum, let it slide. I'll just drift along." Here's one problem with drifting: **you can't drift your way to the top of the mountain.**

The second enemy we face is **indecision**. Indecision is the thief of opportunity and enterprise. It will steal your chances for a better future. **Take a sword to this enemy.**

The third enemy inside is **doubt**. Sure, there's room for healthy skepticism. You can't believe everything, but you also can't let doubt take over. Many people doubt the past, doubt the future, doubt each other, doubt the government (OK, maybe that one is rational), doubt the possibilities, and doubt the opportunities. Most find it *safer* to doubt someone than to first trust them. This will cost you inside and out. Worse of all, they doubt themselves. I'm telling you, doubt will destroy your life and your chances of success. It will empty both your bank account and your heart. Doubt is an enemy. Go after it. **Get rid of it.**

The fourth enemy within is **worry**. We've all got to worry some. Just don't let it conquer you. Instead, let it alarm you. Worry can be useful. If you step off the curb in New York City and a taxi is coming, you've got to worry. But you can't let worry loose like a mad dog that drives you into a small corner. Here's what you've got to do with your worries: drive them into a small corner. Whatever is out to get you, you've got to get it. Whatever is pushing on you, you've got to push back. **It is better to apply pressure than to feel it.**

The fifth interior enemy is **overcaution**. It is the timid approach to life. Timidity is not a virtue; it's an illness. If you let it go, it'll conquer you. Timid people don't get promoted. They don't advance and grow and become powerful in the marketplace. You've got to avoid overcaution.

Do battle with the enemy. Do battle with your fears. Build your courage to fight what's holding you back, what's keeping you from your goals and dreams. Be courageous in your life and in your pursuit of the things you want and the person you want to become.

Worry, doubt, fear, and anxiety are traits of those whose ego has gotten out of control. They have become positive that they control every aspect of the universe (not the same as creating your world). They have to learn to let go and stop worrying about the HOW.

Remember, **keep the faith, fight the good fight, and finish the race.**

That is your job. That is how you succeed.

Wishing you all life has to offer,

From Ken's desk 🎭

Ten Leadership Lessons

If you have kids who play sports, you probably have given them all the tools necessary to succeed, including your guidance, your leadership, if you will. You then apply certain principles or steps to your own behavior with regard to their sports. And what of those steps to your leadership on and off the field? Can they be put into play at work? Specifically, these ten steps you follow as a parent can be directly applied and serve as a great guide for being an effective leader. Let's examine them one by one.

#1: Be supportive of your child by giving encouragement and showing an interest in his or her team. **As a leader, you need to constantly give encouragement** to and show sincere interest in your staff if you want to motivate them and boost their performance.

#2: Attend games whenever possible. If you cannot attend, ask about your child's experience, not whether the team won or lost. **Great leaders see what's going on in the workplace.** They walk around. They attend meetings, and they speak to their people to understand how things are going.

#3: Be a positive role model by displaying good sportsmanship at all times to coaches, officials, opponents, and your child's teammates. **Effective leaders are positive role models.** If you don't act in the manner you'd like your employees to act, they won't.

#4: Let your child set his own goals and play the game for himself/herself. Be your child's "home-court advantage" by giving him/her your unconditional support regardless of how well he or she performs. **Great leaders allow their employees to set goals.** Sure, those goals need to align with the organization's goals, but people are much more successful and dedicated to achieving goals that they set or helped establish. And those who do not meet their goals should be supported and helped so that they improve and meet their goals the next time.

#5: Let the coach, coach. Refrain from giving your child advice when he or she is playing. **If your organization has multiple levels of management, this comes into play.** For example, if a manager tells an employee one thing, the organization's president needs to be careful not to tell that employee conflicting information. All management needs to be on the same page. This is simply done via effective communications.

#6: Respect the decisions of the referee or umpire. This is an important part of honoring the game. Your child will pay more attention to how you act than to what you say. **Things will not always go right in organizations.** Some battles you will win, and others you will lose. When you lose a battle, the answer is never to point fingers or complain about external reasons that caused the failure. Rather, you must accept the failure and figure out how to improve and avoid failure next time.

#7: Read the rule book. A full understanding of the rules will help you enjoy the game and educate others. **In my opinion, the only real rule book in business is the ethics rule book.** By being a positive role model (see #3) and showing a high degree of ethics, your employees will most likely do the same.

#8: Get to know who is in charge. Meet with the leadership of the program, whether it's school sponsored or recreational, to discuss topics such as cost, practice, and game scheduling, insurance coverage, emergency procedures, etc. **Effective leaders get involved in their industries.** No organization operates in isolation. Understand and get involved in your industry. This will help with setting industry policies, finding partner organizations, and becoming well-known, which will positively influence sales, the number of quality people seeking to join you, etc.

#9: Get involved! A great way to support your child's sports experience is by becoming a volunteer for the program. Some of the ways you can get involved: keep the scorebook, assistant coach, equipment manager, run the clock, etc. **See #2.** Make sure you circulate around your workplace and get involved. **Rule number 1: if ever you believe you are too big to do the small stuff, you have become too small to do the big stuff.**

#10: Sit back and enjoy the game. Remember, it is played for FUN. **Great leaders enjoy the journey and not just the end result.** You should be doing what you love to do.

Remember, life is a game. Learn the rules and play it the best you can. Then you can only win.

> "Outstanding leaders go out of their way to boost the self-esteem of their personnel. If people believe in themselves, it's amazing what they can accomplish."—**Sam Walton**

Wishing you all life has to offer,
From Ken's desk

Fourteen Words to Success

You have magic you're meant to deliver to this world.

"Ken, are you sure? You don't even know me that well," you say. Hold on, dear friend. I do know you because you and I are so much alike. You have a strong desire to help others and make a difference with your life. You've been having troubles with procrastination, perfectionism, and lack of focus (for way too long). You're more scattered then you want to admit, and you're disorganized in areas of your life that are important to you.

I've been there, done that. (Own ten of the T-shirts)

Ever since I was twenty-nine years old, my goal was to create a platform that could positively influence the lives of hundreds of thousands of people, one day millions. How was I going to do that? No clue! At all! I was the king of procrastination, the prince of perfectionism, and the most disorganized person I knew. My own family and friends told me to "throw in the towel." I just couldn't. I couldn't.

I'm going to share fourteen words that changed my life forever. If you take HOLD of these fourteen words, apply them. You're going to increase your results and your self-confidence quickly.

Write this on your refrigerator, computer dashboard, or the mirror in your bathroom.

"You don't have to get it right. You just have to get at it." Let me say that again.

"You don't have to get it right. You just have to get at it."

These fourteen words changed my life. Make them part of your success philosophy. This is why you hear me say, "Ignorance on fire will beat knowledge on ice, all day long." Start this week moving forward just 1 percent. Get going. Move. Act. Make February productive.

Wishing you all life has to offer,
From Ken's desk

A Rich Mind-Set Strategy

Imagine for a moment that there was someone who was willing to:

(a) give you a million dollars in cash; OR
(b) teach you to develop and create a way to have all the money you will ever want or need flowing into your life whenever you want or need it.

Now, if we ask most people what they would prefer:

(a) the million dollars cash; OR
(b) taking the time to develop the consciousness that is necessary to have an unstoppable flow of money into their lives whenever they want or need it—a thousand here and ten thousand there.

What do you think they would go for? I believe most people would take the cash. The reason I believe this is because that is what I would have chosen for most of my life when I was struggling with money.

So let us assume someone is lucky enough to win the lotto. How well off do you think they are going to be seven years later? Are people who win the lotto better off financially or are they worse off? Statistics show us that in fact they are WORSE off two to three years later. Can you believe that? Ninety-five percent of those who win the lottery have less money seven years later than they did when they bought the ticket that won it.

Would they have been better off with the cash or with the ability to create an unstoppable flow of money for the rest of their lives? If you can understand that simple concept, you can do the opposite of what the tribe does.

In order for me to resolve this issue, I had to take my eyes off money and put them on the flow of money, off instant gratification and on delayed gratification. I knew I had to THINK differently. I had to reshape my mind to think in ways that would create such a flow. I had to develop a rich-mind life strategy by reblueprinting my mind, because **the rich mind-set** represents 80 percent of our ability to attract and create wealth.

What most people do not understand is that the actual steps—the "how to" (investing, businesses, jobs, careers, etc.)—only represents 20 percent of their ability to create an unstoppable flow of riches in their lives. Therefore, if we neglect the rich mind-set and focus on the "how to," we will struggle with money for the rest of our lives.

For me, it was to live in my purpose, and from there the opportunities will present themselves. Am I fully there yet? NO. How terrible it would be to have *arrived*. But I am well on my way, and you can be too once you fully buy into a rich mind-set, with a rich-mind-set strategy.

Wishing you all life has to offer,
From Ken's desk

Fifteen Minutes

If you are like most people, your life is very busy. However, I am asking—no begging you—to take just fifteen minutes per day to "check in" with yourself and really look at what you have been focused on.

If you had a "bad" day, then that cannot be changed. But what can change is the way you look at it. Something went "right" today. Something good happened. Record that evidence today.

Find something good that you can focus on. This is what will keep you in the "flow." You are out of the "flow" anytime you focus on or replay things in your mind that are not in alignment with the way you want to live.

Self-confidence is a huge factor in being able to keep your focus on what you do want instead of on what you don't want. How much better would your life be if you had **more** self-confidence?

Wishing you all life has to offer,
From Ken's desk

Adjust Your Radar

When I was young, I remember seeing for the first time this really amazing sports car. It was awesome, and I asked my dad what it was, and he told me it was a Corvette Stingray. I had never seen one before, but over the course of the next week or so, they seemed to pop up everywhere. Has that ever happened to you? Of course, it has. It seems that something that never existed suddenly exists in abundance.

How does this happen?

The truth is, it was always there in front of you, but your radar did not pick it up. When a plane uses radar to help guide it safely, the radar sends out a pulse for something it knows—mountains and metal—and that pulse then deflects off of the thing and back to the plane, telling the pilot what is ahead. The key here is that the radar has to KNOW the thing. If it were an object unknown to radar, the pulse would not recognize it, and the chance of hitting that unknown is very likely.

Well, guess what? Your brain works the same way. You look out and see what you know. As our brains are more advanced, when we are not looking for something, sometimes we see something and either it passes right by us, or for the first time it registers and we say, "What was that?" Now that we KNOW what it is, we start to recognize it all the time, but we think it is new, and someone is suddenly making a lot of them.

So what does your radar pick up?

For sure it picks up what you know, and in abundance. The trick now is to train your brain to pick up new things and new ideas—beliefs.

We live in a belief-driven universe. The beliefs we have, most of which are unconscious, determine what we see. We are interpreting everything around us through the lens of our radar, which are really our filters of belief. Once we become aware of our filter and beliefs we can change. We will see an abundance of everything we are looking for and realize it was there all along.

Everything you want is available to you, but you won't see it until you turn on the perception that allows you to see it—your radar.

Our society is rapidly becoming one of "entitlement," which is the dark side of expectations. I hear some complaining that they are just as good, talented, knowledgeable, or experienced as someone who is very successful in their field. They feel "entitled" to more success and expect that simply by being good at what they do, they will reap the rewards.

The problem is they are not engaged in the active pursuit of that success. Successful people are fully engaged. They start one new book a week, and they go to seminars. They experiment, take risks, and take action every day.

They don't THINK about getting on the ride. They GET on the ride. They don't THINK of getting in the game. They GET in the game. They don't HOPE for or THINK about expanding their business. They become fully ENGAGED in the process of expanding their business.

You don't do this by just using positive thinking or affirmations like "I know I can." You are not the little engine that could. You are the little engine that DOES! I am . . . is also an action.

Start looking for things that are not there. Did you know that every solid is made up of molecules, and these are not solids at all . . . hmmm.

Train your mind to see all things new, and your radar will start to show you where you want to go.

Wishing you all life has to offer,
From Ken's desk

All Limitations Are Perceived Horizons

Not so long ago, people thought the world was flat. They looked out into the horizon, and it appeared to them that the earth ended somewhere far out there, and at the end of the earth, one could possibly fall off the edge and die. Therefore, people did not dare to reach the horizon for fear of falling off the end of the earth, so they stayed where they were.

Their perception that the world was flat, that it had an edge (the horizon), kept them from exploring far away from where they were born. It was a limitation that appeared real to them. However, this limitation was not real at all. It was an error in perception.

The horizon is not an edge; it is not an end.

In fact, you can never reach the horizon because it keeps moving farther away from you the closer you get to it. The horizon is an apparent end, yet it is grounded in infinity (you can never reach it).

All of your limitations are horizons. All of them bar none. No exception.

Even the self has no limits, although it "appears" to be encompassed by a limited body. In fact, is the self a reality or simply an awareness of feeling? The Buddha argued that the self is a feeling that gets mistaken for an identity (that which is "having" the feeling). Anyways, that is another topic altogether. Let us get back to limitations.

Any limit that you think you have, whether it is financial, biological, emotional, or whatever, is a horizon. **For example, you may have the belief that you cannot afford something, and so you forever deny yourself that thing; you never buy it. That is believing in the horizon. You believe you have limited funds, and if you spent them on that thing, you would suffer and die or whatever.** However, if you went ahead and purchased it, you would find that you can indeed afford it, and because you have now created a new gap in your money, you would quickly fill that gap with even more money (so long as you don't believe you are limited). This is the difference between those who have scarcity (poverty) consciousness or beliefs and those who believe in abundance.

So what is the solution to limitations?

It comes in two steps:

Step 1: Replace your perspective. As long as you think the world is flat and the horizon marks the edge of the world beyond which you will fall off, all other thoughts and actions will be in error. So **you must train yourself to see the world in a new way, to know that the horizon is an illusion.** If you skip this step and jump straight to step 2, you may burn your fingers because you cannot act as if you have abundance as long as you believe in scarcity. Your beliefs always become manifest. Thought is more powerful than action in creation.

Step 2: Act in line with abundance. In the above example, we saw that one who believes in abundance knows that the "limited" amount of money in their pocket is transitional; it is a river that flows and is hence not truly limited. But the one who believes in scarcity is convinced that they have a true limit; hence, they don't dare cross it. So what does it mean to act in line with abundance? It means that you will be going beyond the horizon. You will march to it and keep moving, knowing that the horizon will never be reached. Know that all resources are cyclic in nature, so the more you spend, the more you earn, and the more you earn, the more you spend. Keep that river flowing. Don't erect a dam or try to hold it. Keep it flowing. Open both hands wide: the hand that receives and the hand that gives. The faster your rate of exchange (giving and receiving), the better.

Horizons are a mind-set. Poverty is a mind-set. Wealth is a mind-set. Happiness is a mind-set. Depression is a mind-set. Health is a mind-set. Disease (dis-ease) **is a mind-set. It is all a mind-set, with its accompanying emotions.** The secret is that the mind is limitless, so you truly have no limits except those that you have accepted as real. It is all just a horizon, and no matter how much you chase the horizon, you will never fall off the end of the earth. So chase it!

Wishing you all life has to offer,
From Ken's desk

Are You Afraid to Die?

"In the last analysis, it is our conception of death which decides our answers to all the questions that life puts to us."—Dag Hammarskjold

How would your life be different if you didn't fear death? Oh, you don't fear death? OK, but do you truly accept it? Our culture is not very good at accepting death. We really prefer to just not even talk about it, thank you.

Let's talk about it anyway. There are really only two views.

Life is only a physical experience, and once you're dead, that's it, so there's nothing to worry about. (Let's leave your loved ones out of the picture for now and deal only with you.)

OR

Life is a physical and spiritual experience, and the spirit continues on in some form after the body dies. You may take a traditional heaven outlook on this or one of reincarnation. It doesn't matter. The point is, you believe that the life of the spirit, soul, energy goes on.

The first law of thermodynamics says that energy cannot be created nor destroyed, and I view life as both a physical and spiritual experience, so I'm going with the belief that we go on. How that looks, I'm not exactly sure, but it doesn't really matter. I find it comforting and interesting. I like to spin possibilities. And if I'm wrong (I don't really think I'm wrong) and I'm just totally dead when I die, I won't know the difference anyway, so it doesn't matter.

No matter what you believe, there truly is no reason to fear the inevitable. I'm sure you've all heard the adage that "if you are afraid to die, you are afraid to live." Perhaps that even sounds trite to you. But have you really thought about it? How differently would you live if you truly were not afraid to die? Aren't all fears in some way ultimately linked to a fear of death? Imagine the increased freedom that you would enjoy if you accepted death as part of a cycle, as a passage to a new form of existence, a new frontier.

I'm always amused by the question, "What would you do if you knew you were going to die?" Duh. Yes, I know that the question refers to knowing the timing. But timing aside, you do know you're going to die, so use that knowledge to really live in the meantime. How annoying to get to the end and feel like you never dared to be your true self, that you never lived loud and hearty, that you played it safe only to end up dead anyway. I said before that I thought "I can't" were the two most limiting words that we can say, but maybe "someday" is right up there with them.

How would your life be different today if you truly accepted death?

Here's a fun game. Try to pick the age at which you will die, subtract from that the age at which you are now, and whatever that number is, get the same amount of quarters and put them in a jar. On the eve of your birthdays from herein, take out a quarter. It may give you that sense of urgency in your life, unless you feel uncomfortable in knowing that you are going to die. ☺

Wishing you all life has to offer,
From Ken's desk

Are You Dedicated or Committed?

As you stare at your bacon and eggs, note that the chicken was dedicated, but the pig was committed.

You've heard me say it often: the guaranteed failure of "plan A" is by having a "plan B," unless plan B is the execution of plan A.

For you to get all your dreams, you MUST be COMMITTED. The one-foot-in-one-foot-out hokey-pokey approach may seem like you will get 50 percent of your dreams, but in fact, it means they will never materialize at any percentage. It means that you are living in doubt and changing your order. You are turning your dreams into fantasies.

Remember my golden rule?

- Find out what you want
- Find out how much it costs
- Pay it!

If you are not fully committed to paying it, then you have taken your dreams into fantasies.

Imagine you want to lose weight. In fact, you have a dream of that perfect "Bowflex" body. You decide to spend the money on a gym membership, and you start working out. After a month, you see some progress, but the thought of going to the gym seems just too inconvenient or too much like work. You then justify how you'll go next week instead—It's too cold now; it's not the best time for me; it's only $30 per month, so missing here and there is no big deal, etc.—EXCUSES! Otherwise known as justification.

Not only is it true that you can have excuses or you can have what you want, but not both, it is also true that you have changed your order to the universe, but you have said you are dedicated to a better body but not committed to it. You now fantasize of a better body, but you cannot truly see it as you once did when you were committed. You lost your dream.

(OK enough about me. Let's try another example.)

Let's say you want a Bugatti. You read a story about one: *"A 1930s Bugatti has sold for about $30 million to become the world's most expensive car—with dealers predicting more records as billionaires look for alternatives to risky financial investments"* You now know what you want and even know how much it cost. But do you? We are part way there as we know about the $30,000,000, but isn't the true cost created by how you get the $30 million? Now, what are you willing to COMMIT to doing to get the $30 million (legally, morally, and ethically, we hope)? Will you commit to any amount of crappy work if you got you the $30 million?

Or

Was the first thought that came to your head, "It seems like way too much work," or even worse, "$30 million! Yikes, so much for that idea." Either way, you lost your commitment and now have a wonderful fantasy, don't you?

"Oh, but, Ken, that's just dreaming too big. It's not realistic." OK . . . hmmm, I feel bad for you there, but hey, it's your life. Perhaps you could fantasize about a Smart Car. Look, I'm not saying you should desire a $30 million car, but first, NEVER sell yourself short on your dreams, and second, make sure they are YOUR dreams, not what someone else has sold you to want. If you feel deep down like you should have something, GO GET IT!

If this Bugatti is your thing, get committed! It's time to set goals, create a plan, and then all you'll have to do is put in the effort—no biggie.

The chicken . . . well, it is pretty dedicated in giving up possible offspring, but the pig? There's no going back now.

Wishing you all life has to offer,

From Ken's desk

Are You Emotional?

That is a question that can put so many people on the defensive mode, and I want to change that.

Here's why. Our emotions are such a primary factor of our happiness and success. This is the clarity that so many people miss, and when you take the time to get clear and focused on what you actually want and why you want it, that is when amazing things start to happen!

"Don't be pushed by your problems. Be led by your dreams." "Emotions Always Win."

I'm going to say something bold, and this is something I can absolutely promise is true. Emotions ALWAYS win! Everything we experience—and I mean EVERYTHING—is defined by our emotions. Or rather it is defined by our emotional attachment to what is going on. I'm serious about this. There isn't a single thing that is good or bad in itself. Good and bad are subjective. What is good and bad for each of us is different, and how we decide what we define as good or bad is determined by the emotions we attach to it.

Now, here's the good news. Within every negative emotion you feel is the opportunity for the opposite positive emotion, IF you just learn how to do six specific things.

Here's the deal. All strong emotions are calling us to take action in one way or another. When you have strong positive emotions, it is normally pretty clear what the action is, but when you are smacked with a strong negative emotion, you need some tools to be able to take that negative emotion and turn it into a positive experience.

So here are the six steps we are going to go through:

1. **Get Honest**
2. **Get Clear**
3. **Get Interested**
4. **Get Real**
5. **Get Creative**
6. **Get Going**

It is ultimately essential that you realize that you control your emotions, because emotions define your reality. How you feel about your reality defines your life, and when you change how you FEEL about your life, you will instantly start to manifest the things that are in alignment with how you feel.

Let's talk about the six steps you can use to transfer negative emotion into positive experience.

1. Get Honest: The first step is to stop and notice when you are feeling negative. It is too easy just to accept the negative mood without really looking at it.

When you feel yourself in a bad mood or feeling negative about something, stop and notice it because what it means is that something needs to change.

2. Get Clear: The next thing you need to do is to ask yourself what the message is in your emotion. In other words, ask yourself what it is trying to tell you about your situation. I also want you to ask yourself what it is trying to tell you about your perception of the situation, because here's the truth: sometimes a negative emotion comes up because you need to change something, like your approach or actions; and other times, negative emotion comes up because what you need to change is your perception. Often, what you are thinking is wrong isn't wrong at all. You are just perceiving it as wrong because of misinterpretations, old filters, limiting beliefs, fears, and more.

3. Get Interested: Now, it's time to get interested, time to be a detective into what you really want. Ask yourself questions like:
*Right now, I feel _____ how do I want to feel?
*To feel how I want to feel, what do I need to believe?
*What am I WILLING to do to feel that way and believe those things?

4. Get Real: It's time to get real. Chances are good that this negative emotion you are feeling is something you have felt before. I want you to think back to one of those times and remember that somehow you got through it then, which means you can get through it now. Getting real will remind you that you can deal with this because you have done it before!

A great example for this is this as follows.

Remember the first time you had your heart broken. You were young and in love, and when it ended, do you remember feeling like you would never be able to find someone else to love? And the second time you had your heart broken, you thought to yourself, *This sucks and is really painful, but I've been through this before, and I know I'll come out of it and love again.*

Use your past struggles to give you strength and reassurance that you can get through whatever you are challenged by now!

5. Get Creative: Now, I want you to get really creative. Take a few minutes to brainstorm different ways you can turn this situation around. (And by situation, I mean the emotion you have attached to it. Remember, emotions define our experience). Once you do that, take the top idea you came up with a really visualize yourself doing it until you feel that sense of certainty that you experienced before when we went through the difference between hope and certainty.

6. Get Going: Immediately take action to transform your emotion. Remember, you really can control your emotions. It is up to you how you feel in every moment!

And I want to reiterate something here. Even though your emotions are your experience, you ARE NOT your emotions. Let me say it a different way. Your emotions define your experience, BUT your emotions do not define YOU!

Start by giving yourself some distance from your emotions. This is going to sound extremely simple, but stop claiming emotions as a self-definition, which means instead of saying (out loud or to yourself), "I am so angry," give yourself some distance and say, "I am feeling angry."

Like I said, it's a small difference, but the difference here is powerful! So, remember, your emotions define your reality and experiences, but you are NOT your emotions and you are now equipped to change your life by changing how you feel.

Wishing you all life has to offer,
From Ken's desk 🗿

Are You in Your Passion, Your Purpose?

How about this for a life motto? *You are not the general manager of the universe. Your job is to stay open to new possibilities and let go of your concepts of how things should work out.*

I was thinking about you today and wondering if you're anything like me. Have you ever been stuck in traffic and had time to think, time to think back and realize what an incredible journey it has been that got you to this point, a time to think just how grateful you should be for such a wild ride this journey has been? If not, it may be time to steepen life's roller coaster.

There was a time when I didn't choose in favor of my passions. My main criteria were: How much money does it pay? Are there opportunities? And can I get any equity? As a sole broker, life gave me money and lots of golf. While that seemed fun, something was missing. I wasn't working within my passion, and it was gnawing at me. My passion was/is teaching others, and that was no longer part of my life.

It was only when I began writing and teaching you guys about it that I began to again see how passion was an extension of the deep principles of life I had spent years studying. I knew from the past that the more I taught about passion, the more I helped others discover their passions, and the more I found those principles coming alive in me.

As a result, I've come to the conclusion that for anyone who is committed to living a passionate life, there is no greater thing you can do than help others to discover what truly matters to them.

It remains my goal, my passion, to help you find your purpose, your passion, and that is why I continue to write to you. It is my hope that we stay on this great journey. In fact, I hope the journey becomes a wild ride for all of us, a ride where your blood is truly flowing, where we confuse work and play, and where we confuse fear and excitement.

Here is what I ask. Take at least twenty minutes each day to put yourself in a quiet place and think about what you truly want from life, what the "perfect life" for you would look like. What would each day consist of? Where would you go? What would you do? Who would you take with you? Why would you do it? Do this without giving yourself any limitations. What the heck, it's just a dream, right? Go all out and do this for the next twenty-one days. Then let me know what changes you have found.

Wishing you all life has to offer,
From Ken's desk

KEN GRIFFITH

Are You WILLING to Change?

We all know that if you want to get something different from your life, you have to be different. A mentor of mine once said, "If you want to change something in your life, you're going to have to change something in your life." And to be different, it isn't enough to act differently; you have to create different beliefs, the beliefs of the person you want to be. Hmmm.

Willingness is a BIG missing step, and it is time we address it. Willingness needs to be your first step, and here's why. I know you are excited about transforming your life. I know you want it more than anything. But are you willing—I mean REALLY willing—to be different? I want to help you understand the difference between desire and willingness.

When I ask someone if they are willing to be different, they usually laugh, look at me like I'm crazy, and answer yes without giving it a second thought.

Listen, here's the truth. To have a different life, you have to be different than you have ever been before. You have to be the person that has the life you want, and I can pretty much guarantee that is going to seriously push your comfort zone. When it comes to wealth, remember, you don't want to be wealthy. You want to be the person who is wealthy.

Life transformation doesn't come from finding the right business opportunity or falling in love or losing twenty pounds. Life transformation comes in the person that we become as we create the life we desire. So don't be like most people. Give this question a second thought and ask yourself honestly. "Am I willing to be different?"

To help you really get a handle on this, I want to talk about what willingness really is. As I said before, willingness isn't the same as desire, and that is where most of the confusion comes in.

When you look up "willing" in the dictionary, this is what you find:

Willing:
1. inclined or favorably disposed in mind—ready
2. prompt to act or respond
3. done, borne, or accepted by choice or without reluctance
4. of or relating to the will or power of choosing

Notice the key words here—ready, prompt to act, without reluctance, and power of choosing. For our purposes, let's come up with a more specific definition of "Willing":

Willing (the NEW definition), Ken's dictionary:

1. Ready to use the power of choice to think, believe, and act differently, quickly, and without reluctance.

I like that. With our new definition, can you see how being ready is different than being willing in the old pretense?

So are you willing to be different? Are you really willing to let go of the attachment to the thoughts, situations, people, actions, and more that are keeping you where you are?

When you know you desire something, you are ready, but change doesn't happen until we become willing. I know this goes against every instinct. I know how easy and common it is to feel that if you just knew what to do to change your life and live the life of your dreams then you would do it.

I know that because that used to be what I said. I said things like "If I just knew the right people . . ." "If I just knew what action to take . . ." "If I had more money . . ." "If I had the right connections . . ." Then I would do whatever it took to make it happen!

Let me share my journey into willingness. I was ready for years before I was willing. And it was only in the moment that I became willing that my life finally started to transform.

The day I became willing was the day I realized that I was about to lose everything I valued—my relationships, all of my money (or what was left of it is more like it), my dignity, my business (again, or what was left of it), and probably my health. I was going to lose everything if I didn't find a way. And all I had was proof that there wasn't a way.

All at once, when it seemed like it was all over, the strangest thing happened. In a single moment, I decided. I didn't decide anything profound about what I would do or how I was going to change my life. I just decided to become willing. Because if I didn't become willing, if I didn't decide that even though there didn't seem to be a way and even if there was I didn't have the time, energy, or resources to do it, I decided that wasn't an option. I decided to be willing to stop paying attention to the reasons I couldn't. I decided to stop paying attention to how I wasn't getting what I wanted no matter how hard I tried and how much I worked and how much I worried and tried to think of something else. And I decided to be willing to accept that everything that seemed to be true wasn't, and that despite all appearances, if I just let go of what seemed to be true and accepted that I didn't really know what was going on, that a new way would be revealed to me.

Talk about a leap of faith. I literally decided to not accept all of the things that were threatening my very survival as the truth because they were the symptoms of the choices I had made so far in my life and I needed to make different choices.

The day I became willing was the day I decided to do things differently than I had been doing them all along. I had to became willing to let go of everything I

KEN GRIFFITH

thought was true and realize that even though I had been saying I would do what it takes, there were many times that, if I was completely honest with myself, I would have to admit that I did know what to do, but instead of finding a way to do it, I found a bunch of very realistic and understandable reasons why I couldn't do what it took.

The reasons why you can't do what it takes will always be there. That's the truth. So here are four steps you can take to help you starting right now!

1. Use your history. To help me on my journey, I looked for a period of time when things had gone right and asked myself what I did differently, and the answer was that I said yes, not yes to everything that someone asked me to do, but yes to opportunity, even when I didn't know exactly what the opportunity was.

2. Stop looking at everything that is wrong. There were a lot of things in my life that were wrong, but constantly looking at them and saying, "See, it's all wrong and no matter what I do or how much time I spend, it stays wrong" wasn't working.

3. Ask yourself one question over and over again until you have successfully started to transform. "What would I normally do in this situation?" And then I did the opposite to make myself act differently and focus differently.

4. Give up trying to figure out HOW something is going to work and only focus on WHY you desire it. Remember, HOW people will always work for WHY people. Know your WHYs.

Once you open up your willingness to see and believe and act differently, your whole world will change. And if you are wondering where you need to be willing, you only need to look as far as where something isn't working. Start there, and willingness will become your way of being and so will abundance and prosperity and joy!

Wishing you all life has to offer,
From Ken's desk

All Things Are Energy.

All things are energy. They are not "made up of" energy. They ARE energy. All things. It is only your set of senses that gives the illusion of form depending on how these senses perceive this energy.

Now, how does this energy work? Well, much can be said about it, but for now, let us look at one of the biggest laws of energy. We will look at it stated scientifically and spiritually:

Scientific:

* Like energies display harmony, resonance, construction, and attraction. Unlike energies repel, have dissonance, and destruction. For example, sounds that are in tune with each other form harmonious music. Sounds out of sync with each other destroy each other (wave motion). By nature, like energies attract; unlike energies repel.

* All objects have a vibration, a frequency. Even a human body has a frequency. Brain waves have various frequencies. DNA has a frequency range. Your words have a frequency range. Colors are merely expressions of certain frequencies. Each energy particle has its own frequency. This vibration is what sets off the LOA mentioned above. This vibration is the one that dictates whether a particular energy body is in or out of tune with another, and therefore whether it will disrupt or build on the other, attract or repel it. Keep this in mind. We shall be referring to your vibration many times throughout this book. Just before we move on, it is appropriate right now to mention that every state of being you get into changes your vibration frequency. That is why you tend to feel lighter when you are happy, heavier when you are sad and gloomy. The more you move toward love and joy, the higher your vibration. The more you move to fear, the lower it is.

Spiritual:

* As you sow, so shall you reap.
* Karma.
* Law of Cause and Effect.
* Do unto others what you would like to be done unto you.

Sound familiar?

As we proceed, you shall see numerous ways that this LOA comes into play in ways that you would never before have considered. For example, how does criticism and judgment of others hinder your progress? Why do all our religions tell us not to judge one another? That very thing that you are so angry about that is making you feel like judging and criticizing someone else about is setting of a certain vibration in you. Do you see that? And that vibration that you put out will bring back the effects to you, the source. Whatever you try to deny another, you automatically attract that denial to yourself. It is not a punishment being handed down to you. All it is, is this:

All vibrations that you offer come back to you as perfectly corresponding manifestations.

The "down side" of this for you is that any critical thought and emotion that you have toward another person will unfailingly limit your own progress.

The upside is that once you remember to always, in your thoughts, words, emotions, and actions, give the best to others, nothing will be denied to you, simply because you will no longer be blocking your own progress, and you will be having a new vibration of abundance hanging around you. Now, don't forget that you also count. Give yourself the best and drop all judgment and criticism of yourself. You cannot clearly create what you desire in your mind if your emotions contradict your thoughts.

The other upside is that no one can enforce anything on you. You will soon see very clearly that nothing you see or experience can be caused by a source outside of you. Your free will, and the LOA, guarantees this. You see, at the moment, you may not be conscious and aware of all the thoughts and feelings you have on all levels twenty-four hours a day in your conscious, subconscious, and superconscious parts of you. Therefore, this lack of awareness may make things seem to come from a source outside of you. But in reality, they all spring from either your conscious, subconscious, or superconscious. And you can learn to raise your awareness so that more and more of your decisions are conscious. However, it is absolutely liberating to know that the whole idea of external assertion is false; it does not exist.

So how do you tell what your vibration is? Simply look at what you are feeling. At every moment, one of the most important questions you should always ask yourself is this:

What Am I Feeling Now?

This determines what follows in your life. Always be aware of your feeling and know that you can change it at will. Your feelings indicate to you your vibration, and they predict what will come next, unless you change it before the manifestation that would normally follow occurs.

Now that you are getting better at this, here is a simple puzzle that you should be able to solve. Let us say that you are unhappy about your current state of finances. Will that create more or less finances for you?

The answer should be obvious to you by now. It will create less. Why? Because your vibration, your feeling, is unhappy about finances. This will attract whatever gives evidence of that, meaning that you will find even more events and people that you "think" are making you even more unhappy about your finances. All the time, it is you who is in control. This brings us to another secret about conditions:

Conditions do not exist as external, independent entities. Conditions arise out of a state of being. They do not cause a state of being. They are effects, not causes. Unhappy conditions are created from an unhappy state, not vice versa. You are unhappy because you are unhappy, and you are happy because you are happy.

Therefore, if you are unsatisfied with your finances, the first step to changing that is to have a new attitude of gratitude and satisfaction. From this new state, coupled with new thoughts of wealth and positive expectations, your finances will miraculously and quickly turn around.

This is why I named my company what I named it. People close to me think the KSG, in KSG in Motion Inc., is due to my initials—Ken Steven Griffith. It isn't. Sure I used it cleverly, but it stands for **Knowledge, Service, and Gratitude** in Motion.

Gain knowledge, serve people, and act in gratitude. As for the *motion*, well, we've all heard "knowledge is power," right? It is a fallacy! Knowledge in **action** (motion) is power! While in motion, you are the cause, not the effect. And yet the effect is being realized while in motion. Awesome.

Wishing you all life has to offer,
From Ken's desk

Be as the Kid You Were

What were you like when you were a kid? I mean before you had heard words like "limitation" or "disappointment" or "can't" or "practical." Do you remember?

Even if you can't remember, here is what I can tell you. There was a time—even if it was a short time and even if you were really young—when you weren't scared of failure, in fact, when you didn't even know what failure was. There was a time where anything was possible, purely because you didn't know what impossible was.

There was a time when you laughed—a lot—and sometimes, even, for no reason.

As adults, we long for the days when we were open and everything was possible while simultaneously judging it as an impractical fantasy. We don't realize we are ignoring a great power, within us, that is so strong it can move mountains and make the impossible possible.

You know, according to the American physicist, philosopher, and management expert Danah Zohar, doing what you really want with your life requires what she calls "spiritual intelligence." It's about your own, personal, deeper actuating motives. Zohar says that self-development and purpose/meaning are principles that are central to spiritual intelligence. When you're in touch with your own "inner universe," you can develop your talents and give full scope to your natural gifts.

As such, you'll live the life that fully matches *who you are* (which is not necessarily the life that others think you're supposed to live). Within yourself, you'll discover your own actuating motives and what really inspires and animates *YOU*. Zohar says that when you manage to live your life from that inspiration, you're quite a happy and fulfilled person. This is pretty much in line with what the famous American psychologist Abraham Maslow (who came up with the so-called "hierarchy of needs" that's designed to explain human motivation) called "self-actualization." According to Maslow, self-actualization is the ultimate state of human development, a spiritual condition in which people are creative, "playful," and tolerant. And if you've read my articles and other materials, you know that these are the very conditions that facilitate the extent to which you can "work" the "laws of the universe" (if you want to call them that).

And you know what? There's actually a specific group of people who can teach us a lot about this state of "creativity," "playfulness," and "tolerance," or rather "spiritual intelligence." Guess who they are. Children! Kids are almost the very paragon of spiritual intelligence.

Of course, this doesn't mean we should all start behaving in infantile ways. However, we can start to look at the world more like children do. We could start to reinvent and rediscover the qualities that we so often lose in the process of what's called "growing up" and "becoming adults." Those qualities are:

- Being open;
- Trust;
- Sincerity;
- Being genuine;
- Curiosity;
- Eagerness to learn;
- Generosity;
- Feeling adventurous;
- Wonder and astonishment at the smallest of things . . .
- And not to forget, *unconditional love.*

And let's face it. People who are living life like this are pretty pleasant company, both to themselves and to others, right?

"Spiritual intelligence" has got nothing to do with religion or faith. Of course, both are fine if pursuing them makes you feel good inside, and if it's your own choice and it's not imposed on you by others.

But "spiritual intelligence" is really about self-reflection and intuition. As such, there's a difference between "spiritual intelligence" and what many consider "being spiritual."

I mean, think about it:

- You can do Reiki, qigong, meditation; burn incense; play with your Ouija board and your pendulum; do rain dances in wildlife outfits; and read books about "spirituality" all day and night. And, of course, that's all fine if that makes you feel good.
- But "spiritual intelligence" rather refers to making the choices that suit *you* and to actually consciously experience the satisfaction and feelings of genuine fulfillment and self-realization that come with that.

And guess what?

That's what'll make you happy, which also happens to be the fundamental state from where deliberately manifesting your intents happens more easily and playfully.

So in that context, what's potentially the greatest advice of all time? **REMAIN CHILDLIKE!**

Be open. Be adventurous. Be genuine, not least to yourself. Be curious. Be tolerant and allow other people to be their unique self, just like **you** like to be **your** unique self. Instead of judging people, be curious and interested in their deeper motivations and drives. Be eager to learn. Acknowledge the wonder of life and the amazing experience it brings. After all, it seems so real, doesn't it?

But in the words of the late comedian Bill Hicks:

The world is like a ride in an amusement park. And when you choose to go on it, you think it's real because that's how powerful our minds are. And the ride goes up and down and round and round. It has thrills and chills and it's very brightly colored and it's very loud and it's fun, for a while.

Some people have been on the ride for a long time and they begin to question, is this real, or is this just a ride? And other people have remembered, and they come back to us, they say, "Hey—don't worry, don't be afraid, ever, because, this is just a ride..."

And we kill those people.

"We have a lot invested in this ride. Shut him up. Look at my furrows of worry. Look at my big bank account and my family. This just has to be real."

Just a ride. But we always kill those good guys who try and tell us that; you ever notice that? And let the demons run amok. But it doesn't matter, because it's just a ride. And we can change it anytime we want. It's only a choice. No effort, no work, no job, no savings, and no money. A choice, right now, between fear and love.

So what's your choice?

Mine is this: I try to remain childlike and to enjoy the ride!

Wishing you all life has to offer,

From Ken's desk

Being in the Moment

Focusing on the way you want your life to be when things not going your way in the present moment is not the easiest thing to do. But if you have the determination to focus your attention in every area of your life as you want it to be, rather than as it is, your life will change dramatically.

As you begin to notice the instant, benevolent, cooperative response of the universe responding to your desires, you will in very quickly be one who is willing to let go of everything and anything that is not part of your vibration. You will let bygones be bygones, ex-partners be ex-partners, grudges and mistakes of others and your own, complaints and ill wishes, injustice and bad behavior all become non-issues.

You will purify your vibration from the stuff you don't like and will replace it with the things you do like, appreciate, and want. And with far less trouble than you think and in far less time and effort than you think, you will begin to offer a vibration that will net you evidence of your thoughts. That evidence is nothing more than the indication of the improved story you are telling.

Remember, you are Source Energy, who has come here to create, and you are worthy of every idea that comes to you. The resources of the universe are here to assist you in your creation just as surely as they assist the earth in spinning in its orbit in perfect proximity to other planets. There is no greater creator than you and no greater reason to create than the things you desire in your life. Everything you create is for the purpose of the joyous satisfaction that it gives you as the Source within you expands.

It is my desire that you think enough of yourself to want to feel good and do whatever it takes to feel good, even if that means ignoring those who lie to you, ignoring those things that you disapprove of, and turning your undivided attention to the things you desire. With every thought you think and with every desire you give birth to the universe expands. And it is only through your joyous quest that all is possible.

Wishing you all life has to offer,
From Ken's desk

Belief

This is a time of year when people starting thinking about what they desire and everything that they want their life to be. And, because there is a whole new year in front of them, there is that feeling that maybe, just maybe, it is all possible.

Well, you know me well enough to know that I absolutely believe that EVERYTHING is possible when you BELIEVE that it is possible. And that is where most people hit a bump in the road. Just because you want something doesn't mean you believe you can have it.

The key is taking your current belief sets and growing them one step at a time. There is a certain bravery in being willing to take the small steps in order to grow your belief sets, and I promise you, that bravery will be rewarded with unstoppable momentum.

Do you really "believe" that it's possible to have anything you want?

Hmmm, big question, isn't it? But isn't it true that whatever you believe today just came from someone teaching that belief to you? Some believe man did not land on the moon but only because someone suggested it and then found (created) all the evidence to suggest it. Most believe man did land on the moon but only because there seemed to be evidence suggesting that. Our belief sets have created cultural disharmony because *we* believe *they* do things wrong and vice versa.

Our beliefs have, without a doubt, gotten us to where we are today. It is our belief that allows us to sell, and it is our belief that gets shaken when we don't. You know you can sell and you know you can sell our product, so it's not you and it's not the product. In other words, it's not the facts, so it must be your belief level. So how about your belief in what is possible for you?

For instance, if you wanted to create abundant wealth for yourself, then "holding the belief" that you can achieve abundant wealth is even more important than having the actual skill to do it.

And again, just for clarity, that doesn't mean you don't need any skill, because the skill is still extremely important, but what it does mean is, your belief in your ability is even more important than the skill.

Skill can always be learned. And when you have the right belief in yourself, you will attract the right people to teach you the skills that you need. Just like my skiing buddies had attracted the lesson they needed into their life!

But training your belief is something that's often overlooked by many people. They will train their skills and pay little (or no) attention to training their beliefs about their ability to implement those skills. Olympic athletes not only have coaches to train their skills, but they also have coaches to train their mind-set. That's how important they believe it is.

It's just like when I was helping my friends push through their barrier. I knew beyond any doubt each of them had the skill that they needed to ski one of the toughest runs in Austria that day.

But I also knew that if I took them to the top of the toughest run, none of them would ski down it, because they didn't believe that they could.

So an obvious question is, "How do you train yourself to believe that you can do anything you put your mind to?" Start by trusting yourself in small steps—one step at a time. Try to believe in a goal you know is a stretch. Just start by believing at least that goal is now attainable. Convince yourself of this one thing and then work on it believing it to be done.

Remember, the only difference between fear and faith is the expectation you gave to any situation. Neither has evidence to support the fear or faith; you just made up a story of how it will work out.

You see, by taking many small steps, you're pushing yourself just outside your comfort zone a little bit at a time. And with each step, comes a new improved confidence and self-belief that allows you to take the next step, and as you move forward, you gain momentum, which builds to "Unstoppableness." ☺

On the other hand, if you sit and contemplate the enormity of the total task, it's more likely that you'll never make it or take any steps toward it. When faced with what feels like a huge challenge, for instance like becoming abundantly wealthy, it's better to take slow small steps toward the goal than none at all.

I hope that's given you some food for thought, and I'd love to hear your story about any huge challenges you've overcome in your life and how you did it, at least your story of a small step you thought not possible in the past.

Wishing you all life has to offer,
From Ken's desk

Better Sorry than Safe

We always hear people say, "Better safe than sorry," but is that true for life?

Look, no matter how safe you play life, isn't it true that sometimes a wind comes along—it may be cancer, it could be the drink, it could be a family fall-out, it could be a woman/man—but that wind picks you up, no matter how grounded you are, and takes you to where you don't want to be.

And despite the bravado that appears to be confidence, we become lost. More so, think how lost we become when we spend our lives always being safe, and then the rug is pulled out from under us. Sorry or safe? Sorry comes after a mistake. The best way to avoid mistakes is to sit on your couch and do nothing.

Think of how lost those people who thought they had jobs for life became when the likes of Lehman Bros. went belly up. These people played it safe and now have no clue as to how to repair their lives.

Years ago, I left Bell Canada, thought to be the safest job outside of a government job. I left because I feared I would be stuck in that rut for the rest of my working days (a rut is a grave with the ends kicked out). Did it all work out for me? NO! I went from a good income to under the poverty line for the next six years. Most would consider that a mistake, a mistake to which I should have been sorry for, right? I went from safe to "Oh, crap, what have I done? Miissstaaaaakkkkkke." Truth . . . THE BEST MOVE I HAD EVER MADE ☺

Here's the best part. As I announced my intention with Ma Bell, those that worked with me came to me with such statements/questions as "You are our hero. How did you do it?" and "You escaped" and "How can I do that? This is all I know." (The amazing part with that one is that these guys had been doing this job for only three years, and prior to that, they hadn't known of the job's very existence.) But I digress. The point here is that if you look back to all the mistakes you've made in life—all the times you've had to say sorry—you'll soon understand that they were great learning lessons and that for a time you lived outside of the parameters set out for you by someone else. You dared, you explored, you risked, and you took a chance. You lived.

Now, that wind has come by, has picked you up, and has taken you to that place you did not want to be at. Well, life will not say sorry, will it? No, but you know how to deal with it. You grew from other ventures, and now you are about to grow some more. Be grateful your journey is not so boring that you did everything right, the way someone else told you it should be done. Imagine a life that's predictable. Where's the excitement in that? Or a life where you have "arrived." Now what? Besides, after the great accomplishments, the inevitable and expedient question comes up: what's next?

Stay in the question and never stop imagining. Albert Einstein said that if you want intelligent kids, read them fairy tales. If you want them to be very intelligent, read them more fairy tales. Let your imagination fly and create your own world, knowing that when that wind picks you up, it is just part of the story of you that you created. Don't be sorry unless you've hurt someone, and don't allow yourself to get hurt by thinking you must do what "they" say.

They told you not to dream (you did and for now you are losing); dream bigger!

They told you not to work so hard at being a success; while failing, succeed anyway!

They told you to do what society wants you to do; be different!

They told you to go to school and then get a good job; live bigger!

They told you to love what you do; do what you love!

They told you to play it safe; say, "Sorry, I want a life!"

"Better sorry than safe."

Wishing you all life has to offer,

From Ken's desk

Blaming, Excuses, and Accountability

When we discover something is going wrong in our lives, we have two choices. We can complain and blame, or change. I have learned not to beat myself up when things go "wrong" because that creates a very low vibration, and by doing that, I attract more of the same thing. Instead I ask, "How can this serve me?" In other words, if things did not turn out the way I wanted them to, I at least want to pull one good thing out of the experience. So my focus is on what I can take away from the experience that will help me next time, then I move on.

Remember, if you think your problems are "out there," then you will continue to look "out there" for the solutions. Keep in mind that if you blame someone else for your problems, then THEY have to change in order for you to have what you want and be happy. It never works.

Too many people take the victim road and end up in a ditch. When you play the victim, you feed the victim, and the universe sends you more opportunities to be one. When you play the victor, you feed the victor; and, well, you get it now, right?

If you look around and see a lot of what you don't want in your life, you're experiencing "negative attraction" —debt, bills, stress, a job that leaves you unfulfilled (or perhaps no job at all), strained relationships, lack of passion, or creativity.

Nobody "wants" these situations or problems, but most people spend a lot of time THINKING about them, and we know from the LOA that what you think about, you attract. So how do you stop thinking about your problems and start attracting your desires?

Riches flow to those who are accountable. In fact, let's take accountability to the next level. Let's talk about being accountable for every single thing in our lives. That's right. I said everything. Even when you are convinced it is not your "fault," you will always experience the greatest results when you become fully accountable. Only when you become accountable for everything can you be responsible to change anything.

As T. Harv Ecker put it, "You can have money or you can have excuses . . . but you can't have both." This goes for more than money; it goes for anything.

Wishing you all life has to offer,
From Ken's desk

Breaking Bad Habits

Here's the truth. We all have habits that support our desires, and we all have physical habits that sabotage our desires. Habits are driven by emotion, and I call emotional habits "habits of expectation."

Now, the thing of it is, we all get the concept of physical habits, but when it comes to emotional habits, we forget that we have the same power.

Let me give you a perfect example from an article I found:

Breaking Bad Habits, by Marcia Wieder, CEO and Founder of Dream University

What's stopping you from achieving your dreams?

Is there some habit or behavior that you keep repeating and all the while continually complaining about it? There is strength in recognizing our weaknesses and power in changing them. If you want to make a serious change in your life for the better, identify your so called "bad habits."

For some, when the pain gets too intense, the loss too great or they can no longer tolerate a situation, then they'll do something about it. I get like that when I hear myself whining and complaining about the same old thing over and over. That's when I must make a change. The more I can't stand something the more motivated I am to change it.

So being honest with ourselves is an essential first step. When I coach people on the obstacles that may be slowing them down or even sabotaging their dreams, often it comes down to behaviors that can be easily corrected. But it begins with honestly assessing and recognizing what it is.

Common bad habits often include: over scheduling, over thinking, over analyzing. Other behaviors that may stop you include procrastination or never completing anything, saying yes when we mean no and vice versa. The next step is to choose to change or break the habit. Once you choose to change it, you can create a "personal practice" to help you.

A personal practice is something that you can easily do with the intention of changing or eliminating what no longer serves you. I also recommend these practices to develop or strengthen your "Achilles heel" or weak spot.

Here's an example. One of my clients is a talented artist who complained that she never had time to paint. She lamented that she couldn't stay focused and often felt distracted.

I suggested a simple practice where for one week, one hour every morning, whatever she was doing, she would complete before she moved on to something else. That meant if she was checking her email and the phone rang, she wouldn't answer it. At first she thought this was crazy and that this would stifle her creativity. Nonetheless, she agreed to give it a shot.

The first day she couldn't stay focused and was quite upset. The second day she noticed she was having all kinds of self-judgment, baling and making the practice wrong. She questioned her own willpower, but even more than that, her own personal value and worth. Was her dream worth making a priority? By day three she lasted almost the full hour. By the end of the week, she was enjoying it. She claimed to be feeling freer and breathing a little easier.

She decided to expand this personal practice to 30 days. At the end of the month, she was receiving so much value from her new found clarity, that she expanded the length of her practice to the entire morning. Mornings are now office time and every afternoon becomes quality time to paint. After three months, she had completed more art then she had in the previous year. At the end of six months she had sold many new pieces. She was on track with her dream of being paid for doing what she loved. A little structure actually allowed for more creativity. That's often the case.

Identify what bad habit you are ready to transform. Create a simple practice that you can do every day or a few times a week. Recognize and celebrate your success, however small.

I send you such articles to allow a slightly different perspective on things. It's funny, isn't it, how sometimes you listen to the same thing over and over again and you "hear" it, but you don't "get" it. But the same thing, presented in a slightly different manner, with slightly different words, or a slightly different perspective suddenly makes the penny drop; and everything you've heard for years finally "clicks" and you "get" it. That's why reading many books may seem like reading the same message, but they are all put differently so that you can see things from various angles, perspectives.

It's SO not easy not to think about what you're afraid of, but to consciously "change the channel" or "change the order" is brilliant. Give it a shot.

Wishing you all life has to offer,
From Ken's desk

Change Is Good!

Do you have a love/hate relationship with change?

Change is such a strange thing. On the one hand, we crave it, and on the other hand, it scares us. Change is essential. Change is inevitable. Change is constant.

Everything changes. Bill gates once said, "Change or be changed." In other words, if you are not willing to change, someone will do it for you. I am reminded of when ATMs first came out, and all the hell the banks had to do get people to use them. They tried offering $20 bills upon your first try. They stood in front of the bank offering to teach. Finally, they started to charge $2 every time you used a teller (funny how that has since reversed, eh). In the end, they were going to have you use this card whether you liked it or not.

Either you accept, change, or you will become beautifully equipped for a world that no longer exists.

We must accept change. People die. Kids grow up. Stocks fail. Friends get married. Companies shut down. The things that bring us safety and security alter and rock our worlds.

This cycle of life, this process of continual change, is actually a basic premise in the Buddhist religion. Buddhists appreciate that everything has a beginning, and everything has an end. It's not just limited to human change either—trees, mountains, airplanes, T-shirts, champagne bottles, televisions. Everything has a start point, and everything has an end point.

So when you witness change in progress, you are merely witnessing things passing from one state to another in that journey from beginning to end.

Look around you right now. Everything around you was created, and everything around you will ultimately be reduced to dust. That includes your body too. Such is the transience of life. Nothing is forever. The world is in a constant state of change. Indeed, the *only* constant on earth is change itself.

At first, this may seem disconcerting, but by understanding what is actually happening and knowing that this cycle is written in stone, we're no longer "shocked" when these things occur. Instead, we're able to appreciate the time we had.

So do you fully embrace change in the world right now?

Try this. Go and get your favorite household ornament or painting right now. Mine is a painting I recently picked up. Observe its color, its artistic design, and the workmanship that went into making this wonderful piece of work.

Then imagine it broken, smashed on the floor, or, in my case, ripped to shreds. While doing that, try to keep in mind the thought that everything changes. Everything has a beginning, and everything has an end. So rather than fighting

KEN GRIFFITH

against that transition—with screams, anger, and weeping—we can instead simply shrug and understand that's the cycle of life.

So ask yourself, do YOU resist change in your life?

Are you fighting against the natural cycle from beginning to end?

Think about the last time you really got annoyed at how something changed. Perhaps you lost money in an investment. Or a relationship went sour. Or maybe you crashed your car. How did you respond?

Can you even try and *appreciate* more of what you actually have right now—rather than waiting to miss it—once it has left your life?

This process of constant change can also be reassuring in times of need and grief. Because when you find yourself in bad situations, you can always be reminded that the next step in that constant cycle of change is not far away. In truth, when we mourn the loss of a loved one, be it by death or separation, we are actually mourning the change in our lives. Our lives are different now, changed. Yes, "even this shall pass."

So don't fight against the constant cycle of change. It happens.

Appreciate the time you have with the things that are important to you and know that, ultimately, everything is reduced to dust.

This is not a cue to be passive toward life and cease to pursue the positive, but rather, it's a technique for making peace with the world and its many, many inevitable transformations.

Being aware that everything is change gives you an understanding, an awareness. It gives you perspective when facing situations we find hard to get our heads around.

Yes, everything changes, but learning to accept that natural cycle will bring you much greater peace and acceptance, and is worth a million self-development boot camps in your personal journey toward freedom.

If you are really struggling with something and you feel yourself in resistance, it could be a tough diet, quitting smoking (yikes! ☺), or seeing that relationship die, here is a great tip and power question to use;

"What about this change can I feel good about?" Change is good is your new mantra. Whenever you are faced with uncertainty, say it to yourself, "Change is good!"

Wishing you all life has to offer,
From Ken's desk 🎭

Changing Your Vibration

In the past, I have talked to you before about indicators. The indicator we receive most is negative emotion. But it can be any type of indicator that tells us we are out of vibrational alignment. Health issues, relationship problems, and business problems are all indicators of vibration. Change the vibration, and the indication must change.

Anytime you are in some situation where it is not as you want it to be, it causes you to ask for a change. In that moment of asking, energy (the Source) moves quickly and instantaneously toward the fulfillment of EVERYTHING you ask for. The question is, "Are you up to speed with that energy stream?"

In these days of fast-moving energy, the stream is moving so fast that if you get a little out of alignment with it, the results will show up fast and usually in a big way. In other words, when you are in a car going 100 miles per hour, you pay more attention than if your car is going 5 miles per hour. If the car you are driving at 100 miles per hour hits a tree, it is a much bigger problem for you than if you were driving at 5 miles per hour.

We are living in a world of fast-moving energy. You cannot be sloppy with your thinking in an environment where energy is moving so fast. You have got to pay attention to your thoughts.

But paying attention to your thoughts is nearly impossible. Let's face it, most people can't even control their kids, let alone control their thoughts. Monitoring your thoughts is hopeless. So don't monitor your thoughts; just monitor the way you FEEL. Decide right now that you want to feel good as much as possible, and you are going to use the power of your mind to focus on better and better feeling thoughts.

I am sure you are determined to think more deliberately and focus on things you want. I also realize that can be a little tricky when you are in the middle of something you don't want. You can't just pretend it does not exist or pretend it is not happening. You can't just withdraw from your work or withdraw from your relationships. In other words, you cannot just withdraw from where you are because it has your attention. You must work out of it one step at a time. Start with your feelings and know that faith is to expect.

Wishing you all life has to offer,
From Ken's desk

KEN GRIFFITH

Accountability

Consider the implication of this idea.

What would happen if I were to follow you with a camera crew twenty-four hours a day, seven days a week for the next one hundred days while you went for your goals?

I bet three things would happen . . . .

1. You would START doing the things you say you need to do.
2. You would STOP doing the things you know you shouldn't be doing.
3. You would MAKE monumental performance gains and change your life.

How is this possible?

Through the power of accountability!

Accountability will serve your character, as well as your credibility, and more importantly, it will get you to accomplish all your goals (whether that is being debt-free or even a multimillionaire).

What stops most people from accomplishing their goals is one thing: their lack of accountability.

Wishing you all life has to offer,

From Ken's desk

Charlie "Tremendous" Jones

Years ago, I attended a seminar where the headliner was Charlie "Tremendous" Jones. I had read a book he had written and listened to a CD of one of his talks. Wish I still had that CD. The seminar and most particularly his talk had a deep impact on me, one I still carry.

What follows is some terrific advice from Charlie on having the courage to take on the role of leadership, not just in business, but among your family, friends, and the many places where leadership is found or should be found. Put the lessons to use in the ideas below; and, friend, you'll be better for it!

Loneliness Is Tremendous
by Charlie "Tremendous" Jones

Leadership begins with loneliness. What is leadership, what does a leader do? A leader is simply one who goes ahead, one who sets the pace, paves the way. I think it needs to be said too, that any company, church, community or agency must have at least one courageous person who is willing, I said willing, not able. There are many who are not willing, and others who could do the job better, if they would.

Many never arrive simply because they really never get started. Once you decide to set the pace and move ahead, you discover why many refuse to pay the price of leadership.

It's lonely leading and so many return to the pack to lead with the gang, only to discover too late that the gang isn't going anywhere. They want to make sure of the end before going off into the terrible unknown where it is lonely.

Another phrase we often hear, "I won't go ahead until I know I'm right." Seems strange how slowly we realize how many times the very things that appeared so wrong, turned out so right, and the things that appeared so right, turned out so wrong.

I've come to the conclusion that we won't know for sure what is the right or wrong until the end, and the end is a long way off. The aloneness of the leader is far better than the loneliness of the follower.

Tremendously,
Charles "T" Jones

Leaders/teachers like Charlie "Tremendous" Jones, Zig Ziglar, and John C. Maxwell have created so many other greats to learn from: Blair Singer, Bill Chaffin,

Burke Hedges, Tom Hopkins, and the likes. And I cannot stress enough how much your life can improve, and your sales will improve when studying these giants, reading their books and if at all possible attending there seminars.

In addition to breaking many sales records in the insurance industry throughout his career, Mr. Jones is the founder and CEO of Tremendous Life Books. For more information on Charlie "T" Jones and Tremendous Life Books, visit http://tremendouslifebooks.org.

Wishing you all life has to offer,
From Ken's desk

Circle of Friends

Here is something that I find holds most people back from achieving the riches they deserve, but it is one of the most difficult things to change. It concerns relationships.

As you expand and grow, so will your relationships. When you choose to become great, people around you will line up in force to convince you to stay where you are and keep you stuck. Not because they are bad. They're not. It's because they value security and dislike uncertainty.

If your objective is to vibrate at a higher level and attract higher and higher results in your life, you will find it difficult, if not impossible to do so, if everything around you is reinforcing the contrary.

If you look at the people you are close to and they are not going in the same direction, or at least not supporting you in the direction you are going, then they are most likely not thinking the things you are thinking or doing the things you are doing. They will hold you back, plain and simple. If you want to grow, you must surround yourself with like-minded people.

Are you spending time with people who support you and are helping you move toward your intentions? Or are you investing your time and energy with people who are holding you back?

This was a hard lesson for me to learn. At one point in my life, I tried to "ration lies" in my mind that I could still surround myself with the same people that I had outgrown. I tried to make it work, but in my heart, I knew they were bringing me down to a level where I was no longer comfortable.

I decided I no longer wanted to spend high-quality time with people I didn't want to be around with. It wasn't easy, but I have never regretted it. I started spending time with people who aspired to values, traits, and accomplishments similar to mine. It wasn't long before I had new friends who supported who I was becoming and where I was going. It is without a doubt one of the most empowering things I have done.

Just accept that when you choose to pursue a greatness that your peer group doesn't possess, they will try to stop you or slow you down. Surround yourself with people who share the vibrations that you are giving to the universe, and you will find that you will achieve your dreams and desires much faster and much easier.

Wishing you all life has to offer,
From Ken's desk

Committing to Being Bigger than Your Obstacles

Like the achievement of any worthwhile goal or objective, your ability to tap into your potential as a leader (or to-be leader) will likely be met with a few hurdles and obstacles. Successfully navigating those obstacles will ultimately mean the difference between success and failure, frustration, and celebration.

You may not have the ability to predict how many, what kind, or even when or where you'll encounter your obstacles, which puts your first obstacle—and it's a BIG one—directly on your path.

Uncertainty

Not knowing what to expect can and often does place a big brick wall on the path of many would-be leaders. It's been my experience that most people would rather deal with a "less positive" outcome NOW rather than wait and have to face the unknown even if the outcome might be more positive down the road.

This is one of the reasons why, unconsciously, most people slip back into the comfort and certainty of their familiar habits and behaviors rather than face the uncertainty of

"what might happen" even if they were successful at achieving their objective.

Uncertainty has an additional residual effect. It can and generally does invoke doubt, and the two—uncertainty and doubt—together will likely spawn fear.

Fear is the second hurdle, and although it tends to show up again and again, it may be your most challenging hurdle. It's the "thing" that stops most people from pursuing, much less achieving, their potential or stepping up into their leadership role.

Getting Over the First Two Hurdles

It would seem, therefore, that as leaders we must eliminate fear from the equation in order to perform at our potentials outer edges, and in order to do that, we must feel a sense of certainty. But since we can never predict with any real level of accuracy what unexpected obstacles we're going to encounter, fear, to one degree or another, will always be part of the leadership success equation.

As Mark Twain once said, "Courage is the mastery of fear and the resistance of fear, not the absence of fear"

Therefore, the mind-set needed to get over your first two hurdles and all the other unpredictable obstacles you will encounter at the helm of your life and business is one of faith—faith that no matter what you face you can will and MUST find a way to get over, under, or around it . . . period!

Here are my five principles for developing a hurdler's mind-set.

(1) **Never ever, ever give into frustration.** Know that with enough behavioral flexibility, there is always a way over, under, around, or through the obstacle. Maybe all you need is a fresh perspective.

(2) **Commitment is key!** When you're 100 percent committed to the goal, nothing can or will stand in your way . . . period!

(3) **Steady the wheel.** Not all obstacles will come at you head on. Like a strong starboard wind threatening to blow you off course, you may get blindsided now and then. Keep a firm grip on the wheal and keep your eyes on the road ahead.

(4) **Develop staying power.** Even though size may matter, it is staying power that will ultimately get the job done. Remember, persistence is the one talent you need to develop.

(5) **Get over it.** When dealing with the internal emotional obstacles like fear, doubt, uncertainty, and lack of worthiness, the best advice I can give you is to get over it and keep moving forward.

Make them your five principles and overcome your fears, doubts, and uncertainties.

Wishing you all life has to offer,
From Ken's desk

Conquering Yourself

Here are a couple of affirmations to live by:

> *Always will I strive to be greater than I am. I must SURPASS MYSELF. In each successive act, test, encounter and thought. I will be GREATER than in the one previous. I am what I am now, but in an hour I must be MORE than I am now. In everything I must exert more power to surpass myself.*
>
> *From now on I vow I will try to act the part of a person TEN TIMES bigger than I am now, for by so doing, I construct greater powers in my own brain which will actually build me into such a leader. I refuse to longer be confined by the shadowy walls which heretofore have cramped me into a narrow sphere. From this day forth the word "limit" is banished from my mind.*

A powerful stuff from the book, *Conquering Yourself*, written in 1917.

Wishing you all life has to offer,
From Ken's desk

Courage and Initiative

Wouldn't we all want to live a life filled with courage and initiative?

Last night while driving home, I noticed a billboard that proclaimed, "Courage and Initiative Come When Knowing Your Purpose." *Awesome*, I thought.

Think of it. When you know your purpose—the reason you are here—why wouldn't you act with so much more courage and initiative? So do you know your purpose?

In truth, we have a few purposes—to create a family, to provide for and protect that family, to do what you were hired to do at a job, to help others or at least others in your extended family.

But what about the BIG purpose? Do you know what that is? Are you at least curious or do you believe you are here to exist and then die? If the former is your belief, then you have no worries. You will exist till death.

The great news for you seeking a purpose is that you have no worries either, just excitement. You are indeed on a journey. You are exploring, no different than you did as a child and no different than those traveling to far-off places. In fact, your journey in its self has direction, a direction into the unknown but direction nonetheless.

Too often you hear people say they want to go out and find themselves. I suggest to you, go out and make yourself. That is how you will find your purpose. It is not written on some chalkboard of the universe. You are to create it from within.

Find out what you are passionate about. Find out what it is you do that when you look up you are amazed at how time flew. Find out what it is that when you are doing it, you feel real joy. This will show you your unique ability and lead you to your purpose.

From there, allow things to happen for you instead of trying to control each step. Your job is to simply know what it is. Leave the rest to the "universe" for direction, and when to act, you'll know.

To help explain, look at the honeybee. The bee has a purpose. Now, most think that purpose is to get nectar, and for the bee, it is. Upon closer examination, we then realize that by the act of collecting nectar, the bee inadvertently pollinates flowers, creating so many more flowers, a bigger purpose.

You may see your purpose as one thing and try to force it, but if you allow forces to guide you, you may end "pollinating" your purpose to its rightful direction.

My point is, get to know what you want to do and then help as many others as possible to do what they want to do. What becomes apparent is that those you found will be aligned in your purpose, and you'll be living that purpose with courage and initiative.

Wishing you all life has to offer,

From Ken's desk

Defining Success

As I have worked with people over the years, I have seen an amazing thing. People often get frustrated because they aren't achieving "success." There are lots of possible reasons for this, but one reason I have found that sticks out is that many people allow their definition of "success" to be driven by someone or something else. That's why you hear me say, "Write down **your** definition of success."

We ought to be looking at our own, skills, opportunities, life situations, etc., to determine what it would mean for us to be a success in our own mind rather than someone else's.

Thus, the key to "success" is all in the head—our head! We develop our own thinking about what it will mean to become a success. The frustration comes in when we look at what someone else thinks is a success and try to attain it, only to find it elusive.

For one person, being a success may mean to make $100,000 a year. For another, it may be $1,000,000. Another may not be concerned with the yearly income but be more concerned with a net worth. Still another may not be motivated by money and may consider himself a success by how many street kids he gets pointed in the right direction and into a productive life.

Now, the temptation would be for the person working with street kids to think they aren't a "success" because they don't make much money. The temptation for the person making $100,000 may be to think they aren't a "success" until they make $250,000. And the temptation for the person making $1,000,000 may very well be to think they aren't a "success" because they aren't helping street kids! And "round and round" it goes when we are gauging ourselves by another's measure of success.

So my advice is this: Set your own course and stay on course. Don't measure yourself against any other standard of success. Do what you do best, and the rest will take care of itself.

Here is the truth. Being a success is doing **your** best, not being the best. When we get to that point, we will experience a lot more joy and a lot less frustration. And that sounds good to me!

Wishing you all life has to offer,
From Ken's desk

The Secret of Deliberate Creation

Beliefs are so ingrained into our lives that we consider them to be truth. In reality, they are just a perspective you are living through. We each have the power to change our belief systems and, therefore, change our lives.

So take a look at your life.

Review your repeated experiences, and they will reveal to you your belief systems.

- Are you always broke or just getting by financially?
- Do you always tend to date the same type of person?
- Do you work a job you don't like but stay for the money?
- Are you happy where you live?
- Do you do the things you enjoy?

Each of these beliefs has served you at some point in your life. Now, it is time to decide if you would like to continue with them or make a change.

Your experiences will reveal your beliefs. Putting those beliefs to work for you is using the secret of deliberate creation. This is going to be an individual process, but I'll give you an example. Look at the experience you are having. Let's continue with relationships and say you can't find the right partner.

Write down your answers to the following questions:

What beliefs do you currently have about relationships? How do you view the opposite sex (or same sex)? What types of people are you attracted to? What qualities do you find attractive? What are your expectations from your partner? What do you bring to a relationship? How do you feel about yourself? What do you love about yourself? What do you dislike about yourself? Why do you want to be in a relationship? What turns you on in a sexual partner? How do you feel about the things that turn you on? Is it easy to find your perfect partner?

This process is to gather information from yourself. The answers will start to show you beliefs you have that are creating your experience of relationships. Remember, understanding your beliefs will allow you to change your life and put the secret of deliberate creation to work for you. After answering the questions, you should have a clearer understanding of your point of view. This point of view has been your creation point.

Now, we start to change.

Conjure up in your imagination a personality that has the perfect relationships. This person has no concept of a bad relationship. They have always attracted loving people into their life. This person doesn't know what it's like to wish for the perfect person, etc. If you complained to them about your relationship problems, they couldn't "relate" to you.

Now, what beliefs about relationships does this person have? Go back through the above questions and answer them as the other personality. When you have the list of new beliefs, you are at a new point in life. Things can now start fresh if you will let them.

So now what? Take action.

Start to live like the person you've imagined would live. How would they act, what would they do, how would they speak? What perspective would they have about relationships, dating, and meeting new people? Live into the new you. It can happen all at once or a little at a time, but if you allow it to, it will happen.

Here is another tip.

Don't look to the reality outside yourself to see the change. You must know you've changed first. It starts from the inside out. The reality will shift, sometimes right away, but usually not until you have fully decided to accept the new you. You are given opportunities to revert back or stay course. This will happen by being given old circumstances to express the new you.

Key point: **circumstances don't matter; only your state of being matters**. Choose your state of being and live it. Then your state of being will materialize the life you desire.

Now, you know the secret of deliberate creation, put this process to work in your life and start creating the life you desire.

Wishing you all life has to offer,
From Ken's desk 😊

Deliberate Creation

Deliberate creation is about learning how to give up the struggle. This is why we will talk about it frequently. Struggle is trying to rearrange the world so that it aligns with the way you think it should be. It is the greatest source of unhappiness in our world today. It happens when you focus on what you perceive you don't have, instead of embracing what you do have.

The need to struggle and effort to get what we want is an illusion; and like all other illusions (or assumptions), by their very nature, they keep us from seeing the truth that is right before us.

We live in a time of striking contrasts. There is tremendous prosperity, and at the same time, there is also tremendous poverty. Why is this so? The reason is that we (meaning all of us on this planet) must change our paradigm and see abundance as a mind-set. Abundance is waking up to the reality that you are already the person you yearn to become and that you already have everything you need.

The denial or more accurately the resistance to your true nature is what keeps you struggling. Abundance is about lovingly accepting WHO and WHERE you are IN THIS MOMENT. It is focusing on all that you have and not losing yourself in all that you don't have. In the end, it is this thought that allows us to live in the flow of unstoppable riches in every area of our lives.

Wishing you all life has to offer,
From Ken's desk

Discipline and Commitment

Engaging in genuine discipline requires that you develop the ability to take action. You don't need to be hasty if it isn't required, but you don't want to lose much time either.

Here's the time to act: when the idea is hot and the emotion is strong.

Let's say you would like to build your sales library. If that is a strong desire for you, what you've got to do is get the first book then get the second book. Take action as soon as possible, before the feeling passes and before the idea dims. If you don't, here's what happens. You fall prey to the law of diminishing intent. We intend to take action when the idea strikes us. We intend to do something when the emotion is high. But if we don't translate that intention into action fairly soon, the urgency starts to diminish. A month from now, the passion is cold. A year from now, it can't be found.

So take action. Set up a **discipline** when the emotions are high and the idea is strong, clear, and powerful. If somebody talks about good health and you're motivated by it, you need to get a book on nutrition. Get the book before the idea passes, before the emotion gets cold. Begin the process. Fall on the floor and do some push-ups. Whatever. You get the idea.

You've got to take action; otherwise, the wisdom is wasted. The emotion soon passes unless you apply it to a disciplined activity.

Discipline enables you to capture the emotion and the wisdom and translate them into action. The key is to increase your motivation by quickly setting up the disciplines. By doing so, you've started a whole new life process.

Here is the greatest value of discipline: self-worth, also known as self-esteem. Self-esteem is directly connected to discipline.

Once we sense the least lack of discipline within ourselves, it starts to erode our psyche. One of the greatest temptations is to just ease up a little bit. Instead of doing your best, you allow yourself to do just a little less than your best. Sure enough, you've started in the slightest way to decrease your sense of self-worth.

That's the problem with even a little bit of neglect. Neglect starts as an infection. If you don't take care of it, it becomes a disease. And one neglect leads to another.

Once this has happened, how can you regain your self-respect?

All you have to do is act now! Start with the smallest discipline that corresponds to your own philosophy. Make the **commitment**: "I will discipline myself to achieve my goals so that in the years ahead I can celebrate my successes."

Ask yourself this: Will I do today what others won't, so that I can have tomorrow what others can't?

Wishing you all life has to offer,
From Ken's desk

Do You Have What It Takes?

Some great advice on what it takes to succeed. Take the questions asked below seriously, because the time you take with them and the answers you come up with can help you to attain what you set out to achieve.

Ten Questions: Do You Have What It Takes?

Have you ever thought about what you must be prepared to endure and do in order to be successful in your career? I jotted down ten questions you can use to gauge whether you already have what it takes, or if you need to do a little "work" to get there. As you know, you either pay the price of discipline or the price of regret.

Discipline weighs ounces. Regret weighs tons!

With that said, here are ten questions to ask yourself:

1. Are you disciplined?
2. Do you take rejection personally? What about criticism?
3. Do you bounce back quickly from making errors or failing over and over again?
4. Are you a planner, or do you do things by the seat of your pants?
5. Are you prepared to take risks? Moderate or big?
6. Do you stay focused on one thing and one thing only until the result you want is achieved?
7. Do you have the stamina to keep going long after everyone else is tired?
8. Can you delegate well, or are you the only one who can do things right?
9. Do you wait for things to happen, or do you aggressively go after what you want?
10. Do you do whatever it takes to achieve your goals or just what's convenient?

These questions are critical for you to ask yourself in order to get a true picture of your nature and behavior. What I have found is that successful people are aware of the consequences of not being efficient in these areas and find other ways, resources, or people to manage for them. This is just some food for thought.

Wishing you all life has to offer,
From Ken's desk

Do You Want More?

We are surrounded by messages in the media, from friends and family, and even from strangers that constantly tell us we should have more—more wealth, more success, more love, and more health. And there is nothing wrong with wanting more of those things (in fact, I think it's great), but it is easy to receive these messages from outside of ourselves and simply accept them as true without really evaluating what is right for you.

I want to tell you a secret. You need to listen to what YOU want more of. You need to get in touch with what that means to you instead of believing it "should" be something that is told to you.

This is the clarity that so many people miss, and when you take the time to get clear and focused on what you actually want and why you want it, that is when amazing things start to happen!

This issue is centered on helping you find that clarity so you can remove any resistance you have to what you want more of and finally allow it to flow to you, in abundance!

What does it mean to you to have more? Exactly what do you want more of? Do you even know?

This question requires you to schedule a short date with yourself, for the purpose of exploring what really matters to you and what you are willing to do about it. The Irish political activist Bernadette Davis reminds us, "To gain that which is worth having, it may be necessary to lose everything else."

I know this takes unbounded courage and strength. Just remember, life is short. Live it your way.

If you could create your life the way you want it, actually live by your standards, exactly what would you want more of? How about starting with some of the essential basics? Would you like more time, more joy, more ease? How about some added extras: more money, romance, travel, friends, fun?

For some, having more is about material stuff. Not only is there nothing wrong with wanting a new car or home or taking a vacation, but in this process, you are empowered by deciding what you want. Perhaps you have plenty of material wealth, maybe even more stuff than you need or want. Your "having more" list may actually turn into your "having less" list, as you purge and clear out the clutter.

Keep in mind that too much of anything can be burdensome. Excess weight, whether it be in the form of pounds, people, or worrisome thoughts, can be a drain. Are you aware of where you are being weighed down or overwhelmed? Can you feel where you are being pushed and pulled? Where has "more" become too much?

Beware of old programming that might immediately surface to squelch your creative process. Are you already starting to feel selfish or guilty? Does even the possibility of a life filled with more of what you want bring up doubts, fears, and concerns?

Here's one thing I know for sure. If you create a dream or a goal that you are more committed to than your reality, which includes your worries and doubts, and if you do something to move your dream forward every day or even weekly, *you will transform your life.*

Wishing you all life has to offer,
From Ken's desk

A Transference of Belief

Selling is a transference of belief. If you don't fully believe, your prospect surely won't.

Let's examine how you believe in all areas of your life.

Did you know that if you move a goldfish from a small fishbowl in your home and take it to a lake, he will continue to swim in the same small circle? Why? Because he has accepted the belief that if he swims farther, he's going to bump his nose. He's always done it this way. Any other way is "impossible."

When you question your beliefs, you question your limitations. If your beliefs serve you, they can withstand the scrutiny. If they don't survive the questioning, it is time to drop them and replace them with beliefs that serve you.

Examples: You may have the belief that you need money to make money. It's hard to succeed in a recession. That you will never get out of debt. That there are too many obstacles in your way to succeed at . . . (you fill in the blank)

Like the goldfish that has been freed to swim in the lake, you still think you are limited. Your limitation is set by your beliefs.

If you are asking yourself, "How can I tell for sure what I believe is true or not?," this is actually quite easy. You've asked the wrong question. The question to ask is simply:

"Does this belief serve me?"

It doesn't matter whether your beliefs are "true" or "false." What matters is that are they moving you toward or away from what you want? If they don't serve you, now is the time to replace them with beliefs that do.

This works for all of life. Can you see how it might help you in selling? Remember . . . you are always selling yourself.

Wishing you all life has to offer,

From Ken's desk

Dream Bigger

Are you ready to stop just dreaming about all the things you'd like to do or have, and start actually doing or having them?

There is no better time to start than right this moment, and start with defining your dreams. Write them down on a note card or journal and keep it in front of your face at all times.

Dream bigger! No, even bigger than that!

The best goal-setting advice I've ever received was to dream bigger than you think is even possible. When you dream bigger, you'll achieve more than you ever thought possible. Do not limit yourself or your imagination!

This is not the year to underestimate yourself and what you are capable of. The time is now to really dig deep and find out what it is you really want for your life in the three major categories: health, wealth, and relationships. If you want to shed thirty pounds, but something inside you says "you can't do it," then you need to go for it. If you want to make a six-figure income this year, then there is no time like the present to start planning.

With a big goal, you need to have a series of little goals (milestones) that lead up to that one big goal. Little goals are ones you know you can achieve, either easily or with a little effort. Little goals keep you motivated because you'll feel excellent right after you achieve it, and then you'll be motivated to keep going toward that bigger goal.

Wishing you all life has to offer,
From Ken's desk

Dreams Are Your Why

"Goals are dreams we convert to plans and take action," Zig Ziglar.

If you allow someone else to create your world, they will make it much smaller than you would.

Remember, the true path to success is DREAM → GOALS → PLAN → EFFORT.

You won't do anything if you don't have a WHY. Why else would you do it? For most, they go to work because they have to pay bills, so that they may exist in comfort till death.

Is that your plan? Is that your WHY?

To live the life of expected success, you first must know your WHY. What do you want out of life? What do you want to do and have and be?

Once you figure that out, it will do you no good to simply sit on the couch and desire. You must set goals to achieve the things you want—long-term goals, medium-term goals, and short-term goals. Your goals must be all inclusive—business, personal, and entertainment.

It is only once you set your goals (sign and date them) that you can now set out a plan to achieve them. And as soon as it feels like a struggle, go and visit your dreams, your WHY.

Also remember your daily goals, which are broken down to the hour and minute.

But, really, none of it matters if you don't have a clear picture of that wealthy life your spirit yearns for. So get details, get emotional about them, and get moving.

Wishing you all life has to offer,
From Ken's desk

Dream Time

In our very full lives, we spend so much time doing what we have to do, that rarely is there time "left over" for our dreams. If you want to end this year right, begin to plan for next year.

I'm not encouraging you to map out your days and hours or obsess about strategy. But I am suggesting that you carve out one hour of dream time for yourself. If you like this process, you can then do another round with your spouse and family. But let's begin with you. After all, once you connect with your passion—what you love—you'll have more energy (and perhaps even time) for the people you love.

Making time for your dreams is not selfish. Since people with passion and dreams actually live longer, healthier lives, it's actually an act of generosity to make time for dreams that make you happy.

For most of us, the critical first step is to quit something. Do a quick survey of your life and dump at least one activity, group, or bad habit that drains you. It could be that hour of TV, the stopover at the pub, that time on a computer game, or the old surfing the Web for useless information, etc. (unless, of course, you do have plenty of spare time). If you don't have to do it and don't want to do it, perhaps it's time to say bye-bye. If you can't make that leap yet, you can still move ahead. Perhaps going through this simple process will fuel your desire to make time for your new or important dreams.

In the comfort of your own space, and at your own pace, answer the following questions. Do it on paper or with a good listener. They key is to get it out of your head. As you are writing or speaking, allow more and more detail to come. This stream of consciousness may open you to new ideas and insights. Here are the simple but important questions for you to answer.

1. What do you love or what matters to you?
2. What do you want/desire?
3. What do you believe?
4. What are you willing to do about this?

After you answer these questions, create at least one simple, yet essential, action step to set yourself up for success. What is the single most important thing for you to do this week or, even better, today?

If your dream is to write a book, join a writers' group, clear a physical space where you can write and be creative, draft your table of contents, or hire a coach.

KEN GRIFFITH

Demonstrate that you're more committed to your dream than to any fear, doubt, or limiting beliefs that might get in your way. Take the essential first step so you know and can declare that you are in action on your dream.

Wishing you all life has to offer,
From Ken's desk

Procrastination Tip—Eat the Frog!

Eat a Frog! Go ahead and have one for breakfast, with eggs, of course. It's a great way to start your day. OK, I know. Nobody wants to actually eat a frog, well, not a live one anyway. But what if you had to eat a one?

For a moment, let's pretend you start your day, and from the very beginning you know at some point, you have to eat a frog. So what do you do? You procrastinate.

Most people will put off eating the frog as long as possible, hoping something will save them or maybe the frog will disappear. As the day goes on, the frog starts to haunt your thoughts. While working on other projects or trying to relax and have fun, thoughts of the frog surface. This starts to create a sense of anxiety and stress. Your enthusiasm and satisfaction will wane, and your feeling of empowerment will lessen as you feel enslaved by the impending doom awaiting you. My friend Joanna knows this all too well.

OK maybe not impending doom, but you get the idea. This one thing has a negative effect on your whole day.

Procrastination Tip:

Eat the fog! This is the radical idea. But take a lesson from Nike and **Just Do It!** It may taste nasty or be an annoying or frustrating task, but accomplishing it will lighten up your mood and give you a surge of energy and enthusiasm for the day. It's an empowering feeling, and it will spread into your other activities.

The Lesson: As we work on projects and organize our day, there may be tasks we have to do, things we know must be accomplished, but we are not excited about. So we put them off, procrastinating and dreading the inevitable. We wind up being tormented by them all day rather than just once and getting it over with.

Shakespeare said, "Cowards die many times before their deaths. The valiant never taste of death but once."

Be brave, oh soldier of life. Use this procrastination tip to eat the frog first thing in the morning and be free of it. Live your day with passion, inspiration, and courage.

Wishing you all life has to offer,
From Ken's desk

Fantasy, Theory, and Fact

Here is an interesting concept that I have used if you're interested in setting a sizeable goal. I know it will help you too!

I want to talk about fantasy, theory, and fact. The basis for this concept is that everything has its origination in the form of a fantasy, which some adventurous soul dares turn into a theory and then becomes bold enough to turn into a fact. This entire transition, of course, is the result of the highest form of no-limit positive thinking available yet. The cautious may construe this as erratic behavior.

Give this serious thought for a moment. The idea of moon landings, communicating via a fax machine, traveling on supersonic jets, or wearing synthetic garments was, a very short time ago, sheer fantasy. Today, they are almost considered commonplace. Why? How did these things come about?

Fantasy

This entire cosmos is filled with thought stuff, a creative form of energy. Imagination is one of our mental faculties, and it is the one we use to fantasize. An active imagination is able to build clear and vivid images. The most important step in building your fantasy is that you not concern yourself with how your fantasy is going to become a reality. Where the resources will come from is of absolutely no concern to you. Let the image evolve freely in your mind. Build the picture in color, feel it, smell it, taste it, touch it, all through the aid of your imagination. Remember, Einstein, perhaps the greatest mind of our times, once said, "Imagination is everything." A simple, short sentence.

Theory

Once you've built your fantasy, turning it into a theory calls for you to answer two questions: Are you able? And are you willing?

You could very easily be thinking, "Yes. But!" At this point, it's important to remember that you are stepping out of your comfort zone and attempting to go beyond the limits that your old belief system dictates. And whenever that happens, doubt, immediately followed by fear, enters the picture. To be able to answer this question in the affirmative—"Yes, I am definitely able"—does not mean that you have to know how it will happen. There is no way that you could know how it will happen. You have never done it before. It's a brand new experience. The Wright Brothers didn't know how to fly when they fantasized themselves doing it! They just believed they could.

The second question is, are you willing? Are you willing to pay the price? Are you willing to make the sacrifices that will be required to turn your dream into a reality? And you know that there will be sacrifices. My mentor, Don, shared with me that most people think sacrifice is giving up something. That's not true. Sacrifice is merely releasing something of a lower nature to make room for something of a higher nature.

The minute you answer, "Yes, I am able!" and "Yes, I am willing!" your fantasy moves to the next phase of creation and becomes a theory in your consciousness; and, at this point, it turns into a goal.

Fact

The process of turning your fantasy to theory is ready to move into the final stage—fact. From this point on, it becomes a lawful process. As you turn the image over to your universal subconscious mind by getting emotionally involved with the image, the laws of the universe kick into gear and begin to turn that image into physical form.

The law of perpetual transmutation takes that image and begins to move it into form with and through you. Your vibration starts to change, and that causes your behavior to change. Your new vibration sets up an attractive force and begins to attract to you all things requisite to the fulfillment of the picture, through the harmonious vibration of the LOA. Although you have no way of knowing exactly how it will move into form, faith and your understanding of the laws will create a knowing within you that it must move into form.

This is the very process that has taken us out of the cave and into the condominium. Let your mind play. Fantasize a much better form of life than you presently enjoy. Do it a lot, as much as possible with an emotional attachment, and see where life takes you. Be present and look for clues. After all, what really do you have to lose?

Wishing you all life has to offer,
From Ken's desk

Fear and Excitement

"It's alright to have butterflies in your stomach. Just get them to fly in formation."—Dr. Rob Gilbert

The tendency for most people is to get into a comfort zone and build a nice little nest there. The comfort zone is made up of all the thoughts we've had and all the things we've done often enough to feel comfortable thinking or doing them. Anything that threatens to push us out of our nest makes us feel uncomfortable.

"Uncomfortable" is a catchall term that encompasses many emotions: fear, unworthiness, doubt, anger, hurt, and distrust, to name a few. Since we have labeled these emotions as "bad," we don't want to feel them, and so we crawl back into our nests.

It can be argued that there are really only two human emotions, fear and love, and that all other emotions are variations on these two themes. Any negative emotion is a spin-off of fear. Except for rare occasions, most of the fear that we experience is over imagined circumstances or consequences. But since fear keeps us from doing things, we never really check out the validity of the fear itself. A feedback loop of fear →not doing → ignorance → back to fear develops.

When something pushes us out of our comfort zone, we feel some variation of fear. The bodily sensations that go along with fear are something that we have come to label as "bad," and we want to avoid them at all costs. Let's look at what happens when the body feels fear: adrenaline, glucose, and other energy-producing chemicals are released into the bloodstream. Our senses actually sharpen when nonessential fears—such as "Did I remember to turn the TV off"—pop up, and we gain an instant ability to focus on the task at hand.

When we are outside of our comfort zone, most of the time, the only thing we are in danger of is learning something new. What is helpful in learning something new? Energy, clarity, and the ability to focus—all available to you via your friend, fear.

Now, am I saying that fear is the best motivator? No, but I am saying that you can change the way you look at the sensations that fear produces.

Do you realize that, at a somatic level, excitement feels pretty much the same as fear? So what I'm suggesting is that the next time you get pushed out of your comfort zone and you feel the adrenaline of fear, instead of crawling swiftly back into the safety of your nest, change the way you look at it. Choose to experience the sensations of excitement and use the clarity, energy, and increased focus at your disposal to say "YES" to the experience and learn something new.

Wishing you all life has to offer,
From Ken's desk

Fear of Failure

Does your fear of failure or fear of criticism rule or dictate your actions? Did you know that fear of criticism is more common and bigger than the FEAR of death? It's OK to admit it. It is that fear of criticism that holds people back from public speaking.

Let me be completely frank with you here and admit something I consider to be very personal. I used to fear that people didn't like me. I think it all started in elementary school. I mean, I had to go to school. it wasn't really an option, so I made the decision to just deal with it.

Yes, I had friends And, yes, I had a lot of good times, but I will never forget the occasional taunting about my attire (I once had home-made pants) and my reading incompetency or so I thought.

The fact is we shape our image early on by the reactions of others, and those become fears that show up in other ways. I'm not saying it didn't bother me, or I never let it affect my decisions. I'm saying that eventually I didn't care if people liked me, which has its own set of consequences (another time ☺)

The bottom line is whether we like it or not, **we have to move forward**, and we will most likely be judged by others. Others will have their opinions and their "ideas" of you that won't always be sparkly or "feel good."

It took me years to really "like" myself, and then it took me years later to realize that when others had a problem with me it was NOT usually about of me as much as it was about them.

If you can get to that stage, that understanding, that concept, and embrace it, you will begin to grow and maybe even grow beyond what others around you are capable of. You see, when you grow, you begin to acquire more compassion for those that have not yet come to love themselves. The wonderful thing about this is that you begin to care and love others as opposed to resenting their judgments.

You realize that it's OK, and they may have not yet crossed the threshold of "self-love."

What I'm getting at here is that the key to overcoming your fears is understanding, loving, and accepting yourself for what you see, not for what THEY see and think.

Even as an adult, I am sometimes faced with sneering, objections, and overall misunderstanding about what I am doing with my business Hey, I talk about money. It's a subject that brings up a lot of "emotion" and insecurity in people.

I was once sent an e-mail by someone I once worked with that most would consider not only irrational but also obscene, and that should have torn at my insecurities. It was downright cruel, in fact. This person chose to take a quote that I had posted in the wrong way about my views regarding "money" and decided to vent. What came out of their mouth (in the form of an e-mail) was a reflection of how they felt about themselves . . . NOT me.

I have earned that mind-set, and I know that what I am doing is useful, and because they don't "understand" and chose to berate my mission and objective, it doesn't change anything. It doesn't shape who I am because I don't chose to let it.

You see, what I do is these three steps when faced with the same challenges.

Three questions to ask yourself when faced with procrastination and fear:

1. What will I lose from overcoming this fear and "just do it?" (a friend, money, love?)
2. What will happen if the worst-case scenario happens? (Am I alone? Homeless? No one will speak to me? Ostracized?)
3. What now? Then what will happen? (Usually, the answer is nothing.)

You see, these simple questions can actually be a way of preparing you for what is truly happening in your mind, which more times than not is empty FEAR with nothing to back it up. The fear most of the time is put to rest when you begin to chip away at the "WHY" and the "WHAT NEXT" set of questions.

Isn't it funny that in the end the FEAR that is preventing us from what we really want is simply a figment of our own imaginations? Fear = False Evidence Appearing Real.

Start asking yourself these questions and working through them when your progress starts to waiver or you feel procrastination setting in. It's usually caused by FEAR, and then you can begin to take note of the real reasons you aren't gaining any momentum.

The best part is that this new found confidence will show through to your prospects and they will gravitate to you and your ideas.

Wishing you all life has to offer,
From Ken's desk

Rejection

Everyone hates rejection, especially people who must sell for a living. However, there is one thing that's worse than the rejection itself: the fear of being rejected.

Rejection is just an event that's quickly over. But the fear of rejection, ah, that can last a lifetime.

It's this *fear* of rejection is true, the bane of sales success. If rejections scare you, you'll find it difficult, or even impossible, to do whatever it takes to make your company successful. You'll avoid calling on customer, you'll balk at hard bargaining, and you'll hesitate to close.

In my experience, the best way to deal with the fear of rejection is to remove the sting of the rejection in the first place. Here's how:

STEP #1: Realize that most rejections aren't real.

Suppose you make a cold call and the prospect hangs up on you. While that feels like "rejection," the truth is that the prospect's reaction has nothing to do with you. You had no way of knowing that the prospect was busy and that the prospect thinks it's OK to hang up on unfamiliar callers.

Maybe if you said something different or called at a different time, you might have gotten a different reaction, but that's just a story you're making up in your own mind. If you had called at a different time, the prospect might just as easily have added an expletive before hanging up.

Most "rejections" don't have anything to do you with personally. Anybody else taking the same action that you did, at the same time, would have gotten the exact same reaction. The "rejection" is simply a hallucination that your emotions have created to "explain" the event.

STEP #2: Understand the source of the "sting."

According to Art Mortell, author of an excellent book, *The Courage to Fail*, there are three situations that make rejection sting:

- When it happens too frequently. It's one thing to shrug off a bad cold call because, after all, that's only one person's opinion. But after twenty, thirty, forty "rejections," each call starts adding weight on your shoulders.
- When you care about the rejecter. If you've got a relationship with somebody, it hurts more if they reject you than if a stranger does the same. As your level of emotional involvement increases, the pain of being rejected increases.

KEN GRIFFITH

- When you consider the rejecter to be important. If you feel that somebody is "better" than you or of superior intelligence, talent, etc., you tend value their opinion. So if that person rejects you, you'll take it more to heart.

Your job is to identify the specific circumstances that are causing the "sting." Then we can begin work on neutralizing it.

STEP #3: *Map the parameters of your fear.*

Take out a pad of paper (or iPad or yellow pad, if you prefer) and write down the answer the following three questions:

- How many times can I contact a qualified prospect and get a negative response before I begin to take it personally?
- How emotionally involved can I become with somebody before I feel that the other person knows me so well that criticism hurts?
- How famous or "important" must a person be before I begin to feel that a rejection from that person would be impossible to shrug off?

Take the time to honestly answer, because you're now pinpointing the exact limits of the fear that's crippling your sales success.

STEP #4: *Change the beliefs that create your fear.*

If you look deeply enough, for each of these thresholds, you are holding onto a unspoken belief (about life, business, people, etc.) that is creating the fear. Examples:

- "After about the fifth bad cold call, I'm ready to call it a day."
- "If I'm close enough to ask a customer for a favor, rejection would hurt."
- "C-level job holders are important, so their opinion of me matters."

To remove the sting of rejection, you need to explicitly and consciously replace those limiting beliefs with better beliefs that create confidence rather than fear. Examples:

- "Every cold call is a new opportunity. The past is the past."
- "A relationship that's not worth risking isn't worth having."
- "Coping with cranky executives means I'm playing in the big leagues."

It's really that simple. Reframing the "source" of the fear expunges the fear, thereby extracting its sting. Here's what Art Mortell once said about dealing positively with rejection.

> "Five words. DO NOT TAKE IT PERSONALLY. Things happen. Customers have lousy days. The economy goes down. It rains. It snows. Sometimes it snows on you. It's up to you to decide whether or not those events are an excuse for failure. In the end, only four things are under your control: your beliefs, your attitude, your emotions, and your actions. If you take care of them, good results are inevitable."

Wishing you all life has to offer,
From Ken's desk

Fear of Success

Sometimes you find yourself with a goal you think you should want to achieve, but you just don't seem to be taking enough action to reach it. You aren't really afraid of failure or rejection. The path to the goal seems clear enough and might even be an interesting challenge, and occasionally, you'll make some progress. But most of the time, you can't seem to get into that flow state, and you're not sure why. This often happens with long-term goals that require intermittent action, like losing weight or transitioning to start a new business and eventually quit your job.

One question I've found helpful to ask in these situations is this: What will happen if you succeed? Forget about what you hope will happen or what you fear might happen, but realistically consider what probably will happen. So you achieve your goal. Then what? What else will change?

I'm not talking about giving a five-second cursory answer, like "If I lose the weight, then I'll be thin." Set aside at least fifteen to thirty minutes just to think about how your life will really change once you achieve your goal (with no TV, radio, or other distractions). There are often unexpected side effects that you may not be aware of consciously, but subconsciously, they can be enough to prevent you from taking committed action. For example, if you lose a lot of weight, here are some possible side effects: people will notice and will comment about it, other people will ask you for diet advice, you may feel you need to continue with a permanent lifestyle change to maintain your new weight, you may need to buy new clothes, you may become more attractive to others and thereby attract more social encounters (wanted or unwanted), overweight friends might become jealous, your family may resist your changes, you may feel stressed about whether you can keep the weight off, you may worry about the loss of certain favorite foods from your diet, and so on.

It's rare that a goal is all roses. Success requires change, and change has both positive and negative consequences. Often while people claim to want to succeed at something, the reality is that the negatives outweigh the positives for them. But one way to overcome this problem is to consciously think about what those negatives are and then uproot them one by one. Uprooting a negative side effect could mean figuring out how to eliminate it completely, or it could mean just accepting it and learning to live with it.

It's certainly helpful to focus on the positive side of a goal, but don't forget to take an occasional survey of the dark side and accept that you're going to have to deal with that too.

Unlike fear of failure and fear of rejection, fear of success can be far more insidious because it's almost always unconscious. But it's not fear of success itself that is the problem but rather fear of the side effects of success, many of which may be genuinely unwanted. Fears that are never evaluated consciously have a tendency to grow stronger. The reason is simple behavioral conditioning. When you avoid something you fear (either consciously or subconsciously), you automatically reinforce the avoidance behavior. So when you (even unknowingly) avoid working on your goal because of a hidden fear of success, you actually reinforce the habit of procrastination, so as time goes by, it becomes harder and harder to get yourself to take action. Insidious!

Asking "What will happen if I succeed?" can solve this problem because it focuses your conscious attention on those fears. Fear has a tendency to shrink under direct examination, making it easier for you to take action. When I say that fear shrinks, another way of stating this is that subconscious behavioral conditioning weakens under conscious scrutiny. I know some people dislike the word "fear" with respect to their own behavior. Don't get hung up on the exact wording; call it "avoidance behavior" if that's more to your liking.

But an additional benefit is that you can also devise intelligent work-arounds for those fears made conscious, some of which may indeed be valid signals of unsolved problems. For example, going back to the weight loss example, if you lose a lot of weight, you probably **will** need new clothes. And if you don't have the money to buy new clothes, then that is a real problem you'll need to address (unless you don't mind wearing oversized outfits). Left unacknowledged, even a simple problem like this can be enough to subconsciously sabotage you from achieving your goal. But once you examine the situation consciously and figure out a way to deal with it in advance, you're sending a message to your subconscious that you needn't fear this problem because you have a practical way to solve it.

Now let's consider the opposite side. Suppose you ask, "What will happen if I succeed?" And upon considering all the side effects, you realize that you don't actually want to achieve the goal at all. The negatives outweigh the positives. I encountered this when I made a plan to grow my games business but didn't seem to make as much progress as I wanted. When I asked this magic question, I realized that I didn't really want to achieve the goal with all its side effects. What I really wanted was to transition to writing and speaking full time, and further building my games business would actually take me farther from that more important goal. Growing my games business seemed like a goal I should want, but when I really thought about where I'd be if I achieved that goal, I realized it wouldn't be the success I truly wanted. That was a difficult realization for me, to recognize that my original ladder of success was now leaning against the wrong building. So I actually had to "unset" that goal once I really understood the likely consequences of achieving it.

Even now as I set goals in the direction of writing and speaking as my new career (don't tell anyone ☺), I recognize that there are big side effects. I simply don't have the mental bandwidth for two full-time careers. One of the hardest side effects for me was letting go of the goals and dreams I had for my personal life now. I wanted to pour myself into a rich life of driving my dream car and chasing down my boat. I wanted to create a brokerage where I sat on the beaches of the world while working deals. However, being able to help people grow fulfills me even more. I found it a very enlightening process to review all these side effects and one by one to acknowledge that I accept them.

What will happen if you succeed, if you lose the weight, get the date, earn the promotion, start the business, get pregnant, quit smoking, become a millionaire, stretch yourself?

Tomorrow we'll deal with it in more detail.

From Ken's desk

Fear of Success

http://ezinearticles.com/?expert=Jeanne_MaySome people have a real fear of becoming successful. Yes, it is true! Some people actually fear success.

And for the person who is afraid of succeeding, the fear is real. Others around the person may not understand. They often think the person is being illogical and ridiculous, but the fear is very real and can be a major stumbling block for any real success in life.

How do you recognize a fear of success?

- When you feel that something is holding you back
- Deep down you know you are getting in your own way
- When you feel everything is out of control
- When you easily find distractions to keep you from what you are meant to be doing
- When you have trouble focusing your energy for very long
- When you lose your motivation
- When your confidence takes a knock

Any combination of the above can indicate a fear of success!
Why does it happen? What is fear of success about?

1. You find change frightening and prefer to keep the status quo. In other words, you prefer to keep things as they are. Change often involves new experiences that can be seen as scary, the fear of the unknown
2. A belief that once success has happened, the expectation will be is that it will happen again. This is particularly real for some students. They are aware of their ability and have a belief that they can do well, but they also have a belief that if they do well this time, it will be expected that they would do well every other time. To prevent that from happening, they don't try very hard in the first place. This can happen in all areas of life and at all ages
3. Once success has been achieved, expectations are increased! People expect more from those who have been successful, and the successful person tends to expect a lot from him or herself and from others. Some people cannot handle pressure of expectations they put on themselves or the expectations of others
4. Attention success can bring may be overwhelming particularly if the person is a very private person and does not like being the center of attention

5. Success is often associated with a lack of privacy in personal life, e.g., TV celebrities, sport celebrities, royalty, etc. The lack of personal life privacy may be too higher price to pay for success

6. Success, particularly in business or work, often leads to major changes in schedules. Some people afraid of success fear their family life will be disrupted, fear they will need to work unreasonable hours, and fear their social life will come to a halt

7. Success may attract negative feelings such as envy, jealousy, and anger from others. Friends and family may suddenly treat the successful person differently. They may be envious of the benefits of success and may ostracize the successful person. For many people, this would be extremely uncomfortable, therefore needs to be avoided at all costs

8. Success may change your personality and confidence. Success brings about certain feelings of accomplishment and achievement. Successful people are typically more confident, more outgoing, and more in control of their life. Some people fear that they will change if they become successful.

(There are others, but they are for another day.)

Now, we are not creating any celebrities or royalty here, and any envy will be hard to notice; but, particularly, number 6 is strong, number 8 is natural, but number 1 is the most hidden.

We think it not likely as we are sure we want our dreams and are in hot pursuit of them, knowing this is not our status quo. Trouble is, don't we all love ourselves? Sure we do. For some, that love is not properly identified, and what we see is a love of who we are and not of who we can be. We have not properly looked into the future. To date, the future looks hazy and a bit scary because it doesn't seem to have the same friends, the same social surroundings, and the people in that future seem intimidating, maybe even lacking in fun. They don't go bowling or aren't on that softball team. In fact, they seem isolated. It's lonely at the top.

None of which is true, but at a glance, it looks that way.

Fear of success is a real problem for some people, and it's a problem that can be dealt with.

Have you ever had a fear of success? I have several times throughout my life, and I know how it has impacted my achievements over the years.

Often, a fear of success is accompanied by a lack of confidence. Developing and strengthening your personal confidence goes a long way in reducing and eliminating a fear of success.

When your confidence is strong, you trust in your own ability to deal with changes that success brings. This is why I spend so much time allocated to self-esteem, the number one scourge on the planet. Low self-esteem causes so many to live lives of regret, fear, anxiety, and doubt. It is ego out of control. It has to be dealt with at the subconscious level, the conscious level, and at the spiritual level. It festers in opinion and falsehoods to the point where facts don't count.

Oddly enough, in getting all your dreams, the facts won't count either, but in the reverse way.

We'll continue along this message throughout, so strap on to the edge of your chair and take this ride to find the real you.

Truly caring for your success,
From Ken's desk

Focus

When we were born, we didn't get an owner's manual for our minds. We created reality through our focus of attention and our thoughts.

Your point of focus determines your point of attraction. Let me put it this way. If there are one hundred things surrounding you and one of them is good and the other ninety-nine are rotten, if you focus on the one, the other ninety-nine must leave you.

If you are surrounded by one hundred things and ninety-nine of them are good and one of them is rotten and you focus on the one that is rotten, in your quest to quell the problem, the other ninety-nine will become rotten too. That is the power of your focus.

So use the power of your focus and the guidance that comes from within and work every day to stand wherever you are and see the world through the eyes of Source Energy. As you do, you will attract people who will resonate with your desires, and those who have been annoying you will annoy you less or go away altogether.

You cannot hold in your experience unpleasant things when you are looking for that which is pleasant. You cannot bring to your experience pleasant things when you are fixated on something unpleasant. It is as simple as that. Tune yourself in to what you want and watch how cooperative the LOA and this universe will be for you.

Dale Carnegie once said, "It is not who you are, who you are with, what you are, where you are or what you are doing that makes you happy or unhappy. It is what you think about." Your focus.

Today will bring you a new awareness once properly focused.

Wishing you all life has to offer,
From Ken's desk

Freedom from Yourself

What you really want most in life is freedom—freedom from resistance. However, you will never find that freedom by trying to control the behavior of others. You will only find it when the behavior of others becomes a nonissue because you are able to focus your mind in ways that allow you to be in alignment, in the flow, and this gives you that feeling of well-being.

The feeling of making others come into agreement with you in order to get what you want will render you powerless every single time. Even people who want to agree won't agree with if you are worrying about them agreeing. Instead, LET IT GO! Say to the universe, "You know what I want. Give it to me in the path of least resistance. Give it to me in whatever way is appropriate." And then watch how many vortexes open for you.

Everything you want can come to you, and you don't need to demand the cooperation of others. When you come into alignment with what you want, the cooperative universe yields it to you endlessly and other uncooperative people become irrelevant to your creation. You can have everything you want if you don't make what other people want seem like it is in opposition to what you want. If you don't make it a big factor in your vibration, the universe will find a way through the path of least resistance to bring it to you.

Watch out for the nonessential things that you are trying to control. When you clean up your vibration, you can see that not only can you have everything you want, but everyone else can have everything they want without stepping on your creative toes at all. You don't get in each other's way unless you fixate on something you don't want them to want and use that as an excuse to mess up your vibration. The universe has the ability to give everyone what they want without anyone getting in each other's way.

Wishing you all life has to offer,
From Ken's desk

Freedom

"When you can embrace all of life, not holding onto anything beyond it's time and not avoiding it once its time has come, you will know the meaning of Freedom."—Unknown

The dictionary defines freedom as "the quality or state of being free; the absence of necessity, coercion or constraint in choice or action; liberation from slavery or restraint or from the power of another."

How would you define freedom for yourself? To be free from your stories, free from your past, free from "shoulds" (some people are full of should), free from need.

Remember, you cannot control the circumstances or people around you, but you can always choose how you react to them. Much of what is difficult about difficult situations is not the situation itself but how you react to it. Have you ever made a situation worse by overreacting? What if you had kept from getting knocked off balance by what was happening, would that have changed anything?

The goal of deliberate creation is to be able to consciously set your point of attraction. That means that how you feel is not dependent upon external circumstances. Your point of attraction is determined solely by you, by what you believe, think, expect, and feel. No one and nothing else is ever to blame—ever. No one makes you unhappy. You do that. No one can make you happy. Only you can do that. It's your choice, always! Think about this. What is easier, to become happy or to be happy? To become happy, all kinds of things must fall into place, but to be happy is just a quick decision, right?

When you can stay centered and balanced no matter what is going on around you—when you can consciously choose instead of letting circumstance dictate how you feel—then you get how to consciously create your life.

I think the quote above sums it up quite eloquently. If we are truly letting all of life in, without judgment, without labels, embracing all of it, not clutching at what is no longer ours nor pushing away what is, then we truly are free.

As you go about your day today, see in what ways you can set yourself free.

Wishing you all life has to offer,
From Ken's desk

Practicing Gratitude

Have you ever noticed that we tend to attract into our life those things that we focus on most? Granted, that's not exactly rocket science, and more than a little obvious. That said, because it is true it only makes sense to give pause and really think about what it is that we want so we can lessen the possibility of ending up with a whole lot of what we don't desire. Makes sense?

If we want to experience a greater sense of fulfillment, we need to really explore the things that we're grateful for. What I'm suggesting is really getting down to the nitty-gritty and looking back on the successes that you and I have experienced at different points in our lives.

The reality is if we're not careful, it's very easy to look at our lives and miss out on the many achievements we have experienced. It's incredibly important to acknowledge our accomplishments because that is one of the main things that helps us grow our belief system, the same belief system that will allow us to overcome and conquer any and all future challenges that will come our way.

Here's a simple strategy to get in touch with the things you have to be grateful for:

Take a piece of paper and write down the things that you're thankful for, both past and present. Resist the urge you may have to edit out anything that comes to mind. Just write it down. Simply practice free writing—simply write down what comes to mind—your past achievements no matter how menial they may appear in this moment. In reality, each and every past accomplishment is incredibly important because in some way it's helped to craft you into the amazingly talented person you are.

After you have written down your list of previous accomplishments from your life, just read over it. Think back on each of those positive experiences, reliving them as best as you can. Just close your eyes, take a deep breath, and to the best of your ability think back on how great you felt for having succeeded in each of the past experiences you wrote down. Take just a minute to remind yourself that you have everything you need to meet with success in all your current endeavors.

Look back on your list of achievements at the beginning of every day. Doing so can be a powerful source of encouragement and a great way to kick off your day.

Now, here's the key to real success: once you've done this enough to keep it to memory, write down all your future accomplishments. Feel them and act in gratitude for them coming true. And they will!

Wishing you all life has to offer,
From Ken's desk

Goals and Visions Unlimited

It is about time your business, heck, your life even, started working out successfully and predictably, isn't it? How are your plans working out? Your marketing plans, your business plans, your presentation plans, your life plans, and all other sorts of plans? Do they work out exactly or do they resemble a list of things that do not come true?

Oftentimes we hear business, marketing, and life gurus tell us that planning and goal setting are the key to creating a successful life. They tell us also to visualize and have vision. That is all well and good. But it is about time someone told us exactly how to exactly set those goals so that our results are exact. And it does not stop there. How do you visualize and think after that? Your goals and visions, in the presence of right thinking and certainty, are the prophecies of what you shall one day become. Here is a most effective technique.

Let us start with the goals and visualization then move on to thinking. These are the goal-setting steps to follow. These steps are the same whether you are doing it for your business or for life. In fact, try not to separate your life. Life is a whole, and it works out that way. Separation only exists in the mind at the level of the ego. Make life goals that include your business and marketing. Do not make business goals only by themselves on the side and forget life goals as this will actually short-circuit the business goals. Everything works together as a system. So here we go:

1. List what you would like to have, do, and be between now and the next thirty years. List everything you can think of, small and large—places to visit, things to have, residences, experiences, partners, skills to acquire, things to do, people to meet, projects, charities, health, habits—everything! This is not a list of what you think you can achieve. It is a list of what would give you the most incredible life of your liking, whether you think you can achieve it or not, a life that is unbelievably fantastic for you. Your list should have at least one hundred things in there. It is not hard to come up with at least one hundred things for thirty years. To be very wealthy, have about five thousand things—even small details regarding your desires should be in there.

2. For each goal you listed, write the reasons why you wish to have it. If for **example** you wish to have a large home, write down the reasons why. In other words, what will you do with and in this home? Put emotion into it. Reasons empower your goal and make it easier to imagine and visualize and attain it. They give life to it and make the subconscious accept it a whole lot better.

3. Get cuttings from magazines, brochures, the Internet, photographs, etc., of the items in your goals and stick them in your journal or dream board. Start a goals and visualizations journal on paper or computer. In it, place pictures of the things you wish to have—cars, stocks, buildings, boats, land, travel, clothes, or anything else. Refer to it often. Twice a day is highly recommended. The more real and detailed your visualization and imagination is, the faster and more accurately you will realize your goals. Pictures are very important to have in your life.

4. **Every day**, read your list, look at your pictures, and then **spend at least twenty minutes twice a day imagining, animating, and visualizing in detail all your goals.** If you meditate, and it is highly recommended that you do, your goal visualization, do your goals visualization in meditation as well. Meditation puts you closest to the Source, the best place you can be to plant your seed of visions into the field of infinite possibilities and creation.

5. Then, here, now, do something that takes you closer to your goal. There is always something to do now, however small. It will open the next step to you, a step that may be unseen until that first act is taken. Every act is an act of self-definition and creation. Act deliberately and with awareness so that each act takes you closer to your goals, not further. Act with purpose.

6. Do everything with gratitude. Think, speak, and act with gratitude, the gratitude of knowing you are guaranteed success if you act in the ways of these laws. Gratitude is a statement of certainty. That is power. Be genuinely grateful and excited about the fact that you already have your goals realized, for they will be by universal law, guaranteed, and so they are. This type of gratitude works wonders.

7. Enjoy your fruits, enjoy experiencing your goals when they manifest into your reality! They are sure to do so, guaranteed by universal law. The reason they are guaranteed is that every moment of your life is created by your mind (and, in a lesser extent, the collective minds of people around you). Your life is images of your mind, expressed, translated, and crystallized into form. You are literally the source of your life, although it may not appear so, especially if you are not present and aware of your daily thoughts, worries, desires, and beliefs. Most people are unconscious and engulfed in their mind in one huge day dream. Wake up and watch yourself!

"I am ... I am ...' No matter what you are trying to create next in your life, find a way of putting it into "I am." For example, if you wish to lose weight, do not think or say "I will lose ten pounds" or "I want to lose ten pounds." Instead, say, think, and write "I am x pounds now." Do the same with wealth. The only time that exists in the universe, scientifically and spiritually, is now. Hence, "I am."

Do not worry how your goals will be fulfilled. There are powerful forces at work in all of nature, with infinite intelligence and coordination. Things, people, books, places, TV shows, movies, etc., will start appearing and helping you to achieve your goals. In other words, "coincidences" will happen. Simply visualize your goals believingly.

The trick is in the details and in consistency. For example, if having a new home is a goal you have, write it down in detail. Write down where the house is located, how many rooms it has, the size of the compound, the size of the home, the furnishings in it, and so on. Then visualize it that way. And do not change your mind. This is very important. Understand that the universe is in activity manifesting into physical form all your thoughts. Every single one of them turns into some amount of physical form somehow and somewhere. If you change your mind, you will be undoing your work. Just hold your thought until it becomes fully physical.

You are almost done. All that is left now is to know a little bit about creation and thinking, so that you maintain your vigilance and confidence.

8. All thought has an effect. Therefore, imagine your life exactly as you wish it to be and be it. Become it. Do not let another thought ever come in that contradicts or weakens that vision. If you notice one coming in, immediately block it, change it for a positive one, and declare that you shall never let yourself think something like that again. This is the ultimate in positive thinking. It is focused and filtered. Do the same with your words and actions. Never let anything you say or do go against your vision, your highest wished for life. This is because life is created through thought, word, and action; therefore, you must guard all three. Do not stress over this. It may take effort at first, but it will soon become normal to you. And if you are in a "bad" spot, remember that all conditions are temporary, as is the nature of everything in the universe. Conditions do not define you, for you are beyond them. In fact, only you can determine how long you remain in a "bad" spot by the way you handle that situation in terms of your thoughts, words, and actions.

9. The final thing is to be present. Stop day dreaming all the time. Be present, be here, now. It is the only time that exists, the only place you can be, the only place where life is. And it is the only place where you can do anything anyway. Be grateful for the present moment, as it resolves itself always at your command, and for that, be grateful or else you miss its fruits and "lessons." Stop chasing your dreams in your mind (i.e., sitting on the couch wishing), for such a place is a phantom world that does not exist. Instead, call them forth into your present moment, now.

That is about it! A mouthful but that should get you going very well, indeed! Be present, be vigilant, be certain, and be clear.

Wishing you all life has to offer,
From Ken's desk

Handling Fear of Success: the Hard Part

What are the solutions to address a fear of success?

- Suppressing anxieties of not being good enough
- Uniting all talents and virtues for a greater good
- Confronting and dismissing existing fears in an appropriate manner
- Recognizing and welcoming the chance to triumph over competition without feeling unworthy or undeserving
- Expressing views and opinions without hesitation
- Setting sights on a goal and achieving it with both sacrifices and rewards; these make up the rough climb, the seemingly impossible.
- Steps that if completed always lead straight to success, rewarding those who persevere

Fear of success is the following:

- Fear that you will accomplish all that you set out to, but that you still won't be happy, content or satisfied once you reach your goal
- Belief that you are undeserving of all the good things and recognition that come your way as a result of your accomplishments and successes
- Opposite of fear of failure, in that fear of failure is the fear of making mistakes and losing approval. Fear of success is the fear of accomplishment and being recognized and honored.
- Lack of belief in your own ability to sustain your progress and the accomplishments you have achieved in your life
- Fear that your accomplishments can self-destruct at any time
- Belief that no matter how much you are able to achieve or accomplish, it will never be enough to sustain success
- Belief that there are others out there who are better than you, who will replace or displace you if you do not maintain your performance record
- Belief that success is an end in itself; yet that end is not enough to sustain your interest and/or commitment
- Fear that once you have achieved the goals you have worked diligently for, the motivation to continue will fade
- Fear that you will find no happiness in your accomplishments—that you will be perpetually dissatisfied with life.

What are the negative consequences of the fear of success?

Fear of success can result in:

- A lack of effort to achieve goals you have set for yourself in school, on the job, at home, in relationships, or in your personal growth
- Self-destructive behavior, such as tripping yourself up to make sure that you do not sustain a certain level of success or achievement you once had in school, on the job, at home, in relationships, or in your personal growth.
- Problems making decisions, being unable to solve problems
- Losing the motivation or the desire to grow, achieve, and succeed
- Chronic underachievement
- Feeling guilt, confusion, and anxiety when you do achieve success; this leads you to falter, waver, and eventually lose your momentum.
- Sabotaging any gains that you have made in your personal growth and mental health, because once you become healthier, a better problem solver, and more "together," you fear that no one will pay attention to you. You are habituated to receiving help, sympathy, and compassionate support.
- Your choosing to do just the opposite of what you need to do to be happy, healthy, and successful
- Reinforcing your chronic negativity, chronic pessimism, and chronic lack of achievement since you cannot visualize yourself in a contented, successful life
- Denouncing your achievements and accomplishments, or seeking ways in which you can denigrate yourself enough to lose what you've gained

What do those who fear success believe?

- I have worked so hard to get this far, yet I need to keep on working hard; I'm not sure the effort is worth it.
- I know people care about me when I am down and out, but will they like me when I am on top and successful?
- I've never been happy before, so how can I be sure I'll be happy once I achieve my goals?
- I am nothing, and I deserve nothing.
- How can people like me if I succeed in reaching my goals in life?
- I can't sustain the momentum I would need to achieve my goals.
- How can I be sure that my good fortunes won't go sour and be destroyed?
- There are always more demands and more needs that have to be met in order for me to be successful. No matter what I do, it will never be enough.

- They are all better, brighter, smarter, and more talented than I am. I really don't deserve to be successful.
- It's hard to be at the top.
- Everyone is out to shoot down the head man.
- No one really likes a winner.
- Everyone goes for the underdog.
- I am happiest when I am under pressure and challenged.
- Hard work, no play, and constant effort make me happy. What would I do if it were different?
- I feel so guilty when I realize how much I have been given in my life.
- I'm always afraid I'm going to lose it all.
- Starting over again gives me meaning and a sense of mission and purpose.
- I'm so bored with what I've accomplished. What's left to do?
- Everyone has the right to fail in life, and I have the right to choose to fail if I want to.

What new behavior patterns can help in overcoming your fear of success?

- Learning to reinforce yourself for the hard work, effort, and sacrifices you have made to achieve success
- Being able to honestly appraise your level of achievement, success, and accomplishment
- Accepting yourself as being healthy, "together," happy, successful, prosperous, and accomplished
- Not giving yourself any excuses for being unsuccessful
- Giving others in your life permission to give you honest, open, candid feedback when they see you self-destructing or backsliding
- Monitoring your level of commitment and motivation to reach your goals
- Visualizing your life when you are successful
- Giving others credit, recognition, and support for their personal achievements, successes, and accomplishments
- Honest, open, realistic self-talk that encourages you to work your hardest to achieve the goals that you have set for yourself
- Accepting the compliments and recognition of others with an open heart and mind

Steps to overcoming fear of success

Step 1: You first need to identify the fear of success in your life. To do this, answer questions A through J in your journal for each of the following twelve areas:

1. At school
2. On the job
3. With family
4. In marriage
5. In relationships
6. With friends
7. In your career
8. In your emotional life
9. In your hobbies
10. In sports
11. In your physical health
12. In your spiritual life

a. What do I think will happen if I achieve success here?
b. What would success in this area of my life look like?
c. In what ways do I feel undeserving of success here?
d. Who am I afraid of hurting or intimidating if I achieve success here?
e. What do I think is lacking to keep me from sustaining success in this area?
f. What are my biggest concerns about succeeding in this area?
g. Who do I believe is more deserving of the success I have or will achieve here?
h. How motivated am I in the struggle for success in this area?
i. In what ways do I think that once I achieve success here that I will lose focus or direction in other areas of my life?
j. In what ways do I think that I'll be unsatisfied or feel unworthy if I achieve success in this area?

Step 2: Once you have completed step 1, answer the following questions for the same twelve areas:

a. What evidence is there that I have not sustained enough effort to achieve my goals in this area?
b. What are my long-range goals for this area?
c. In what ways do I self-destruct achievement and success here?
d. How much of a problem do I have in making decisions here?

e. In what ways has my motivation been diminished in this area?

f. In what ways have I been an underachiever in this area?

g. Have I ever felt guilt, confusion or anxiety when I did achieve a level of success here?

h. Have I ever feared losing people's attention, sympathy, or concern if I achieved success here?

i. Have I ever chosen just the opposite of what I needed to be successful in this area?

j. Have I ever put myself down for achieving success in this area?

Step 3: After looking at the negative consequences of the fear of success in each areas of life, identify the beliefs that lead you to fear success. Once you identify the beliefs for each area, refute them if they are irrational and replace them with rational beliefs. If your beliefs are negative self-scripts, replace them with positive self-affirming scripts. Use the "I Am" and "I have" lead-ins to each affirmation to assist in this effort.

Step 4: After you have identified your irrational beliefs and replaced them with rational beliefs and self-affirming scripts, identify what new behavior you need to develop in each of the twelve areas. Answer the following questions in your journal:

a. How can I improve the ways in which I reinforce myself?

b. How can I make a more honest appraisal of my accomplishments?

c. How can I accept myself as being successful?

d. How can I eliminate all excuses for being unsuccessful?

e. Who needs to have permission to give me honest feedback when they see me self-destructing?

f. How can I monitor my level of commitment and motivation to succeed?

g. How can I improve the ways I visualize what it will be like when I achieve my goals?

h. How can I improve the ways in which I offer others reinforcement and praise for their individual success and achievements?

i. How can I improve my self-talk to assist me in achieving my goals?

j. How can I learn to accept the compliments and recognition of others for my success?

Step 5: Once you identify the behavior traits you need to develop in your life, make a commitment to accomplish this. If you continue to have a fear of success, however, return to step 1 and begin again.

Please note that this was my number one fear. I had to do more work in this area of my being than any other. I found out that I was afraid of the life to be had if successful and the work it would take. It takes a lot of work, a lot of self-examination, and a lot of honesty about ourselves; but it is worth every bit of pain.

Truly caring for your success and with thanks to Jake Lawson,
From Ken's desk

Happiness

We convince ourselves that life will be better after we get married, have a baby, then another. Then we are frustrated that the kids aren't old enough, and we'll be more content when they are. After that, we're frustrated that we have teenagers to deal with. We will certainly be happy when they are out of that stage.

We tell ourselves that our life will be complete when our spouse gets his or her act together, when we get a nicer car, are able to go on a nice vacation, when we retire.

The truth is, there's no better time to be happy than right now. If not now, when? Your life will always be filled with challenges. It's best to admit this to yourself and decide to be happy anyway.

One of my favorite quotes comes from Alfred D. Souza.

"For a long time, it had seemed to me that life was about to begin, but there was always some obstacle in the way, something to be gotten through first, some unfinished business, time still to be served, a debt to be paid. Then life would begin. At last it dawned on me that these obstacles were my life."

This perspective has helped me to see that there is no way to happiness. Happiness is the way. So treasure every moment that you have. And treasure it more because you shared it with someone special, special enough to spend your time, and remember that time waits for no one.

So stop waiting until you finish school
> until you go back to school
> until you lose ten pounds
> until you gain ten pounds
> until you have kids
> until your kids leave the house
> until you start work
> until you retire
> until you get married
> until you get divorced
> until Friday night
> until Sunday morning
> until you get a new car or home
> until your car or home is paid off
> until spring, until summer
> until fall . . . until winter
> until you are off welfare
> until the first or fifteenth

until your song comes on
until you've had a drink
until you've sobered up
until you die

Until you are born again to decide that there is no better time than right now to be happy.

Look, we all know that fear is our number one enemy. That is what is truly stopping us.

Here are a couple of things you can do to help alleviate fear:

- Creating a concrete, kickass vision of your life—I realized that when I made it visual, I could REALLY see what I chose to create from within. After all, it's an inside-out job, isn't it?
- Surrounding ourselves with inspiration and listening to music that lifts us up. After all, "what you put your attention on grows stronger in your life," right?
- Spending time with powerful mentors. What a difference it made when I met people who'd been through the same stuff I was going through and had made it through to the other side. Not only did it give me hope, but they also taught me the shortcuts and how to avoid the pitfalls that are inevitable as you pursue your passions.

Go now and experience life.

Wishing you all life has to offer,
From Ken's desk

Your Mirror

Having the courage and patience to put out the vibrations of what you desire to be, as opposed to where you are in the present, is the hardest thing you will ever have to do. Keep in mind where you are and who you are in your life right now is based on your past intentions, thoughts, feeling, and actions. But you can change your future by changing your thoughts, feelings, and actions.

Your current level of results is nothing more than the residual outcome of your past thoughts, feelings, and actions. They have nothing to do with what you are capable of or who you are capable of becoming unless you continue to make decisions based on those results. If you do, you will continue to create the same things over and over again in your life.

Here is an interesting way of looking at your life. If you look at your current results, you can see what you have been up to for the past five years or so. What you have been thinking, feeling, and acting upon is reflected in your current results. Look at your body, your bank account, your house, your car, your relationships, your job or lack thereof, and what vibrations you have been offering, because your results are nothing more than a feedback mechanism, a mirror of what you have been thinking, feeling, and acting.

Think about a mirror for a moment. A mirror does not judge; it does not say if something is "good" or "bad," "right" or "wrong." It does not edit or delete. A mirror just reflects back whatever is put in front of it. Do you follow this metaphor?

The universal mirror is exciting because when you get what you desire, you know you are on your game. When you have less than pleasing results, that's just the universal mirror reflecting back to you where you have the opportunity to adjust your thinking, feeling, and actions. Getting upset because you have messed up your life in any area is wasting precious time. The mirror is there to give you a wake-up call. It is saying, "Hey, you're broke. Are you ready to do something about it?"

Wishing you all life has to offer,
From Ken's desk

Hope

I've often heard such lines given to me as "Ah, you're just trying to sell them hope" when referring to the possibilities here and in life, like somehow hope is a bad thing or perhaps I should be selling despair. Duh.

Truth is, hope can be a form of scarcity, which is not good. Any form of scarcity is not good and is usually a sign of error in thinking. With hope, there are those who live in hope and those who produce hope. What does it mean to be a producer of hope? People who produce hope are creators. People who live in hope are those who just wish and wait for things to change.

Hope is essential because without it, life would be a daunting task, a living hell. However, there is a dark side to hope that very few people talk about. The difference is in what we do or don't do with hope.

For most people, hope is characterized by waiting for other people or events to change so that we can be happy or get what we want. In this respect, hope is like the dark side of positive thinking. Positive thinking alone rarely brings about change because it is a passive activity. Hope then becomes a waiting game.

What people fail to understand is that hope is only a small part of the equation for success. Without action, hope leaves you in a negative reinforcing cycle of expectations, disappointment, and stagnation. Hope is then the longing and wishing for things we think we don't have. However, the energy we put into wishing and waiting actually prevents us from receiving what we want.

Hope can be a prison. It is a conditioned belief that there is nothing we can do but sit back and "hope for the best." The dictionary defines hope as "the desire for something to happen while expecting or being confident that it will come true." This is nothing more than a waiting game.

Many people create a dream and then wait for a sign from heaven that they are on the right track. When the sign fails to come, they give up and go off onto some new adventure, again waiting for a sign that this is finally "it." Worse yet, they give up on hope entirely.

We are conditioned to wait. We wait for the bus; we wait in line at the grocery store and the bank. In school, we raised our hands and waited to be called upon, etc. We wait until our parents, teachers, or some other adult tells us that it's OK to do what we want to do. We wait for the weekend (not us, of course ☺) or for our paychecks. We "can't wait" for the Superbowl.

People that are into hope feel powerless. Powerlessness is a conditioned pattern. Why is it that we can read about people who overcame great odds to accomplish some fantastic feat, but we can't manage to get to an appointment on time (or for the sales meeting)? We are powerless because of heavy traffic, weather, kids won't cooperate, or some other excuse. At worse, this powerlessness brings us to sloth. (Sloth is often thought to be laziness but, in fact, is an old English term that means to become so fraught with fear that one becomes frozen, unable to move.)

If we really faced the truth of the situation, we would see that this supposed powerlessness is a clever disguise to keep us resisting what we can do in the moment. Read: procrastination.

We allow hope to become an excuse for inaction. And with all the skills of justification, we stay positive in hope, we tell others of our faith in our future, and yet we are trembling on the inside, knowing that this hope is fading away.

Hope isn't fading away. The time to act is fading away. Opportunity is fading away.

You see, when you become a creator, a person who produces hope, then hope becomes faith and faith becomes expectations (the true meaning of hope). Your hope is real because you gave a reason for hope to live. As a creator, will all things work out? NO. But at least there's hope, right? Real hope. The hope that makes you a ray of sunshine for all because you walk with the confidence of someone who creates, which allows others to see you as their hope.

To have hope is awesome! When you transform from **belief** to **faith** to "**know**," that "I know" attracts others on similar missions, and your job becomes clear. Learn-do-teach, That is the process for success. Learn what you need to know to act. Do until you know enough to teach. Teach enough to master.

Hope is awesome, to be someone else's hope more so.

Be a creator, be a mentor, be . . . hope.

Wishing you all life has to offer,
From Ken's desk

How Not to Go from Success to Failure, Riches to Rags

The riches to rags story is as old as the hills. It happens to corporations, countries, communities, families, and individuals. One day you are up, the next day down. It may be short term or long term. And we have well-established names for these states: broke, poor, bankrupt, and so on. This story is so common that it has been woven into our economics and legal systems. That is not important. What is important is this: why does it happen, what is the real cause, and how does one not get into it? I had to learn this the hard way. Here's hoping you don't.

We are now going to analyze the steps that people unconsciously take to get from success into failure. As we do so, you will see how simple they really are, and at first, you may be tempted to dismiss this analysis, as it does appear to be very simple. But consider what you read here as a whole, and you will see the mechanics better once you take it all in.

All things in our lives arise from our thoughts. It therefore serves us well to observe the thought pattern that leads to failure. It starts off as an unrecognizable creep, unless you are aware of its mechanics, and swells into a mental panic that seems to take over your life. We now have scientific, psychological, and spiritual evidence that shows us that we become what we think about, believingly. Our thoughts create our next experience, our next moment. Quantum physicists have proven beyond a doubt that the material world is fully dependent on its observers. They have proven that all matter is made of energy, and this energy "arranges" itself into the matter we see based on the expectations of the observer. In other words, it is our intentions, attention, and observations that "collapse" this energy into matter. This is not scientific speculation any more. Nobel-Prize-winning scientists have proven this without a shred of doubt. All our religions, all of them, tell us that what we believe we become.

If you analyze any time you have ever personally gone down the road to some sort of "failure" in your finances, relationships, or health, you will notice that the road always had a particular chain reaction. Stop reading now and think of a particular instance when you did go through some sort of "failure" in the past. Do you have one in mind? OK, now trace its beginning to its end, and you will see that it had the following trend:

Stage 1: First, you were OK before the "failure" started to happen. You did not even have your attention to the possibility of this failure happening. It may be something that may have popped in your mind before, but you did not particularly have it in your constant attention at all.

Stage 2: Then something made you start paying attention to the possibility of failure, of a "bad thing" happening. For example, assuming it is a marketing failure or a business failure, you may have seen a newspaper article saying something about the economy going into recession, or you may have missed a payment on a bill, or a particular bit of marketing you put out did not return the amount of results you initially "hoped" for, not expected, but hoped.

Stage 3: You observed this one instance of "failure" or "bad news," and you somehow got hooked onto it. Something in your mind said, "Wow, this is bad. I am afraid of it. I hope it doesn't become worse." Or something to that effect. At this point, it is still a minor idea in your mind. But notice here what happened. You saw something out there in the world. You looked at the world, asking "What is your truth?" You looked at the world for evidence of truth. Think about that for a second. People are used to looking at the world to get their definition of truth, and whatever they see out there, they accept it as truth. OK, so you looked outside, and you saw this small failure. You accepted it as a truth and a possibility that may happen to you. You took it in. This is where the downhill trip all starts. Remember, the world becomes from our thoughts, our beliefs. That is why positive thinking works, why faith works, and so on. The external world is a reflection of our internal state. When you change, it changes. We now have solid scientific evidence of this fact.

Stage 4: The world does not know who you are. It only reflects upon who you are. Failure now starts to pick up speed when you look more and more upon the world, asking "Who am I? What is my truth?," as you always do unconsciously, and then accept whatever it says. So now the small failure you observed and accepted as truth sets off some more thoughts of failure possibilities. So you think, *Gee, I hope this next bit of marketing I do doesn't fail* and so on. But what are you doing then?

You are declaring internally that you have no control, that you are under the mercy of little things, and you are on the side of failure, hoping to succeed. So you do the marketing, and because the world reflects you, it most likely doesn't work out as you hoped. You are always telling the world who you are, and it is always exactly reflecting that. If you come from a standpoint of failure, it will prove you right and vice versa. We are the sum total of our thoughts and so is each of our worldly experiences.

Stage 5: You observe this new failure, and because now there is more failure, you go into panic. You believe it more and think more and more that you will really mess up. And because you think of it so often, with so much worry, the failures in your world happen more and more. And you look upon them and accept them more and more. This chain reaction goes until your mind is out of control, in a panic, and you

KEN GRIFFITH

feel as if you are in a daydream, a web of thoughts and emotions all tangled up. But do you see how you got there and how easy it is to get out?

The world does not know who you are; it only manifests what you are. Do you see this little vicious cycle? You are the cause; therefore, you are the evidence. But when you believe you are not, you look upon the effect and let it determine your cause. And because it came from your cause, it will mirror what you feared was true, and you will think it is true, so you will cause even more harm unknowingly, and the cycle continues.

This is what will free you: do the opposite. Instead of accepting the "failure" you see in front of you as truth, simply choose not to accept it. Remember, it is only there because you brought it there at some level. You may not have been conscious and aware that you were doing it. It cannot be without you empowering it to be. It is now merely asking you, "What next, boss?" And whatever you say, it will do. Yet you ask it what the truth is and accept its answer as truth. Its answer is the answer that you have given to it. By your acceptance and reaction to it, you empower it even more. And as you react, it moves to match your reaction. And because it moves and you observe the change as having matched what you feared, you accept the change as truth and just for you. Simply stop this. You are the truth of your world. You never have to accept external truths. You have a choice.

Now that you know that our world patterns itself on our thoughts and beliefs; you can take back the power you gave away to your fears. At first, it may be hard to change the way t\you think, from a partly conscious way to a fully conscious and directed way, ignoring any "truth and evidence" offered to you by the physical world. But know it works, and you can do it, and with practice, it will soon become normal to you and everything will flow. Haven't you ever noticed how the most successful people today all did what everybody said was "impossible"? They stood against the "evidence" and declared their own truth, and the universe moved with them. It cannot fail to move. If you are in a tight spot, remember that this spot is not the truth. It is just a reflection of what you hold to be true in your mind and heart. Free your mind and heart, holding them free no matter what, and your external will miraculously change. Cause and effect are instantaneous; time only coming between them to the extent of your clarity and certainty!

Wishing you all life has to offer,
From Ken's desk

How One Man Risked Everything and Made It Big

This inspirational story will show you how one individual achieved his dreams against all odds. The result: he is a successful businessman making much more than he ever thought possible!

Tony Lee always dreamed of owning his own business and sending his kids to college. Today, he's co-owner of Ring Masters, a company that makes engine rings for industrial use, and his daughter is heading to college next fall. Tony is hoping she'll be the first college graduate in the family.

Tony has achieved some of the biggest goals he set out for himself and his family, which are impressive, given he grew up in a low-income neighborhood with limited opportunities and never went to college. But what's even more inspiring is Tony Lee's journey to get there.

After leaving the army in 1997, and a short stint at American Steel, Tony took the only decent job he could find. Tony accepted a janitorial job at an Eaton Corp. factory in Massillon, Ohio, in the heart of the rust belt. Like a lot of U.S. manufacturing centers, Massillon has suffered from closed factories and thousands of lost jobs. Tony was grateful for the opportunity and made the most of it, rising from janitor to foreman in four years.

But Tony was just getting started.

In 2002, Eaton started shutting down divisions of the factory, one by one. Soon, over one thousand workers were down to just thirty-five in Tony's division, which was slated to be closed at the end of 2002.

But Tony refused to let the factory die. He spent hours at night in the local public library studying. Despite never going to college, much less business school, Tony wrote a business plan detailing how his factory could survive and prosper.

Against all odds, he convinced a group of investors to buy the factory and keep it running. Members of the investor group and Tony's coworkers all say they were inspired by Tony's leadership, passion for the business, and drive to keep it alive. Everyone, it seemed, was rooting for Tony to succeed.

But there was one big catch: The investors wanted Tony to have some "skin in the game," so he had to raise $25,000 to purchase a stake in the factory.

For Tony, this was just one more obstacle to overcome. After taking

KEN GRIFFITH

a second mortgage on his house, selling his motorcycle, and literally scrounging for loose change, Tony had the money and was in on the deal. Actually, he was "all in." Failure was not an option for Tony.

Now, nine years later, Ring Masters *is a thriving business with over $4 million in annual sales. From fifteen workers at the start, the company now has over twenty employees, a growing list of clients, and plans for further expansion.*

Tony says he's recouped his $25,000 investment "several times over" and is now a co-owner of a growing business. For anyone who's ever thought "I can run the company better than my boss," Tony Lee is an inspiration. And he's still inspiring his coworkers and employees by working side-by-side with them on the factory floor. Tony says he "leads by example" and would never ask an employee to do a job he wasn't willing to do.

There is a law in the universe that says if one person can do it, anyone can. Are you will to climb mountains or go through walls to create the YOU that you wanted to be? Is failing not an option for you? Are you all in? Remember, the way to guarantee failure of plan A is to have a plan B, unless plan B is the execution of plan A.

Ego is the biggest barrier to income. Are you letting your ego stop you from getting what you want, or do you have that I-don't-give-a-rip-who-thinks-what-of-me-I'm-going-for-it" attitude? Do you have the maturity to say now is my ,time and nothing will get in the way?

There are lots of Tony stories out there. Will one of them be of you?

Wishing you all life has to offer,
From Ken's desk

How to Harness Your Point of Attraction

"When you can embrace all of life, not holding onto anything beyond it's time and not avoiding it once its time has come, you will know the meaning of Freedom."—Unknown

The dictionary defines freedom as "the quality or state of being free; the absence of necessity, coercion, or constraint in choice or action; liberation from slavery or restraint or from the power of another."

How would you define freedom for yourself? It strikes me that much of what we need is a how-to to set yourself free—free from your stories, free from your past, free from "shoulds" (I should have . . . [some people are full of "should" ☺]), free from need.

You cannot control the circumstances or people around you, but you can always choose how you react to them. Much of what is difficult about difficult situations is not the situation itself but how you react to it. Have you ever made a situation worse by overreacting? What if you had kept from getting knocked off balance by what was happening? Would that have changed anything?

The goal of deliberate creation is to be able to consciously set your point of attraction. That means that how you feel is not dependent upon external circumstances. It is not dependent upon your mate doing the dishes or your child picking up his room or your friend calling you or who wins the election. Your point of attraction is determined solely by you, by what you believe, think, expect, and feel. No one and nothing else is ever to blame, ever. No one makes you unhappy. You do that. No one can make you happy. Only you can do that. It's your choice, always.

When you can stay centered and balanced no matter what is going on around you, when you can consciously choose instead of letting circumstance dictate how you feel, and when you choose to respond and not to react, then you know how to consciously create your life.

I think the quote above sums it up quite eloquently. If we are truly letting all of life in, without judgment, without labels, embracing all of it, not clutching at what is no longer ours nor pushing away what is, only then we truly are free.

We must remember to question everything and rule out nothing, and to be willing to suspend everything you know. You cannot discover new things until you stop telling those new things what you think they should be. Let them tell you what they really are!

Wishing you all life has to offer,
From Ken's desk

KEN GRIFFITH

Sales Professionals

Sales professionals have a never-ending thirst for ways to improve their game. They desire to be the best, and they desire the best from life. They are willing to go through whatever it takes to master their life and often come against walls. Some of these walls are short in height, and some seem too high to scale. Sales professionals know that walls are not only there to stop them from getting their dreams but are also there to see how much they want their dreams. Will they go over, under, and through the walls?

It is critical to the sales professional that they increase their value a hundredfold, if not a thousand fold. They know that their reach must surpass their grasp, and they know that they must be under constant construction. They, more than any, know they must go through failure after failure, self-examination after self-examination, and simply get up one more time than they fell.

Look at it this way. As a seed is planted in the darkness of the earth, so too are your failures, your despair, your ignorance, and your inabilities are in the darkness in which you are planted so that you may ripen. As clay, touched by the genius of man, becomes pottery or a castle, its value has risen a hundredfold. Can it not also be that your value should increase a hundredfold? Aren't you more than a lump of clay?

Look, a wheat seed has three options applied to it. It can be put in storage and eventually fed to the pigs, it can be ground to flour to make bread, or it can be planted in the earth to produce a new head from which a thousand more grains will be produced.

You too have three options, much like the grain of wheat. You can sit waiting for something to happen, ultimately failing life and being fed to swine. You can be shaped by others to perform a job in the support of others. Or you can create your own life, a hundredfold of your current self. The difference between the grain of wheat and you is that you get to choose which course you take.

Increase your value and increase it at least one hundredfold. Remember, it is your choice! Keep learning, keep growing, keep going through the walls; and remember, look to what you are going too, not to what you are going through.

Wishing you all life has to offer,
From Ken's desk

Do You Enjoy It?

I have a question for you today. Ready?

When you achieve a goal or manifest something you desire, do you enjoy it?

Or do you just check it off your mental list of things you want to achieve and then move onto the next thing?

Obviously, it is important that you take the time to enjoy what you manifest and create in your life. It's important because, cliché as it may sound, life is a journey, NOT a destination.

But there's another reason it is so important for you to take the time to recognize and relish what you manifest and create, and that is because when you do, you grow your belief sets and gain momentum toward everything else you desire!

I want you to take five minutes today to do something that will significantly increase your power as a master of manifestation (remember, you created your world). I want you to write down the things that you have created and manifested in your life that you haven't taken the time to really appreciate and celebrate!

As for commission salespeople, this is critical. When you make a sale, you manifest something you desire. You must celebrate each win, no matter the size. Take yourself out if that's all you can afford, but celebrate.

Remember, though, your life is bigger than what you do Monday to Friday. You have many more achievements to celebrate. So write them down and take a minute to expand your belief sets and increase your momentum! Life mastery will be yours.

Wishing you all life has to offer,

From Ken's desk

Input and Output

How many times have you heard someone say that it's all about energy? Well, I'm going to agree with that. It really is all about energy. Everything is energy. But if you are still struggling with keeping your energy positive and attracting what you want, then there is more you need to know.

Here's the deal: what most people don't realize is that there are two powerful aspects of energy that must be in agreement for you to manifest what you want in life (or better).

If you are struggling in any way, these two aspects are either misaligned, or they are aligned toward what you don't want, instead of what you do want.

Can you see why this is important for us to talk about today?

That's why I wrote this issue and focused it on helping you get your input and output aligned toward what you desire—so that the positive manifestation can begin!

When it comes to successfully manifesting the life you desire, your input MUST match your output and vice versa, or else you are going to run into some serious roadblocks that include (but are certainly not limited to):

Procrastination
Feeling Stuck
Banging Your Head against a Wall (proverbially speaking, that is)
Hitting a Success Plateau
Indecision
Doubt
Worry
Frustration
Inaction
Overanalysis

Sound familiar? And the list goes on and on.

Now, let me be clear. Everything on the list I just gave you is normal and to be expected at times, but what I want to point out to you today is that when you are experiencing any of these things, that is a great indicator, or clue, that your input and output aren't matching.

Let me define what I mean by **input:** Input is anything that comes to you in any way, shape, or form that colors what you experience, view, and believe about yourself, the world, other people, animals, God, cars, umbrellas . . . ANYTHING!

The Most Common Forms of Input Are:
Friends and Family
Media—Visual, Auditory, and Written
Strangers—Anyone you cross paths with but don't know or anyone in the public eye
Animals
Subconscious Beliefs
Conscious (Chosen) Beliefs

Let me define what I mean by **output:** Put very simply, output is the energy you give out.

Here are the most common ways that you output:

Conversations
Energy—what mood you are in
Internal Thoughts/Self-Talk
Nonverbal Interaction

Here is why it is so important that your input and output match. When they match, you get whatever the match creates.

So if your input and your output are both primarily negative and full of negative expectation, then most of what you get in your life will match that negative energy and expectation.

On the other hand, if your input and output are both primarily positive and full of positive expectation, then most of what you get in your life will match that positive energy and expectation.

And when your input and output don't match, you get a whole bunch of crossed wires and mixed signals, feelings, and contradictory beliefs.

In other words, you get the list I gave you earlier: procrastination, feeling stuck, banging your head against a wall, hitting a success plateau, indecision, doubt, worry, frustration, inaction, and overanalysis.

Obviously, if you want to get positive results in your life, you have to make sure that your input (what you take in) is primarily positive and also that your output (what you give out) is primarily positive, and you have to be diligent about it.

How do you make sure your *input* is primarily positive?

The first step is awareness, so start by taking a good and honest look at your current inputs with this two-step process.

KEN GRIFFITH

1. Assess each input area (from the list below) and write down the most influential factors/people in each area:

> Friends and family
> Media—visual, auditory, and written
> Strangers
> Subconscious beliefs
> Conscious (Chosen) Beliefs . . .

2. Write down if each influence is primarily positive or negative.

I'm not telling you to cut everyone and everything out of your life that you discover is a negative output, but awareness makes for amazing change, and you can use that awareness to shift the energy of that output. There may be some people or situations that you choose to limit, but we all have to deal with negative input at times (family), so the power is in how you deal with it and how you can set up your interactions to be more positive in the future.

3. For the next seven to ten days, pay attention to all of the input that you have in your life and pay attention to the input you actively seek out.

How do you make sure your *output* is primarily positive?

Again, the first step is awareness, so start by taking a good and honest look at your current output with this two-step process.

1. For the next seven to ten days, pay attention to all of the output that you give off in your life.

Conversations: Do you gossip a lot or talk about limitations a lot, or do you focus on positive things that you are doing?

Energy: What mood are you in? What energy do you consistently put out there? When someone asks you how you are, what do you say? What do you think? When is your energy most positive? When does it shift to negative? How are you when you are driving, waiting in line (not good for me ☺), etc.?

Internal thoughts/self-talk: Do you jump to negative or positive conclusions? Do you believe in the possible or the impossible most of the time?

Nonverbal interaction: What is the subtle interaction you consistently have with other people, animals, nature, etc.? Are you closed or open? Pay special attention to your physicality with this.

2. Watch your input and your output. Make sure they match and make sure they

match what you want to attract. If they don't, ask yourself what you can do to change your input to help alter your output.

Get into this. Make it fun! Don't judge yourself when you become aware of a negative input or output. Instead, get excited, because with that awareness comes the opportunity to shift to positive input or output.

Remember, this takes time! Take it one input at a time and one output at a time. Don't try to do it all at once. That doesn't work with anything!

Wishing you all life has to offer,
From Ken's desk

Inspired Action

"When was the last time you followed an instinct that went against common sense?"

Seems like most of my life doesn't make sense to other people . . . just to me.

1. When in your life have you had a strong instinct to do something that may have seemed off topic, disconnected, or out of left field, but you did it, and when you did it brought you success in a way that you never would have imagined?

2. When in your life have you ever been faced with a situation, relationship, or opportunity that seemed like exactly what you had been looking for BUT in the pit of your stomach you knew it wasn't? And even though you had absolutely no rational justification to feel this way, and other people thought you were crazy, you decided to walk away; and it turned out to be the best decision you could have made.

It is the difference between forced action and inspired action:

The struggle between forced and inspired action most often shows up when we want something in our lives to be different. Most people look at the things they are dissatisfied with and do one of two things:

1. Ignore it (bad idea)
2. Try to FORCE it to change by taking action (EVEN WORSE idea)

Forced action is anytime you are trying to force something to change or "think" your way out of something. Forced action tends to stem from fear, doubt, and worry.

Inspired action is when you feel a strong instinct to do something. Inspired action stems from openness and trust.

Here are the tricky things about inspired action:

- Inspired action doesn't always seem completely practical.
- Inspired action will often make you push your comfort zone.

Imagine taking one step (just one) of inspired action every single day.

How different will your life be a year from now?

What about a month from now?

Or even by the end of the day?

Are you getting excited yet?

Great! Here's a trick to help you.

Every day, look at your current primary goal (target) and ask yourself this one question:

'What one step can I take today, which pushes my comfort zone, I KNOW will take me one step closer to (fill in your goal here)?'

Now here's the key to this trick.

1. It has to be one step and one step ONLY of inspired action. (Calling Bob to talk about our joint venture is one step. Getting a new Web site up is multiple steps.)
2. You HAVE TO TAKE THE INSPIRED ACTION!

The cool part is that most of the time, the step of inspired action will take less than an hour and will move you forward more than ten hours of JUST ANY ACTION.

Seriously, one inspired-action phone call will normally change your life faster than ten hours of organizing your office.

Make Sure It's Inspired Action.

I know what it's like to wonder if the action you are going to take is inspired or forced. Sometimes it is hard to tell the difference. Let me help!

As I said before, forced action can keep you busy and running in circles every day for the rest of your life, while inspired action doesn't eat up all of your time and definitively moves you toward your goals.

Knowing the difference between regular action and inspired action will eventually become a "gut instinct" for you, and once you tap into your intuition, the LOA will work for you in ways you never imagined.

BUT chances are good that right now you are like most people; and much, if not most, of the action you take is probably inspired by fear. So to help you get in touch with the difference between forced action and inspired action, I have a tool for you.

There is one question you can ask yourself to discover if your instinct is guiding you out of fear or inspiration.

Before you take *any* action, ask yourself this question:

"Will doing this move me toward my goal of _____, away from my goal of _____, or will it keep me running in place?"

IT'S IMPORTANT to name the goal SPECIFICALLY. If you are general and don't get specific, this won't be as effective.

If your honest answer is that it will move you toward your goal, great, GO FOR IT!

But if it will move you away from your goal OR keep you running in place, then ask yourself this question:

'What small action can I take RIGHT NOW to move me toward my goal of _____?"

When an answer pops into your head, ask yourself the first question again just to make sure you aren't fooling yourself.

Then GO TAKE THE INSPIRED ACTION!

Wishing you all life has to offer,
From Ken's desk

Is Your Past Bigger than Your Future?

What do all of the following statements have in common?

- *Ever notice as soon as you get in the express line at the grocery store, the line slows down?*
- *When I was growing up, my mother was very distant, and since then, I have had a hard time relating to women.*
- *Just when I was getting ahead, my ex-wife's lawyer came after me for the unpaid child support.*
- *I'd like to have more money, but I have so many financial problems I will never get out of debt.*
- *I enjoy personal growth, but my husband thinks all that stuff is nonsense and doesn't like me to participate in it.*
- *I'd like to open a business of my own, but my wife thinks it is too risky, so I guess I had better stay at this secure and boring job I dislike going to every day.*

What all these statements have in common is the nature of the person making the statement. As diverse as all of these statements are and as diverse as the people who make them appear to be, each statement reflects the same type of individual, a person with low self-worth and a predisposition toward negative expectations.

The biggest common denominator all these people share is that they are desperately holding on to being a victim. They live at the victim level of awareness. They almost celebrate the fact that they are victimized. Their "stories" are always about their past and the latest problems and tragedies that have befallen them. Of course, they are not really victims but volunteers. They have made a choice—usually unconscious—to remain a victim. Here's some news for you. No one can roll over you unless you give them permission.

You can't be a victim and be a success in life. You can be one or the other, but not both at the same time. This is no different than excuses. You can have excuses or you can have what you want, but you can't have both. If you want to feel like a victim and that's what you affirm to the people around you, you will continue to create a self-fulfilling prophecy. You will repel love, defer happiness, attract illness or injuries, and sabotage any financial or business success. The problem is you tell your story so well to everyone around you that you end up following your own script.

The good news is that remaining a victim is a choice. If the above describes you, then ask yourself this question. "Is remaining a victim moving me TOWARD or AWAY from what I want?" If it is moving you away, then you are paying a very high price to hold on to your victimhood. Now is the time to release it and move up to a higher level of awareness. It's just a decision . . . really.

If your future looks bigger than you past—or you want it to be—then it is always time to move toward what you want, now!

Wishing you all life has to offer,
From Ken's desk

Judging

We talk a lot about developing compassion, both for yourself and for others. We say that when you understand why someone behaves the way they do, then you are more able to feel compassion instead of judgment toward them.

Typically, when we judge someone, we are making a whole host of assumptions. Take a simple judgment: "She should be on time." Is that true?

Do you know:

- If something unavoidable occurred to prevent her from being on time?
- What lessons she is learning in her life by being late?
- If being on time is an important standard for her?
- If her inner guidance was keeping her from a certain intersection at a certain time?

The bottom line is that you don't know. You never really know what someone else's path in life involves. Therefore, the answer is always, "No, it's not true." It's just your opinion.

Having compassion does not mean that you have to condone someone's hurtful behavior, but it does mean that you don't judge the person. Now, I imagine that some of you are thinking, "What about criminals?" I'm willing to bet that the most heinous crimes are committed by people who had heinous things done to them as children. Does that excuse or justify their behavior? Definitely not. But if you knew their story, you would feel more compassion for them. We see this in our work in the judicial system, where judges pass judgment on the action of an individual, while remaining compassionate to the person.

Our day-to-day judgments are typically not of that magnitude. They are mostly about things that we believe other people should be doing based on our own values, standards, wishes, or needs. So the next time you find yourself judging someone, take the judgmental thought and ask yourself, "Is that true?" Can you know with absolute certainty that it is true? If you're not in that other person's skin, the answer has to be, "No, it's not true."

Wishing you all life has to offer,
From Ken's desk

A 1 Percent Junkie

As you may know, I am a complete "junkie" when it comes to advancement or self-improvement. "Junkie" might not be the right word, though you know what I mean.

Here's a quick tip I've been teaching for a decade.

Never go to bed the same person you were when you woke up. Let me say that again. Never go to bed the same person you were when you woke up.

Every day you must make a COMMITMENT to grow at least 1 percent a day. Not 10 percent or even 50 percent a day. Heck, I don't know how to do that either, but I do know how to grow 1 percent per day.

My goals: take two or three actions per day. Complete one thing a day. Take 1 percent action on my fitness and health goals each day. Drink one more glass of water than I usually do.

These are tiny, little habits that if you take each day will transform your life in a week. Yes, that fast. One of my favorite daily habits is reading. Every day I read something that can help me personally and professionally. I can take one or two ideas from any book and apply them immediately into my life. Can you tell I do this?

One percent a day, that's it.

Thoughts

"You want power to succeed; you want power to do and to dare; you want power to deal with others; you strive for power to rise above the commonplaces of life—to be a leader. For instinctive in every person is a great natural desire for supremacy."

"The individual determines his own position in life, according to the amount of intelligent effort exerted. It is for this reason, that people will never be equal, because there are those—the majority—who will not work to acquire this inner power."—Unknown

Wishing you all life has to offer,
From Ken's desk 🗿

Kenisms

Ignorance on fire beats *knowledge on ice* every day.

The people that are in your past didn't make it into your future for a good reason.

The beatings will continue until moral picks up.

We have become a society that knows the cost of everything and the value of nothing.

It is always too soon to quit.

Trading short-term gain for long-term pain is a lousy trade-off.

I have met many people who were educated way past their intelligence.

Attach value to failure. It takes the fear out of it.

Don't let excuses rule your life. When you compromise, you lose a bit of yourself.

If you want to change something in your life, you are going to have to change something in your life.

You are not your circumstances; your circumstances are you. When you change, you change your circumstances.

You are like an iceberg. The 10 percent above the water—visible—is your reputation. The other 90 percent is your character, guided by your integrity.

You are not in charge of your success. Your habits are in charge of your success. The good news is that you are in charge of your habits.

Middle-class people plan to be comfortable. Comfortable will not get you rich, but rich will make you comfortable.

Don't just set goals; strive, drive, and kill for them.

The solution to you and all your life problems are your dreams.

KEN GRIFFITH

The obstinate man does not hold opinions; they hold him.

Show me a good loser, and I'll show you a loser.

Leaders adapt and embrace change.

Leaders are the thermostat, not the thermometer.

Leaders always know it will work out. It is only a matter of when.

Want everyone, need no one.

How much worrying do you have to do to fix something?

If you want to avoid arguments over leaving the toilet seat up all the time, use the sink.

If you have a bad cough, take a large dose of laxatives. You'll be afraid to cough.

To avoid cutting yourself while cutting vegetables, get someone else to hold them.

If you want to train yourself to get up at the first time the alarm goes off, put a mouse trap on the top of the alarm.

If you can't fix it with a hammer, it is an electrical problem.

Always remember, everyone seems normal until you get to know them.

Perhaps the best wedding vow is in the promise to not ruin another woman.

Every day you should work so hard that you come out sweating like Mike Tyson at a spelling bee.

Now get back to work!

Salespeople have the same blood type . . . B+ (positive).

Truism
You have worked your whole life to get to the point where you will have to work the rest of your life.

Jobs I once had include:
Satellite dishwasher
Silhouette for "men at work" signs
Test pilot for unmanned flights
Chairman for the local Ouija board
Before model for a fitness magazine
Obituary humorist
And I once was used to dub Sylvester Stallone movies into English.

More:
I never forget a face, but in this case, I will make an exception.
I used to think I was indecisive, but now I'm not too sure.
Drawing on my fine command of the language, I said nothing.
I like long walks, especially when they are taken by people who annoy me.
Some cause happiness wherever they go; others, whenever they go.
Facts are meaningless. You can use facts to prove anything that's remotely true!

How to fire someone:
"I have no idea how we as an organization would ever get along without you, but starting Monday we are going to try."

From Ken's desk

Knee jerk reactions

At this point, you are probably becoming aware of your typical knee jerk reactions. Those automatic, habitual ways you have of reacting to certain situations. For example, someone hurts you and you clam up and withdraw from them, or your friend is late to meet you and you send her waves of seething resentment when she arrives, or your mate fails to do what he said he would do so you pepper him/her with accusatory questions.

What is your predominant knee jerk reaction? What type of situation sets it off? Can you feel it coming? Can you catch yourself before you react? No matter how long you have had the pattern of reacting the way you do, know that it is a habit and habits can be broken. As you have heard repeatedly, awareness is the first step. Choice is the second step. Once you are aware of what you do, choose to do something different.

Let's take the above examples and choose a different response.

1. Someone says something that hurts you, but instead of clamming up and withdrawing, you let them know you are bothered by what they said. Take responsibility for your reaction and don't blame them. Instead of "You made me feel bad," choose "I felt bad when you said I look like a stork when I dance."
2. Your friend is late for your meeting, but instead of sending eye daggers, you tell her that being on time is a high value to you and ask that if she is going to be late, to please call you, OR if you know your friend is consistently late, be late too (*tough one for me*)!.
3. Your mate fails to stop for groceries on the way home, but instead of questioning his memory and his commitment to you, ask if there is a reason why he was unable to keep his promise. Ask if he is still willing to go get the groceries. React with a smile instead of an accusation and have fun watching his reaction!

In other words, be unpredictable! Be lighter and more playful. Choose a different response. Just make sure the other person is sitting down when you do! ☺

Wishing you all life has to offer,
From Ken's desk

Laughter

"Laughter is an instant vacation!"—Milton Berle

When was the last time you laughed? I'm not talking about a chuckle or a smirk. I'm talking about a good, hard belly laugh. Remember the last time you laughed until you cried? Doesn't just the memory of that feel good?

I read some statistics that said children laugh three hundred times a day, adults only fifteen. Another said children laugh 146 times a day and adults only 4. Whatever the actual numbers are, it's clear that we, as adults, are not having much fun! And I'm willing to bet that many adults aren't making the statistical average these days—even as low as it is—especially if they listen to the news and get caught up in negative conversations, of which there are plenty to be had if you succumb.

Laughter is good for the soul and the body. Science tells us that laughing has many health benefits, among them the release of endorphins and decreased blood pressure and stress hormones (70 percent of diseases are stress-related . . . dis-ease). Laughter truly is the best medicine.

But laughing is not something you should do because it's good for you. It's something you should do because it feels good. Actually, it feels great and it provides an instant connection to the flow. I know that a rich mind strategy can seem quite serious at times, but recognize that you are to be light about your life. Don't take it so seriously. Remember, our best affirmation is . . . **I AM wealth, I AM abundance, I AM joy.** JOY . . . a key ingredient. You can almost always find humor in a situation if you look for it.

What makes you laugh? Rent it, watch it, read it. Who makes you laugh? Call him, meet her for lunch, play with your kids or your pets. Lighten up. Feeling better is just a belly laugh away!

Wishing you all life has to offer,
From Ken's desk

Principles of leadership

The goal of the leader is not to draw a following that results in a crowd. The goal is to develop leaders who become a movement.

Remember, the most expensive workers in a company are not the highest paid. The most expensive workers are the people who are unproductive.

A leader must be the thermostat, not the thermometer. Water boils at 100°C/212°F, but at 99°C/211°F, it's just hot water. The leader must turn it up a notch.

Use the 101 principle. Find the one thing that you believe is the potential leader's best asset and then give 100 percent encouragement in that area. Remember, people will not care how much the leader knows until they know how much their leader cares. Care about **their** needs, desires, and dreams.

Michelangelo said of David, "The sculpture had always existed within the stone." He had simply chiseled away the rock around it. Do that for those you lead, knowing inside is a leader looking to grow.

Here is a test

As a leader, are you committed to personal growth?

Do you have a game plan for personal growth? Yes. No.

Are you the leader of that plan? Yes. No.

Are you willing to change to keep growing even if it means giving up your current position, if you are not experiencing growth? Yes. No.

Is your life an example for others to follow? Yes. No.

Are you willing to pay the price to become a great leader? Yes. No.

A *no* on any of these questions should cause a leader to examine his plan and commitment to personal growth. A lack of commitment on the part of a leader makes it difficult for potential leaders around him to be developed. If you as a leader have not made this commitment, your future is limited, and you will never become a great leader. Now is the time to change!

Wishing you all life has to offer,

From Ken's desk

Letting it go

The concepts of faith and surrender and letting go are all essential to manifesting your desires, and yet our rational (conscious) minds are constantly fighting for us to do just the opposite.

So what do we do? How do we handle it when we know what we need to do, but somehow we just won't do it? I want to give you some specific tools you can start using right now to harness the power (and art) of letting go!

I can't even begin to express how important this is. Make sure you read it all the way through, and when you do, you can start to see instant manifestations! Letting go is not only often thought to be a release of weighted stress but is also for simply allowing your emotions to be free; whatever your reason, this might help. Let it go.

The concept seems so simple—just let it go and trust the universe/God—right? Sure, simple in concept, but then our emotions kick in and the idea of "letting it go" gets thrown out the window.

Why do we struggle to "let it go"? The plain and simple answer is that even though we want to trust the universe/God, we feel much more likely to achieve what we desire if we stay in the driver's seat. It is human instinct to clutch and hold and control. When we operate from the conscious mind, we operate from the knowledge of "what is true" or "realistic" in our physical world. But you already know that the conscious mind is just the tip of the iceberg, and "what is true" in our physical world is only what seems to be true. Similar to "realistic," we made them both up.

When we are looking to our conscious mind to define reality, trust in the universe/God is a tough thing—trust and faith and letting go all rely on our ability to in our believe that despite what may seem true in our external world, there is so much going on in the "unseen" nonphysical world that can bring anything into fruition.

What if this was true?

To start to tap into that belief, I want you to ask yourself, "What if my subconscious mind and the universe/God know EXACTLY how to bring about anything I desire, even if my conscious mind has no idea how?"

Seriously, what if that is true?

Now, I want you to suspend your disbelief for just a second here and answer this question. "If it is true that my subconscious mind and the universe/God know EXACTLY how to bring about anything I desire, am I free to let go how it is going to happen?"

I guarantee that if you knew that your subconscious and universe/God had it all

KEN GRIFFITH

taken care of, you would have no problem letting go. You would willingly surrender because you would KNOW that you were going to be taken care of.

Now, what if this is true?

What if you realized that every time you stop trusting and start trying to figure out "how" and control the outcome, you actually set your subconscious mind back in its job of manifesting everything you desire? Would you get out of the way then?

Of course, you would! If you knew this with certainty, you would make it your job to get out of the way of your subconscious.

Here are the three truths of manifesting:

1. Your subconscious mind DOES know exactly how to bring you everything you desire.
2. Your subconscious mind knows how to access universal energy and manifest anything.
3. Anytime you "hold on," "force it," or "try to figure out how," you get in the way of the process.

How do I know? I take a look at my personal history, and that's exactly what I want you to do to start to harness the power of letting go in your life too!

There are two great ways to tap into your history for this:

1. Think of a time in your life when you wanted something and did let go how it was going to happen (this often happens when we are too busy or are too focused on something else), and then it showed up in your life without you ever trying to "make it happen."
2. Think of a time in your life when you really wanted (or felt you needed) something and you tried to do everything to make it happen, and then finally out of fatigue or frustration, you just "gave up trying," and then it showed up in your life.

Once you have given yourself some proof from your past, letting go becomes easier and makes much more sense to your rational mind. For the next week, I want you to live "as if" it is true that your subconscious mind knows exactly how to bring you what you desire. Here's how.

Anytime you find yourself trying to figure out how you can "make" something happen, I want you to stop and say this to your subconscious mind:

"Subconscious (brain), I know you know EXACTLY how to bring me all of the right people, opportunities, and situations to bring about [NAME YOUR DESIRE HERE] or better in my life, and I know that my job is to pay attention to the people and opportunities and

situations that show up and listen to your guidance so that the inspired action I can take to assist you becomes clear."

Try it. You will be amazed at all of the amazing things that start to show up in your life!

Wishing you all life has to offer,
From Ken's desk

Your Thoughts into Physical Reality

Life, the Source, uses your thoughts as the instructions by which to create your reality in the material world. Life expresses your thoughts into physical reality. To express is to make known, to state, to articulate, to communicate, to convey. The force of life makes known your thoughts to yourself and everyone else by forming them into experiences and objects that can be experienced here in the physical world. You experience your own thoughts firsthand, your images of your mind, so that you may know which ones are suitable and which ones are not. That is how you know yourself, that is how you experience yourself, and that is how you grow. This world is designed to enable you to experience your Self. It is designed to enable you to experience an idea and its effects and consequences.

To the extent that your thoughts are not conscious, deliberate, and focused in any topic of life, you will be affected by the outcome of the thoughts of other people. And to the extent that your thoughts are clear, focused, and noncontradictory, your results will be sped up. A few people are able to perform what many people would call miracles simply by thinking only one way and strongly about a thing. The idea that the outcome of their intention may not happen as they wish it to happen does not even occur to them for a split moment.

You are never denied answers to your questions. Whatever questions you ask believingly and earnestly will be answered exactly, no more and no less. If you earnestly and believingly seek and ask how to earn one million dollars, the universe will conspire to bring you the knowledge, tools, people, and events to give you that answer. If you ask how to earn a billion dollars, you will also get answers worthy of that amount. Einstein was not born a mathematical and physics genius. He simply asked the right questions, believingly. You see, the universe works by a perfect law, which never once errs nor favors particular people. Once you understand the universe's deeply complex yet simple rules, which are perfectly balanced, you cannot fail to succeed predictably. Whenever you see chaos and unpredictability in the universe, you are simply seeing something that you do not yet understand, but something that is organized and predictable by certain laws. Nothing is difficult for the Source, God. And perfection and balance is the nature of the Source. Hence, all laws are applied equally, universally, and unfailingly. Ask the right questions, believingly and earnestly.

Be specific and do not keep changing your mind. All thoughts count and produce results. Changing your mind all the time "confuses" the universe. Imagine walking into a travel agency and saying, "I wish to travel." Then you look at the agent blankly. He or she would be ready to make your reservation, but they cannot until you tell them where you wish to go. Imagine you now say, "Well, I'd like to go to Moscow and Timbuktu, at the same time." Again, the agent cannot fulfill that request. Now, imagine you say, "OK, then book me to Moscow. No, wait, Timbuktu. No, wait, Moscow. No, wait, I am not sure I can afford it. No, I can. No, maybe I don't wish to go there or travel at all." This is how many people think all day. And the universe is "confused" by their thoughts, just like the travel agent is, and it therefore produces "confused" results for them.

Whatever you put your attention to gets energy from you and grows. Remove the attention, and it dies. Be conscious and deliberate in this. Intension goes along with attention. What you intend and give attention to begins to become.

Wishing you all life has to offer,
From Ken's desk 🙂

Abraham Lincoln's Persistence

The following story has become a piece of American history.

Abraham Lincoln was born in a one-room log cabin and overcame numerous failures and obstacles to become president of the United States.

Enjoy the **Lincoln Did Not Quit** story.

Lincoln Didn't Quit

Probably the greatest example of persistence is Abraham Lincoln. If you want to learn about somebody who didn't quit, look no further. Born into poverty, Lincoln was faced with defeat throughout his life. He lost eight elections, twice failed in business, and suffered a nervous breakdown. He could have quit many times, but he didn't, and because he didn't quit, he became one of the greatest presidents in the history of the United States of America.

Lincoln was a champion, and he never gave up. Here is a sketch of **Lincoln's road to the White House:**

1816	His family was forced out of their home. He had to work to support them.
1818	His mother died.
1831	Failed in business.
1832	Ran for state legislature—lost.
1832	Also lost his job—wanted to go to law school but couldn't get in.
1833	Borrowed some money from a friend to begin a business, and by the end of the year, he was bankrupt. He spent the next seventeen years of his life paying off this debt.
1834	Ran for state legislature again—won.
1835	Was engaged to be married, sweetheart died, and his heart was broken.
1836	Had a total nervous breakdown and was in bed for six months.
1838	Sought to become speaker of the state legislature—defeated.
1840	Sought to become elector—defeated.
1843	Ran for Congress—lost.
1846	Ran for Congress again—this time, he won, went to Washington, and did a good job.
1848	Ran for reelection to Congress—lost.
1849	Sought the job of land officer in his home state—rejected.
1854	Ran for Senate of the United States—lost.
1856	Sought the vice-presidential nomination at his party's national convention—got less than one hundred votes.

1858   Ran for U.S. Senate again—again, he lost.
1860   Elected president of the United States.

Remember, the size of your success is in direct relation to the size you are willing to fail. Falling in love with failure pays very well.

Wishing you all life has to offer,
From Ken's desk

Luck

"Success is just a matter of luck. Just ask any failure."—Earl Wilson

Ever heard the phrase, "some people just have all the luck"? The reality is, so many people say this phrase out of frustration, feeling like they are getting a hard deal in life compared with these "lucky people," when in fact it's nothing to do with luck at all. It's a scientific phenomenon known as a personal energetic frequency.

It might sound a little bit "out there," but the idea that energy or vibrations can influence a person's reality is actually nothing new. Different cultures around the world have been tapping into it for thousands of years. Out of China came Qi Gong and Tai Chi that get energy operating at a level for health and relaxation. In India, there's a strong belief that activating what is known as Kundalini energy will result in self-awareness and a deeper understanding of consciousness. Then in Japan, Reiki has healed countless people simply by working with their personal energy fields (a practice becoming more and more common in the Western world too).

Even at the tiniest level, quantum mechanics has discovered that atoms and subatoms are in fact composed of packets of energy. A famous research study showing evidence of people affecting the energy of objects is that done by Dr. Masaru Emoto, where he took water and exposed it to different objects and environments. He then projected a particular thought onto a glass of water and placed it next to a specific object. After projecting his thought (positive or negative), the water was frozen, and the resulting water crystals were observed under the microscope. Amazingly, when a glass of water had a piece of paper with a written word of high energetic frequency like "love" stuck to it, the water crystals formed beautiful patterns that were pure in color and in perfect symmetry. In comparison, when a glass of water had a piece of paper with a written word of low energetic frequency like "anger" stuck to it, the water crystals were rough, dull in color, and in a state of disarray. Crazy, right? But true. It just shows the power our projected energy fields have upon the world around us.

Taking it a step further, in 2002, a psychiatrist and consciousness researcher called Dr. David Hawkins did a study on the connection among atoms, energy, and human awareness, eventually publishing his findings, which concluded that every human has a personal energetic frequency. This is a form of energy surrounding our bodies affecting what kind of circumstances and events we will attract into our lives. Based on his research, Hawkins developed a measurement system identifying the different levels of energy vibrating on what he termed the scale of consciousness.

The scale runs from 1 to 1,000, with 1,000 being the highest state a human can attain (if you reached this level, you'd be an enlightened master teaching all grasshoppers ☺). At the lowest end of the spectrum is someone who is not thriving at all. To determine where people are on this scale, Dr. Hawkins used muscle testing and kinesiology. Feelings like shame, guilt, and fear, the energy created by these emotions all vibrate at low frequencies. And feelings like love, happiness, enlightenment all vibrate at high, uplifting frequencies.

Right now, the average level of energy on earth is around 207, way lower than the maximum of 1,000! And this is because throughout our lives, we accumulate hidden energy blockages and negative conditioning that holds us back from higher vibrations.

The level we should aim for is 500 and above; 500 is the vibration of love. When you vibrate at this level, life becomes drastically different. Because your energetic field acts like a magnet attracting experiences and people on a similar wavelength you start attracting positivity and "high-energy" things into your life, like love, abundance, and wealth. A simple shift in vibrations can have a massive effect on the reality around you.

Of note on Dr Hawkins' study is the discovery that it doesn't just have a positive effect in your own life. He identified that one person operating at a level of 500 (love) can lift 750,000 other people above 200. Imagine the impact you could have in the world if you sparked off so many other people to vibrate in their own lives at a higher frequency!

The great thing is that nobody's personal energetic frequency is fixed or predestined to a certain level. The same way that you can train your body to get them into shape, or train your mind to learn a new language, you can actually retune your frequencies. By removing the energy blockages holding you back, it's even possible for you to elevate your own personal energetic frequency to a higher vibration—a level of love (500) or above! Not all are Pollyanna as many would suspect is it?

To add, you must remember that what goes in goes out. Keep reading books that take you where you desire and throw out the crap in your life. Reading led me to these studies, validating so much of what I believe in, but more so, reading keeps you in the question.

Consistent learning and raising of your energy level will create so much luck.

Wishing you all life has to offer,
From Ken's desk 🎭

Meaning

Imagine you are in the ocean, and you are a poor swimmer. Behind you is a huge wave. Now, what do you think? Do you think what an exciting and fun wave? No! You're scared as hell. Now, imagine you are an experienced surfer, and the same wave comes up behind you. You say, "Cool. Hang ten. What a wave, dude." Did the wave change? Obviously, it was just the meaning you gave to it.

Nothing in life has any meaning besides the meaning we give it. How do we create meaning? In many cases, we are programmed by our culture and the people around us. The truth is that all meaning is subjective. Some of us are taught that having designer clothes, a perfect body, and having a lot of money is the true meaning of success. In other cultures, having a loin cloth, a lip plate, long earlobes, and living off the land is the true meaning of success.

Some of us are taught that death is sadness, and others believe it is joyful because we get rid of our worn-out bodies so our spirit can move on and have more fun! When it's 20°C/72°F outside, some will say it's cold, while others will say it's hot. If three people are looking at one, two of them might say that one is beautiful, while the third says that person is ugly, right? You get the point by now.

So if nothing in life has any meaning besides what you give to it, then your experiences in life have nothing to do with what is happening in your life but with everything to do with the meaning you attach it to.

Understanding that you can choose the meaning to the events in your life gives you a tremendous power to change the quality of your experiences, the quality of your results, and the quality of your life.

If you have a situation you now have chosen as a bad experience, could you not change it to a learning experience? If you feel you are living in poverty, could you not look at the doctor in Cuba who is earning $15,000/year and start to count your blessings?

What can you change the meaning of today? Look around you during your day and notice the things you have given meaning to by way of attitude and give it a new, opposite attitude meaning. How do you view certain cultures, religions, people driving slow or too fast, people who have rejected you or disagree with you, your idea of manual labor, etc. Do this for a week and see how things start to change for you.

Soon you will be properly able to see things from other perspectives, and those new perspectives will open you up to all kinds of possibilities.

Wishing you all life has to offer,
From Ken's desk

Money Wisdom

These days, most of us are caught up in the "rat race."

Put simply, we have to go to work have a job in order to pay the bills and provide the basic necessities of life: clothing food and shelter.

In our materialistic world, we have added to that need to earn money by buying "stuff"—cars, computers, smart phones, tablets, TVs, a "better" house, and so on.

Have you noticed how easily you judge someone by the car they drive? I know I do. There seems to be within me a measuring stick that automatically tells me that "Bob" is successful because he drives a new BMW or an Escalade!

Of course, many of you probably would not know what type of car, if any, a friend or someone you have just met drives. You just don't relate in any way to cars.

But it could be something else that you value and thereby make judgments on.

This, of course, presupposes that "Bob" has a great income, that he is happy and successful, and that all is wonderful in his world. If that could only be you!

On the other side of the coin, I am reminded of the book written by Robin Sharma, called *The Monk Who Sold His Ferrari*.

It's a made-up tale about a successful attorney who had lost his spark for life. He had a "spiritual crisis," was looking seventy years old at the age of fifty-three. He decided to give up his so-called successful life and his Ferrari, go to India, and study with the sages. He learned how to simplify his life, learned to do the things he feared, and to set goals, to live joyfully, and so on.

This is all very wonderful if you are in a position to actually give up your job and go on a pilgrimage to find nirvana, whatever that might be for you. In fact, that ideal might even be a worthwhile goal!

There are, as with all teachings on personal development and spirituality, underlying messages and lessons that you can adopt to maybe make your life a little easier.

Such ideas as:

Suspending judgment—as best you can.

Living as much as possible in the present—not dwelling on the past or worrying about the future.

Living joyfully—again, as best you can.

Believe or at least begin to build a belief that yes you too can develop a "success mind-set," taking some time to walk or exercise outdoors regularly and to pay attention to the sounds and smells and beauty that nature provides.

Be thankful for what you have.

And getting absolutely clear as to what you want from life.

If you are somewhat vague about your desires and then burn yourself up in order to get the things you think you want, only to realize that your new lifestyle actually doesn't "do it for you" and is not what you wanted after all, is all that effort worth the cost to your health or your relationships?

Of course, it is always worthy to set lofty goals that are in alignment with your values; just don't be disappointed if you discover the ladder you are climbing is leaning on the wrong wall when you get to the top!

As a mentor, I emphatically believe in discovering what you want and setting goals and taking appropriate action. I don't know any successful person who just drifted his way to the top (and stayed there).

Just get very clear first.

What do you want, really? Why haven't you got it?

The point being, don't let society set your goals. Too many have dual incomes to keep up with the "Jones" when they would be much happier with less and only one working.

At the same time, those with lofty goals are often judged as being greedy and thinking money buys happiness. That too is poor judgment by the one judging.

Just be the real, authentic, you . . . and question your qualifications to judge others.

Wishing you all life has to offer,
From Ken's desk

More on Hope

Why do we resist doing what we can in this moment? Because we might fail.

If you get right down to the core of it, you will see that people act powerless because it's far easier to blame circumstances than go ahead and do it anyway, and maybe look really stupid in the process. So we give our power away to others. It's like we're saying, "No, please, you take my power. This way, I can blame you if things don't work out."

Hope attempts to prove we're powerless.

We say things like "I am not the one in charge here, so there is really nothing I can do."

"I believe my fate is in God's hands." "They won't let me (government, rich people, or anyone else who appears to have more power)." "What is the use of trying? The odds are clearly stacked against me."

These are nothing more than assumptions. Assumptions are characterized by the habit of taking for granted that something is true when it is not. Questions you must ask are, "Is my assumption true or false? What proof or evidence do I have about my assumption?" What's more stupid than a stupid question? The answer is an incorrect assumption.

Think of this in terms of your return on investment. In business, we focus heavily on the ROI (return on investment), but we forget to use that same concept throughout the rest of our lives. When we fail to do what we want because of an assumption, we are forgetting about the concept of ROI. What would be the ROI for doing it anyway, even if someone somewhere holds the assumption that it is impossible? If all any of us ever did was follow our assumptions, we would still be afraid of falling off the edge of the earth.

Is it wrong to hope or have expectations? Absolutely not. However, the tipping point where hope turns into defeat is when hope keeps us from doing what we can do in the moment.

Wishing you all life has to offer,
From Ken's desk

The "NEWS"

I understand what I am about to say may sound crazy to you, but allow me to suggest the possibility that you have been totally brainwashed and you have unknowingly become your own worst enemy.

In fact, this is exactly what is happening to millions of people. And most likely, you are one of them.

What I am talking about is the subliminal and subconscious programming you are getting, programming that is imprinted on your subconscious without your knowledge.

I am not saying there is an organized conspiracy to program your mind. The people that are spreading these negative messages don't even know they are doing it!

The problem is as you are exposed to these mind viruses, you are likely to be infected. Just as exposure to raw sewage can cause you to be infected with germs, microbes, and other nasty things, prolonged exposure to the media will infect your mind with many nasty viruses. Society spends billions of dollars to protect us from biological and computer viruses, yet a mind virus can be the most dangerous of all.

One of the best things you can do to prevent mind viruses is to stop following the news. Don't watch TV news, don't listen to "talk" radio, don't read newspapers or magazines that have the news in them. Why? Because they all make their money by selling fear, lack, scarcity, and limitation. Bad news is what sells.

Open the average newspaper and you will see that 90 percent or more of what you read is negative news. The percentage is about the same for radio and TV. Do you really believe it is important to find out how many houses burnt down or how many people were robbed or killed in your city, state, or another country? Do you need to know about the bus crash in India that killed four people (not to be insensitive, but . . .)? Do you really need to be reminded of the economic situation every day? Being exposed to all this negativity creates a negative view of the world and negative thought patterns in your mind.

When I tell people to skip the news, they invariably ask, "How will I know if there is a major world tragedy or natural disaster heading my way or terrorists striking near me?" Trust me. You will know about all the big stuff you need to know. Let's face it, the vast majority of your friends and neighbors follow the news so they can do the watching and reading for you. You still won't be able to escape it completely because most restaurants and shops now have the TV news on all day long. Or I get, "The news is necessary for my job." OK, so watch the first five minutes; the rest is likely irrelevant. Besides, if something major happens, you will know about it.

And let's face it. Have you ever gone on vacation for a couple of weeks and skipped all news media then come home and find that nothing happened that affected your life, yet had you been home for that period the news would convince you that all kinds of crap were about to happen? Bunk.

Oh and don't even get me going on such media on Hollywood stars! Remember, great minds think about ideas, good minds think about events, and average minds think about people.

I haven't watched the news for the past ten years. *The evening news is where they begin with "Good evening" and then proceed to tell you why it isn't.* I don't read the newspaper other than to entertain myself on the odd occasion. My life is about creating good stuff. Eliminate the news media from your life for the next thirty days and see what I mean.

Wishing you all life has to offer,
From Ken's desk

Are We the Right Example?

It is not what we give, but the example we set. Life is not just about money. I know that may be counter to the philosophy of society, but there is so much more than making money and climbing the corporate ladder that matters in life. One of the great traps we fall into in life is the edict that we must be great providers for our families at all costs. *"My children will have it better than I did as a child."* This philosophy and notion stems from two places really. One, from the absolute place of love for our children that it truly matters that we provide a great life for them while under our charge. Second, and most important, this notion stems from the push of a society that tells us constantly this is what we should do. *"If we were good parents we would buy them these clothes and take them on those trips and provide this computer and that home and this car and on and on."*

Sadly, the price of that great chase on the hamster wheel of life ends up costing us our hopes and goals, and dreams. If my sole purpose in life is to merely provide for the next generation, then what was this all about? Is this the only purpose my life served? Inadvertently, what ends up happening is that the generation we are looking to provide for loses inspiration for their own future by watching the example of those struggling to provide so much for them. Not only are they not able to be "with" the person they are trying to provide for, but their own goals are also negated almost entirely in this pursuit.

Here is one of the great gifts we can pass on to our children. To strive to lead our own authentic, exciting, fascinating, challenging, fruitful, and successful lives to set the example to show those we love what is possible for the next that will walk the path. Oddly, we seem to be programmed to do the very best we can for our children until they go off on their own. Great, so we helped them for age one to twenty, what about ages twenty to eighty?

If you have traveled, you might remember how the flight attendant tells you that in the event of an air pressure failure to put your mask on. The next bit of advice is that **you are to put your mask on before trying to help with your child's or anyone else in need.** You see, **before you can help anyone else**—including your children—**you must first help yourself.** We must remember that our children are watching us. Even if they don't seem to be, they are. We are their role models more than we are their providers.

Wishing you all life has to offer,

From Ken's desk

Objections Are Not Rejections

How many times in your life have you wished you could rewind the clock, if for only a few minutes, so that you could say what you REALLY wanted to say at some critical moment? It could have been in the face of a tough question by a prospect, your boss or even your spouse. It could have been a comment you made out of being upset, in frustration or in fear. The problem is many times that window of opportunity to make the point you want to make has already passed. Fortunately or unfortunately, our lives pivot around moments where we have the opportunity to shine or to fumble.

You see, we falter for several reasons. First, because a personal objection stimulates the number one fear of most humans, that fear of rejection (even though you are not really being rejected!). The second reason is because in school you were taught to answer questions and not to ask them. You were rewarded for answering, not asking. So when someone hits you with a tough question, you are conditioned to try and answer it, and if you cannot, you feel embarrassed. In school, you did the buying, and the teacher did the selling. You had little choice. Wrong answers were penalized and even laughed at.

So when the question is asked, your emotion rises, and your ability to think clearly falters. It is not because you are dumb or weak. It is because you were conditioned that way. Think about this scenario: You present a multimillion dollar idea to someone and ask if they have any questions, and they say no. That's a bad sign. So you do want questions? You'd just prefer they weren't objections, right?

The problem is that in business as in relationships, you have to be able to face hard issues and deal with them honestly and directly. If not, it is like taking your problems and the objections of others and stuffing them into a closet and slamming the door shut. By repeating that behavior, sooner or later, you open the door and you have an avalanche. And few of us can stop an avalanche.

Worse than that, the mere fear of objections sometimes keeps you from even taking a chance. While you may have great dreams and be a wonderful person, you may live a life of frustration and mediocrity only because of a fear or avoidance of handling tough issues or objections from others.

It is my belief that no one is really afraid to make presentations for their business or their own ideas. What they fear is the possibility of objections. Knowing this, what if you knew you could handle all objections? How would you act and feel differently?

Let's go back to school, not the way you did before but to start to learn to be the seller and not the buyer. To be the one asking all the questions, not the one giving all the answers.

KEN GRIFFITH

Scruffy Murphy's Irish Pub

225 The East Mall
Etobicoke, Ontario
Tel: 416-231-9411
Check #: 679729

Server: POCAHONTAS   Date: 02/01/2013
  Table: 2   Time: 16:37
              Client: 1

5	GuinnessPint	33.50
1	Fish Fry	14.50
1	Beef Burger	11.50
1	Add cheddar	1.25
1	Side Fries	4.95
1	Bud Light	4.50

SUB-TOTAL:	70.20
HST:	9.13

TOTAL: 79.33

GST #862016003RT

UFC!! Sat., Jan. 26 @ 8pm &
Sat., Feb. 2 @ 10pm!
Superbowl Sunday, Feb. 3!
Prizes, beer, wing & spring roll
specials ALL DAY!
Be here every Leaf's game for
your chance to win one of 2
Leaf's jerseys! Draw on the
Stanley Cup final game!
Wireless pswd:4162319411

To excel in business and in life, you need to gain confidence and respect for yourself. You need your mental and emotional strength to soar. Confidence replaces hesitancy, and power will overcome fear. The more you work on YOU, the more money you make, and the more people you influence. It is time to reclaim your destiny, which is to be strong, confident, and bold, and to live out your dreams.

It starts with learning about objections and learning how to handle them, learning to ask questions instead of just answering them, and understanding that your fears are just stories you made up from your past conditioning, none of which are genuine.

Make your focus on learning objections as you go (remember, you learn more from practical mistakes than from theory, so don't freeze in analyzing) and learning to ask questions from questions.

Remember, an objection is a statement that disagrees, refutes, doubts, or negatively questions something that is being offered. A rejection is a flat refusal to accept and disregard the entire argument, a true "no."

Neither is a rejection of YOU.

Wishing you all life has to offer,
From Ken's desk

"Only principles endure and these I now possess, for the laws that will lead me to greatness are contained in the words of these scrolls. What they will teach me is more to prevent failure than to gain success, **for what is success other than a state of mind? Which two, among a thousand wise men, will define success in the same words; yet failure is always described but one way.** Failure is man's inability to reach his goals in life, whatever they may be."

This excerpt comes from *The Greatest Salesman in the World* by Og Mandino, a must-read book!

Mandino's main philosophical message is that every person on earth is a miracle and should choose to direct their life with confidence and congruent to **the laws that govern abundance**.

In this chapter of this book, he talks of a set of scrolls he has found and how he wants to become a slave to the good habits he will learn from them and how the first habit he would create is to read each scroll thirty times each but not move to the next one until he has read the one before thirty times.

Notice what he says of success, a state of mind, and how failure defined even lacks energy.

Notice too that he talks of principles, laws of greatness, and how they will teach him.

Success is a state of mind, and with the right tools and the right habits, you will achieve whatever success you are looking for. You must first define what success looks like for you. Then you must **discipline yourself to learn from success**, to which only then you become the only one or thing that can stop that success. While you are not fully in charge of your success, your habits are, but you are in charge of your habits.

The career you have chosen is laden with opportunity, yet it is fraught with heartbreak and despair, and the bodies of those who have failed could be piled high enough to challenge the CN Tower. Failure can be alien to your life once you prepare for wisdom and principles that will guide you into the sunlight of wealth, which only yesterday seemed impossible.

Remember, you are only six inches (fifteen centimeters) from massive success, that being the distance between your ears. **With new thinking, you can create new habits of reading and learning and doing, which can only lead to success.**

"Sales" comes down to mastering the skills, correcting some thinking, and going to work.

We'll provide you with the "scrolls" to master the skills and offer you the chance to correct your thinking.

You'll have to accept and take on the new thinking; then it's just go to work.

Truly caring for your success,
From Ken's desk

Optimism versus Pessimism

Which one are you?

Do you believe that reasons for failure are temporary, or do you believe that failure is permanent? Do you believe that things will never change?

Do you see that a setback is specific to a situation, or do feelings of inadequacy penetrate and spread?

Do you take rejection personally?

Do you believe that you have the power to improve a situation; or do you believe you have no control over your destiny or work outcomes? "Nothing I do will matter."

Remember, it's not what you say to the prospect that matters most. It's what you say to yourself!

Let's face it, the sales job is difficult and stressful because salespeople work alone and face frequent rejection from potential customers. Successful salespeople are self-motivated people who are able to handle the negative feelings associated with rejection and who ***persistently** work hard until they achieve their goals.

They are optimists who expect that things will ultimately go their way. They become successful because they always persevere. In the face of routine setbacks, even major failures, they keep going.

Pessimists get discouraged and gloomy after a stretch of unsuccessful calls and start looking for excuses to end the day early. Remember, you can have anything you want, or you can have excuses, but you can't have both. Optimists, however, remain enthusiastic and continue to believe that the next call will result in a sale. Eventually, they are right!

OPTIMISM WINS! OPTIMISTS WIN!

Honestly, have you ever heard of a pessimist winning?

From Ken's desk

---

* **Persistence** is the only real talent needed in sales.

Our Thoughts Are Not Secret.

There are messages and all forms of communication coming at us from all angles every day. As a result, we feel that the one bastion of solitude we have to guard ourselves from the world is our thoughts. We believe that our thoughts are silent and can only be paid witness to by ourselves. I have often shared the analogy how different thoughts can be perceived. For the homeless man or woman on the streets of Toronto who stands alone on the street corner speaking their thoughts aloud, we judge and label them with having a psychological problem. If we hear a voice speaking to us all day in our head, we call it thinking. When you consider it just for a moment, the only real difference is the audio (sometimes the visual).

What most fail to realize is that our thoughts do show up in our lives as results and actions for all to see. If the voice in our head plays out negative thoughts, that is what is created, negative results for all to see. If the thoughts we have are of promise and hope and determination, the world gets a clear view into our head connecting the thought to the outcome. Because we believe that our thoughts are our own and the world can't hear them, we allow them to direct all actions and activities in our lives. Think for just a moment if for an entire day you spoke out loud what you heard inside your head. What would the world think of your thoughts then? Know this. They may not hear the thoughts, but the world will witness the results. Focus then on the thoughts that produce promise and prosperity. The world will see the outcome of the thoughts you hear. You see because our thoughts really are not secret.

Wishing you all life has to offer,
From Ken's desk

Outpicturing

Do you know what "outpicturing" is?

To explain it to you, let me ask you a question.

Think to a time when you were really stressed about something and, in your mind, you kept playing out what you were feared "MIGHT" happen—over and over again—so much so that you could see it and feel it so strongly that it started to shift from fear to certainty; and then, sure enough, it happened exactly how you feared it would.

How many times have you done this?

Now, here's the exciting news about this. When you do this, you are already accessing one of the greatest powers available to you.

Now, let's shift my question a little.

Think to a time when you were really excited about something and, in your mind, you kept playing out what you were excited "MIGHT" happen—over and over again—so much so that you could see it and feel it so strongly that it started to shift from excitement to certainty; and then, sure enough, it happened exactly how you were excited it would.

You might have to think WAY back for this one, but I guarantee you have done this before.

Without knowing it, in both examples, you are practicing the law of outpicturing. The power of outpicturing comes when you shift your emotion from "anticipation" (whether it is positive or negative) to "certainty and expectation" (again, this can be positive or negative).

So what can you do with this information right now to start to manifest what you DO want instead of what you DON'T want?

Pay attention to what you are playing over and over in your mind. When you notice yourself playing a fear, doubt, or worry over and over, you need to shift the energy and use that to fuel the movie of what you "DO" want instead.

Here's another tip; The brain doesn't actually pick up negative words, so when you say you DON'T want something, the brain only picks up the "want something" part.

If you say I want to LOSE fat, the brain hears "I want fat." I DON'T want to forget his name . . . to . . . I want to forget his name.

How do you flip this? Try I want to be in great shape. I will remember his name, etc.

Try it. Just the awareness will change your reality!

From Ken's desk

Past Experiences

Each and every day is full of opportunities. Unfortunately, we don't always see the truth in this. In fact, to a large degree, whether we are able to accept this or not, it depends on our past experiences; that is, whether or not we can recall a time in our life where we ventured to try something and achieved it.

It is through each and every accomplishment that we build up the belief in ourselves, which ends up leading to our willingness to attempt again, and expand to bigger challenges, which also hold far greater opportunity for richer rewards.

Past experiences are ONLY there to learn from, not to dwell on, not to sit on your laurels, not to be used to view your future. Your past experiences are your teachers of how you react to things. They teach you about you and allow you to grow.

Make it a point to regularly reconnect with your life's accomplishments—both big and small—knowing full well that in doing so you are nurturing your belief system. Make no mistake. It's your belief system that allows you to achieve your heart's desire.

Wishing you all life has to offer,
From Ken's desk

Patience, My Good Man/Woman

A good friend of mine asked of the validity of deliberate creation as if it were a new fad or the latest diet pill; you know, it makes one wonder when a diet pill comes out, and it says guaranteed success when used with eating less and exercise. Wouldn't eating less and exercise alone cause weight loss?

So what of deliberate creation and the laws of attraction? Are they fads by motivational gurus? Are they the placebo to get you to do what you would have done in any way? And can't we simply say, "See, I didn't get what I wanted. Therefore, it doesn't work"?

Let's break it down. The laws of attraction (not quite what was led to believe in *The Secret*) are not some magical system of sitting on the couch, wanting something, and then just getting it. To be fair, that little video was a teaser to learn more, but most aren't willing to spend the time or money in themselves. They are actual physical laws of nature that through quantum physics were found to be laws not just of this earth but of the universe. What makes it difficult to buy and difficult to sell is when the word God is injected as so many have such hard-wired beliefs that they get turned off quickly before getting to understanding (see how even I remain vague here). That is another topic for another time, but these are real.

The Law of Perpetual Transmutation of Energy
The Law of Vibration
The Law of Relativity
The Law of Polarity
The Law of Rhythm
The Law of Cause and Effect
The Law of Gender

It is the last one that I want to address today along with deliberate creation. **The Law of Gender**—nothing on heaven and earth is created or destroyed, or all success already exists.

The good that you desire is already there. (Desire came from the Latin term *de sire*, which means of the father). This should help you understand your worthiness and that you just have to access your desire, or success, as a spiritual being. Have faith in the unseen and expect the incredible. That is the true meaning of faith— believing in the unseen and expecting the incredible.

-You will see it, when you believe it.

Put it this way. A radio wave gives you radio music or talk. You can't see the radio wave; you just have to tune your radio frequency dial to the right frequency to get the station you want. Some stations make you feel good, while some make you feel not so good; all you have to do is choose the frequency you want. Is there a metaphor here? I think so. If you want to be happy and successful, just tune into the right frequency and lock-on.

New things are created only by changing something that already exists. It needs an incubation period or gestation period; that's all. All things have a gestation period; we just don't always know what that period is.

Think of it this way. If a husband were to come to his pregnant wife in month 3 and say, "Well, come on, where's the baby? Why isn't it out yet?" you'd think this guy is nuts. We all know it takes nine months of gestation to have a baby. Go back far enough in history, and there was a time when we didn't know that. Not everyone knows the gestation period for an oak tree, but it has one. Things on the physical plane are easy for us to figure out, but on the spiritual plane, we don't know so we tend to believe there isn't one.

Those you do not win give up right before the breakthrough because they look only at their current results. Belief in faith plays a big role in the science of success.

Your desires and beliefs make the manifestation of energy to the physical form. You plant the seed then have faith.

Deliberate creation is when you take a vision, make a theory (or creation), and turn it into fact (deliberate). You desire something in your life, you focus on it becoming real, and it appears. Hocus-pocus, you say. Think of this: absolutely everything on earth was created by thought then turned to reality. Someone once thought it would be much nicer to have flushing toilets. Someone thought we should have a place for cigarette butts. Someone had the notion that someone else should come by and pick up our garbage. Someone (you might know who here) thought it would be cool if we could interact whenever we wanted to through computers. And someone thought it would be better if we could drive through a restaurant and take the food home.

All of these were visions that were turned into fact. Through cause and effect, a thought was manifested to reality.

So what's my point here? When you take your vision for how your life should be, there is only one thing that can stop it from becoming so. YOU! How? You lose patience or you don't see it shaping up the way you expected and think it is wrong.

Let's go back to the idea that at three months a baby should be born. Crazy, right? And yet we somehow think we know what timeframe—gestation period—is correct for so many pieces to fall into place for our vision. Now, we lose patience and change our mind, and all the things being put into place have been put on notice and start altering. Hmmm, wonder why that didn't work out. Or we see things starting to form, and during this transformation, we don't like what we see. Caterpillars are not so pretty. Butterflies are. More so, cocoons are definitely not pretty. If you are looking to create a butterfly, you may be real disappointed at the stage of cocoon. Get the metaphor?

KEN GRIFFITH

Let go and let it happen. Your job is to create the vision for your life, never lose focus on that vision, and trust it will come out right. Then get out of the way. Do not lose patience. Do not think you are in charge of the process. Just be in charge of the desire, and by being present, you'll know when to act.

From Ken's desk

In the United States, it was Thanksgiving yesterday, and there is great power in being thankful. There will be many messages sent to you about gratitude and being thankful, and I think that's great. You know I am a big fan of gratitude, especially if you read where I told you about the three G's (gratitude is the first G) and how you can use them to attract money or anything quickly.

But, in this issue, I want to address something different when it comes to gratitude. I want to help you when you really struggle with what you can feel grateful for. I want to help you when you struggle with really turning your emotions around to focus on what you do want instead of what you don't want.

I understand how hard it can be to REALLY shift your perspective. I know that you are here because you are committed to life mastery, and I am fully aware that, even though the ideas and tips and exercises I give you are simple, they aren't always easy. That's why I am dedicating this issue to helping you really shift your focus and your point of attraction, and we're going to do that by shifting your perspective!

If your life isn't working in any way, if you feel like you have been slamming your head against a wall or if you feel you were dealt a really bad hand, what you need is a change of perspective.

I'm telling you this with 100 percent certainty: that getting a fresh perspective is the FIRST step to getting out of being stuck. And I am going to say something that pushes a lot of buttons, but I'm going to say it anyway.

You DECIDE how you interpret everything, and your interpretation defines your experience!

Here's the deal. Your interpretation comes from your perspective, so if you need to change your interpretation, what do you need to change first? You got it. You need to change your perspective!

Let me give you a really simple example of how perspective determines focus and vision.

Picture a racehorse with blinders on. Now, tell me this. Why do they put blinders on the racehorse? They put the blinders on to define the horses focus and vision. They also do it to keep out distractions that would potentially take the horse off track or slow him down. So when it comes to race time, blinders are essential for a racehorse.

BUT...

Later on, when the horse is free in the paddock, those same blinders would actually be harmful and would limit the information he could take in to help him thrive there. In other words, to be successful in a different environment, the horse needed a change of perspective.

Now, here's the thing. Most of us were born, and due to whatever our situation was, we developed a certain perspective. Our perspective when we were young was formed by the people around us. Their words, their thoughts, and their feelings were all soaked up like a sponge by our young minds; and from that, we created filters.

From those filters came perspective. Those filters became our blinders. And, to be honest, those blinders probably served us, in one way or another, at the time. Perhaps they protected us or helped us thrive in the environment we were in. But as we grew older and as we changed and as our desires and influences and environments changed, our filters became outdated; they stopped serving us and started holding us back.

So here's the good news. If things aren't working in your life, you never changed your perspective, and perspective can always be changed, sometimes in an instant.

Let me give you an example. In 2009, Mark Herzlich, a college football player, was diagnosed with a rare form of cancer. After the normal (and completely understandable) reaction of despair and defeat, it is reported that Herzlich closed himself in a room, and when he came out, he had completely changed his attitude.

And he did this (in my opinion) by changing his perspective from wondering why it happened to him to deciding he was going to do whatever it took to prevail over cancer. With that perspective shift, everything changed. He is now (two years later) cancer-free and just had his first start in a professional football game.

I'm telling you, it's all a matter of perspective.

Try this exercise.

1. Look around you. It doesn't matter where you are. Just stop and take a minute or two to really take in your surroundings. Notice what you see, what you hear, what you can feel, etc. Use all of your senses.
2. Now, go find something that is at least one to two feet off the ground—a step stool, a bench, a chair—anything. Put it in the same spot you were just in and stand on it.
3. Now, what do you see? What do you feel, hear, etc.? Pay attention to the different things you notice from this new perspective.

This is exactly what you need to do with anything in your life that isn't working.

Now, try this exercise.

1. Write down one area of your life where you feel like you are really struggling. Write down everything you believe about this area. Write down how you feel, what seems to be true, what it feels like, what it looks like, etc.
2. Write down the story you tell yourself and other people about this area of your life.
3. Write down the proof that you have that makes you believe this story is true.

Once you are done, ask yourself this power question:

"If I looked at this from a different perspective, what might I see?"

Now, from this different perspective, answer the same questions again (remember how different everything looked earlier when you stood at a higher level and looked around):

1. Now, that you are looking from a different perspective, write down everything you believe about this area. Write down how you feel, what seems to be true, what it feels like, what it looks like, etc.
2. From this new perspective, write down the story you could tell yourself and other people about this area of your life.
3. From this new perspective, write down the proof you could find that would make you believe this story is true.

Your most important job from this moment on is to constantly look for a better perspective. If you were trapped in a huge hole in the ground, would you just accept that you could never get out, or would you try to look at where you were from a different perspective to see if there were options you hadn't seen yet?

You get the idea. Your life is the same way. Are you looking at the problem or are you looking for solutions? That is the biggest perspective shift you can ever give yourself.

When you feel stuck, ask yourself, "Am I looking at the problem or am I looking for solutions?"

The second you ask yourself the question, your perspective will shift, I promise!

If you are having trouble finding things in your life to be grateful for, ask yourself this, "Am I looking at what I don't have or am I looking for all of the things I can be grateful for?"

You can ALWAYS change your perspective. ALWAYS! So if something isn't working, look at it from a different angle, look at it through different eyes, get your focus off the problem and onto the possible solutions, start telling a different story, and your perspective will change. And when your perspective changes, so does your life!

I recently looked at a situation in my life that I thought was most unfavorable to me. Once I began to examine it through a different perspective, I soon realized that while I was thinking of how the situation affected me, my new perspective showed how I was positively affecting four other people. That made my old perspective irrelevant and my new attitude, a good one.

Try it.

From Ken's desk

Popularity and Pride

Ever notice how all the cool guys at school ended up working for the nerds?

They don't go to seminars, read books, or get involved in the deeper conversations—you know, the ones on ideas—and why?

PRIDE/EGO

Pride is a killer. It stops you from going forward, from learning, and from growing. To say pride is a killer may seem harsh, but since we know that everything and everybody is either growing or dying, we then know that pride is slowly killing.

In school, it was so important to be popular. Popularity is people liking you; happiness is you liking you. Popularity allows you to become the person that complainers complain to. Sure it makes you feel big, but at what cost?

We are like ketchup bottles. The makers of ketchup pour ketchup into the ketchup bottles, and once we take the ketchup home, we squeeze it, and out comes the ketchup.

In other words, what goes in comes out. What is constantly going in you has no choice but to come out of you. So the question is, if you were to be squeezed, what would come out?

What are you reading? Who are you listening to? How do you spend your downtime? Are you conducting yourself in a manner that gets you closer to your goals? Are you conducting yourself in a manner that your vision of you successful self would? Are you looking to be popular or someone to be admired? Have you checked your ego at the door? Have you become someone to be admired?

It is true that it is lonely at the top, but that is because so few are willing to not be average. Is that you?

If things aren't working the way you thought they should be, maybe it is time for a checkup from the neck up.

From Ken's desk

Positive

Here's the truth: being positive is more than thinking positive thoughts. Being positive is all about the energetic charge that radiates from you. To just think positively is only part of it. To feel positive emotion is the rest.

You've heard things like this a million times:

- Positivity is the key to success and happiness.
- Your outlook determines your outcome.
- Your life is 10 percent what happens and 90 percent how you react.
- When you raise your vibration, you raise the vibration of the world.
- Stay positive and anything is possible.
- Your NOW is all that matters.

The thing is it's true. BUT if you are anything like I was, hearing that it is true isn't the same as **knowing** that it is true. And that best thing I can do is help you know it with every cell of your being. Because when you know it that deeply, making the choice to be negative becomes very difficult, and your mission becomes always raising your vibration.

Let me start by telling you why positive thoughts and feelings really matter to your happiness, success, and fulfillment. It is because we see what is going on differently when we process through a positive filter. We attach a different meaning to what is going on when we process through a positive filter, and we make different decisions when we process through a positive filter.

Keep in mind, a positive filter is more than just **positive thoughts**. A positive filter includes **positive emotion** and **positive expectation**. There is also a certain amount of letting go that comes with a positive filter, because there is the expectation that things will work out for the best, there is less attachment to HOW we will force them to work out.

There is an essential element to having a positive filter. You must be rooted in the NOW. "Now" is where you tap into your source of infinite creation. "Now" is our point of power and choice, and NOW keeps you PRESENT.

Here's the proof: The most powerful kind of proof is the kind you provide yourself, so I have two scenarios that are going to help you do just that by using your own history. Answer these questions, and you will have all the proof you need.

1. Think of a time when you were clearly processing through a negative filter. What were you like? Did you see most things that were happening with a negative take on them? Did you attach negative meaning to most

everything that was happening? What kind of decisions did you make? Were your decisions based in fear, doubt, or worry? Did things seem to only get worse or stay the same no matter what you did? Did you have a sense that "nothing was going your way"?

2. Think of a time when you were clearly processing through a positive filter. What were you like? Did you see most things that were happening with a positive take on them? Did you attach positive meaning to most everything that was happening? What kind of decisions did you make? Were your decisions based in confidence, faith and power? Did things seem to just keep getting better? Did you have a sense that "everything was going your way"?

When you look at both of these times from your past and answer the questions I just gave you, it becomes very clear why a positive filter (positive thoughts, feelings, expectation) is ESSENTIAL. The first step to shifting to a positive filter is to get firmly rooted in the "now." The second step is to start LOOKING for positive proof.

You can shift your filter to positive in every single moment. You REALLY have that power. And once you completely understand why raising your vibration is the first and most important element in manifesting anything and everything you desire, then you will find a new commitment within yourself to always raise your vibration—higher and higher—always. And when you do, you will change your life, and you will change the world. After all, your world is created by you, right?

One final question. Again, remember a time when you were in negative mode and a time when you were in a positive mode, which was more fun?

Wishing you all life has to offer,
From Ken's desk

Procrastination and Motivation

What is motivation and procrastination? Why do we procrastinate?

Let's think about the energy and state of mind you had prior to moving toward your ambitions and goals for starting your business (and yes you are in business now). I imagine there was a kind of excitement in your nature, a feeling of anticipation, and a bit of mystery too. There was an active part of you firmly committed to your goals while taking actions to build your business. At the same time, there were some quandaries as to how everything was going to take shape and manifest (i.e., How many deals would I really close? How would they pay?).

When we are in growing stages, there's a lot of energy present. At times we can thrive on the activities and kinds of energy that it takes to imagine and intend. When we get to the place of accomplishing our goals, we can come to a plateau, including an energetic plateau. The purpose of this energetic plateau is for us to acknowledge our accomplishments, regroup, and conceptualize and imagine the next level of attainment. The reason this is so is because our natures are very goal-oriented. We do not like to be at a place where we are not growing, learning, and enriching our beings. When a person attains something they have been working to achieve, it is time to bask in the sunlight and enjoy the accomplishment. The next stage is to take a look at what the next desire for your life could be.

You are at a marvelous place. You have completed a very important goal. This result shows that you are beginning a new cycle of growth and desire. Does this mean that this business is not right for you? Or does it indicate that because you have achieved success in getting this business under way, you have outgrown it? Well, not necessarily. It may be that you are energetically ready to begin conceptualizing and imagining some new goals, perhaps how your new goals and ambitions could enhance your current business. It also could be that your nature is one that is exceedingly goal-striving. Some people are more this way than others. This is why it is so important to develop an understanding of one's passions in life, as it gives us a better understanding of the kind of innate energies that are a part of us.

Now, may be a good time for some self-discovery, which will in turn help you understand if you are the kind of person who needs more than one ambition at a time. If so, you may be ready to grow and learn while adding some new skills to your life. It could also mean that you are at a place of conceptualizing and integrating. This state also happens after we attain and begin reorganizing our thoughts to establish the next goal.

Now let's talk about motivation and procrastination. Sometimes these behaviors are a sign that something in your nature is feeling out of balance. Perhaps there is an intuitive part that is slowing things down because it has greater understanding of the

KEN GRIFFITH

timing of things than you do consciously. So procrastination is not necessarily bad. It can be telling you to pay attention; that there is something below your conscious mind that your subconscious or intuition is sensing. If this is so, then this is a place to stop and pay attention. Listen to the underlying energy and what it wants to tell you. Once you embrace this energy, the need to procrastinate, or your lack of motivation, will point you to a path that wishes to evoke your inner resources and help you discover your inner voice. It can help you learn what your nature is trying to teach you. Embrace this energy as a path of discovery. Chances are you will find it wishes to make you more vastly aware of other options, help with appropriate timing, or point out other aspects of your nature that wish to learn and grow in new ways.

Some people can sometimes feel like they shouldn't want more than they already have, that they should be satisfied with their achievements. This can create a kind of letdown or an empty feeling, especially after all the energy it took to accomplish a goal. Depending on a person's beliefs, this state can be depressing in a way. Understand that this is just a misconception that often is rooted in old beliefs that may relate to doing "religious" or "spiritual" kinds of things. Nonetheless, we are by nature goal-oriented beings. We are on this planet to learn, grow, love, and exercise our beings. We wish to establish our abilities and contribute to the whole. When we hit a plateau, it can be a wonderful time to be grateful and to challenge ourselves to grow, expand, learn, and embrace more opportunities to express our nature.

Always listen to your feelings, as they do indeed want to point you to something you can learn to value in your nature. Hopefully, this answer will give you a little more information about the dynamics you brought up in your question and help you find a place of peace and balance in your life.

Wishing you all life has to offer,
From Ken's desk

The Power of Your Intention

Let's imagine that you have a seed and you plant the seed with the full intention of it growing into a beautiful rosebush. You have complete certainty that this is going to be the most beautiful rosebush, and you can already imagine sitting next to it in your backyard, relaxing and enjoying its beauty.

In fact, you are so excited that you when your friend (who tends to be a bit negative) comes to visit, you take her out back and show her where you've planted it and tell her how amazing your rosebush is going to be. And she responds by telling you how there is supposed to be a cold spell in the weather and how the ground in your backyard is too rocky for roses.

What happens to you then? Most likely, the power of your intention for that rosebush is released and replaced with doubt. Because your positive intention is now clouded with doubt, you may be tempted to pay too much attention to the rosebush and overwater it or just give up and remove the seed altogether.

How many times has this happened to you? The key is that it doesn't always take someone else to cloud your intention with doubt. Often we do it to ourselves by trying to figure out how it is all going to happen.

All that matters is this. Your intentions are like seeds. They need to be treated carefully. Plant them, give them sunlight and water (otherwise known as faith and belief), and then let the universe do its stuff!

I promise you that when it is time for your intention to be known to the outside world, it will burst forth. And when it does, it will no longer be a seedling; it will be a fully confident idea fueled by inspired action and momentum!

Pay attention to how you treat your intentions. Love them and give them the time they need to grow. When you do, you will be amazed at the things that start happening for you.

Wishing you all life has to offer,

From Ken's desk

I Respect You. Do You?

Seriously, do you respect yourself? If you said yes, I want you to look closer. Do you really treat yourself with respect? Do you treat yourself with the same respect you expect yourself to give to others?

Are you kind to yourself? Or do you think and say things to and about yourself that you wouldn't allow other people to get away with?

So many people struggle with feeling like other people don't treat them with respect—and a lack of respect is a terrible feeling—but here's the powerful thing to see.

Respect starts with you. Respect starts with how you treat yourself. Other people treat you how you teach them to treat you.

Ouch! That last one might hurt a bit, and I'm sure it will push more than a few buttons, but it's true. Truth is, if you constantly undervalue yourself and push your needs and desires to the side, you aren't giving yourself the respect you deserve, and other people will follow suit.

I'm writing this to you today out of the greatest respect for you. You are so valuable and extraordinary and it's time you knew that! :)

Pay attention to how you treat yourself today—ask yourself if that is how you would want someone else to treat you—lack of respect is just an old habit and you can transform it, I promise!

Wishing you all life has to offer,
From Ken's desk

Self-Improvement

I don't believe in "*self*-improvement."

To believe in self-improvement, you must first believe there is something wrong that needs improving. When people believe they are flawed, the natural reaction is to start searching, searching, searching for whatever is "missing," looking for answers, happiness, and meaning "out there."

Here's my message today: Nothing outside you can solve your problems. You were made perfect.

If there was an external "fix" for life, there would be no sad, stressed-out, or depressed rich folks (check out the tabloids to see what I mean). The good news is that you were born with all the resources you need in order to be happy, wealthy, and successful.

Maybe you've heard that before, or maybe not. And I know that can be hard to swallow when you feel in lack, or lonely, or depressed—been there. Or when you can't pay your bills or you hate your job, been there too. But the breakthrough can happen in an instant. It happens every day.

There's a flash of inspiration. And suddenly you are CLEAR, you're taking action, and things start to happen without effort.

And when your life changes overnight, it's not because you suddenly "improved" yourself. No, it's an internal shift. It happens when you "align" yourself. It's the moment when your conscious desires line up with your natural unconscious power to manifest and any conflicts and counterintentions you have instantly dissolve. There's a release of power that sends energy up and down your body, and you KNOW something has shifted.

That's the power of "alignment."

See, it's not *self-improvement* but *personal and professional development* that you seek. That is what will help you "align" to help you see what is truly in front of you and to help you find that "ah ha" moment.

Wishing you all life has to offer,
From Ken's desk

Some Recurring Thoughts from Some Greats

"In reading the lives of great men, I found that the first victory they won was over themselves, self-discipline with all of them came first."—**Harry S Truman**

"To succeed you need to find something to hold on to, something to motivate you, something to inspire you."—**Tony Dorsett**

"Strength is Happiness. Strength is itself victory. In weakness and cowardice there is no happiness. When you wage a struggle, you might win or you might lose. But regardless of the short-term outcome, the very fact of your continuing to struggle is proof of your victory as a human being."—**Daisaku Ikeda**

"Victory always starts in the head. It's a state of mind. It then spreads with such radiance and such affirmations that destiny can do nothing but obey."—**Douchan Gersi**

"Victory belongs to the most persevering."—**Napoleon**

"Victory at all costs, victory in spite of all terror, victory however long and hard the road may be; for without victory there is no survival. History will be kind to me, for I will write it. Kites fly highest against the wind."—**Winston Churchill**

"Far better it is to dare mighty things, to win glorious triumphs, even though checkered by failure, than to take rank with those poor spirits who neither enjoy much nor suffer much, because they live in the grey twilight that knows not victory nor defeat."—**Theodore Roosevelt**

Remember, the only competition you have is your disciplined mind versus your undisciplined mind.

You see, it is in how you think, what you think about, and most importantly your WHY

Wishing you all life has to offer,
From Ken's desk

Something to Ponder

How's life? Really, how is your life?

Is what you're doing right now in your life congruent with who you want to be in the world? What you want to contribute? Is your life rich with love, peace, freedom, and joy?

Are you living the life you TRULY want to live, or are you conforming to what you believe others expect of you? How long have you been doing that?

Are you clear on who you really are? Do you take time each and every day to get in touch with what you believe you're here to be and do? Or are you putting out the fire of "real life"? Handling situations? Living in reaction mode?

Look at your day-to-day activities. Is this the life you always dreamed of, or did you somehow get caught up in patterns of behaviors and decision making that were not your own? Do you make the "important" choices in life based on being "responsible"? To somehow fit in or be accepted?

Validate, if you will.

These things aren't inherently bad, unless they disconnect you from who you truly wish to be.

So who's life are you living REALLY?

If you're not BEING who you truly believe yourself to be, what comes up for you when you think about what might be?

Is there resentment toward someone or something? Are you blaming your job, your marriage, your parents, the economy, or ANYTHING outside of yourself for your current situation? For that matter, are you blaming YOURSELF for your situation?

When you think about the life of your dreams, do you feel exhilarated and inspired, or is there a sense of longing? A yearning to experience a life that you may feel by now is far beyond your reach?

I know that feeling well. I lived that way for many years, pointing "out there" for all the reasons I couldn't be, do, and have what my heart desperately yearned for.

After a while, you may have gotten complacent. Resigned to what you believe is the "fact" that it's too late for you now. You've got what you've got, and you just have to deal with it.

Do you, in fact, still have a sense of yourself, or is it just too painful to look at? Again, I know that feeling. It's not only a horrible feeling, but allowing that feeling to perpetuate is a spiritual death trap.

How did this happen? How do we get so far off track?

Is it in fact possible to create something unreasonably different than what you

KEN GRIFFITH

have right now? To step powerfully into being someone who not only experiences feelings of joy, passion, and inspiration but evokes those feelings in others as well!

To become someone who contributes the full value of who they TRULY are powerfully, without apology, and with full impact.

And do you know what occurs when you do that?

Abundance. Unspeakable abundance. But not just financial abundance. And, in fact, the focus on financial abundance is what causes people to compromise themselves so early in life. The belief that money somehow brings happiness and peace creates decisions that are based on how much money you can make instead of how much JOY you can experience.

Here's my advice:

Choose joy.

Life is NOT about money. It just isn't. Money is great to have, of course. It does provide you with the flexibility to have experiences that you may not otherwise have, but it is NOT the **source** of joy.

You just have to trust me on this. I, like many, didn't really believe that when I heard it. My line was, "But you don't understand. If I could just get out of debt, I'd relax! I'd be happy!"

Not having overwhelming and miserable debt or other financial problems isn't the root of unhappiness, and in fact, it's the other way around.

Happiness, joy, passion, prosperity, they're all "inside jobs." You must first BE that which you wish to experience.

"But HOW can I do this when my life looks like this?"

I get it. Totally get it. But it doesn't change the fact that this view is a distorted perception of how the universe really works.

I'm not going to sugar coat it. A shift like I'm talking about isn't necessarily easy by human standards. It may involve discomfort, tremendous challenges, and even some pain. I had plenty of that. While these unpleasant-sounding experiences aren't REQUIRED for moving into the life I'm talking about, they are going to be the experience for some people.

But ask anyone who's moved through these feelings to the other side, and every one of them will tell you that it was the most powerful and "worth it" experience of their lives, because of the infinite possibilities that open up when you step outside of your box of limiting beliefs about what's "true" about your life.

So, again, what are your limiting beliefs? You're not good enough? You don't deserve it? It's too hard? You don't know how? They won't let me?

Absolutely none of those are true! Now, imagine if you lived a life where you had the OPPOSITE beliefs: "I'm MORE than good enough! I absolutely deserve it! It's effortless! I don't HAVE to know how! No one has the power to stop me!" (a sort of George Kastanza experience . . . the opposite).

It's all about stepping powerfully into who you are while eliminating those negative beliefs that act as resistance to what you desire your life to be. When we do that, we are literally allowing the universe to work in concert with us to bring those things to us.

The not-so-good news is the book of you has been written. The great news is it has been left to you to write the last few chapters.

Wishing you all life has to offer,
From Ken's desk

Negative Attraction

If you look around and see a lot of what you don't want in your life, you're experiencing "negative attraction."

Debt, bills, stress, a job that leaves you unfulfilled, strained relationships, lack of passion, or creativity—nobody "wants" these situations or problems. But most people spend a lot of time THINKING about them. And we know from the LOA, what you think about, you attract. So how do you stop thinking about your problems and start attracting your desires?

The laws of attraction (combined with inspired action) make it possible for you to turn things around, to find love, to lose weight, to attract abundance, to create a new life rich beyond imagining, no matter where you are now. That's why talk about them so much.

But if your mind is focused on your problems, on what's not working—if you spend time feeling bad about yourself, about your life, angry toward others—then what you'll attract will be in alignment with those thoughts and feelings. What to do?

Stay in the moment! In the moment, there ARE no problems. Your energy and emotions turn universally positive, and you connect with your "infinite attraction point." When you are in the "now," everything you manifest is automatically aligned with your desires. The best part is you don't have to meditate or use any special audio programs or hypnotize yourself to put your mind into the moment.

Think about it. When you are presenting to a customer, do you ever think of your problems? No, you are in the moment. Have you ever played a sport and in the middle of a game find yourself thinking of problems? Again, no, as you are in the moment. So stay in the moment throughout your day and watch how things work out.

When you spend a lot of time thinking about your problems, you don't solve them; you attract more of them. Stepping into the "now" instantly dissolves negativity and raises your vibration so you only attract what you desire most. And finally it's easy to do; there's no reason to wait.

Wishing you all life has to offer,
From Ken's desk

Stay Muddy

Don't let the title of today's title fool you. It's an important success lesson. Keep what you learn in mind as you move through your daily routine.

One of the greatest success secrets is something we often miss when studying the greatly successful: Whatever field they are in, whatever business empire they run, the chances are excellent they have done it at some point with their own hands, learning its nuts and bolts, from the ground up.

Abraham Lincoln knew law. He'd practiced it in freezing-cold, bare-floored small-town courtrooms. So did Gandhi. They both emancipated millions, but only because they knew the feel of the craft in their hands.

Before he was a great general or the nation's first (and arguably greatest) president, George Washington worked as a land surveyor. He knew the land he would later govern. As a boy, Sam Walton milked the family cow and sold the surplus milk to neighbors. Bill Gates spent thousands of hours as a teenager programming computers. You get the picture.

People who achieve great things that the world will never forget start out by accomplishing small things that the world will never see. And great leaders don't expect anyone else to do anything they haven't done themselves. They get dirt under their nails and mud on their boots.

Getting muddy is critical not only to building success but also to hanging on to success. Once you start entering the heady atmosphere of big achievement, you find there's a lot of voltage flowing through you—cash flow, recognition, notoriety, influence in high places. Whatever it looks like, it's voltage, and it can easily fry your circuits. The only way to survive, as with any encounter with massive current, is to stay grounded.

For electric wires, that means direct physical conductance to the earth. For human beings, it means humility to stay grounded. If you want to be successful, it's necessary to be humble. And if you want to be hugely successful, it's imperative to stay hugely humble.

Hugely humble. Now there's an oxymoron. Or is it?

There are few terms more misunderstood in our culture. People often equate humility with a lack of confidence or self-esteem, or think that being humble means being weak. But that's backward. In truth, the more humble you are, the more personal power you have. Humility is like underwear—necessary, but if it is showing too much, it is indecent. The word humility shares a common root with humus. Being humble means being aware of your connection with the dust of the earth. The soil is the source of everything you have.

KEN GRIFFITH

Remember your muddy beginnings, and you can accomplish anything.
Be humble and be very proud of it. ☺ Yeah, yeah, very punny.

Wishing you all life has to offer,
From Ken's desk

Stop Changing Your Order

If I could tell you one thing that would shift the LOA from working against you to working for you, this is what it would be: Stop changing your order.

Let me explain how this works.

It is the job of your outer mind (conscious mind) to give direction to your inner mind (subconscious mind), and it is the job of your inner mind to make that order happen.

A good example for this is if you are in a restaurant, it is your job to place your order, and then it is the restaurant's job to make sure your order gets to you in a timely manner in the way that you ordered it.

So, in this scenario, you are the outer mind and you decide what you want by looking at the menu. The restaurant is the inner mind, and the second you place your order, the restaurant uses all of the resources available (waiter, chef, manager, kitchen, ingredients, etc.) to bring you what you ordered.

There Are Two Important Things to Notice Here:

1. Once you place your order, you don't obsess over how the restaurant is possibly going to bring you what you ordered. You simply place your order and know that the restaurant has the resources to deliver.
2. When you place your order, the restaurant doesn't judge your order as good or bad, or right or wrong. It simply takes your order and places all of its power into delivering it to you as quickly as possible.

Now, here is the big challenge (and the key).

Imagine if you place your order and, before your waiter got to the kitchen, you said, "Wait, hold on. I thought I wanted steak, but I just saw the chicken dish go by, and it looked amazing, so I'll have that instead." And then as the waiter disappears into the kitchen, you call after him and say, "Hold on. I know that chicken looked good, but I am really trying to be healthy, so can I have a salad?" And so on and so on.

The result is pretty obvious: if you keep changing your order, you will never get any food!

Pay attention to how often you change your order to the universe on a daily basis AND realize that cancelling your order by thinking that it is impossible or too difficult or because you can't see HOW it can be done causes the same result.

Place your order and let the universe figure out how to bring it to you. There are

KEN GRIFFITH

so many resources that you aren't aware of that are ready to work in your favor and bring you exactly what you desire (and often even more)!

Wishing you all life has to offer,
From Ken's desk

Stories … True or False

Stories are a sequence of thoughts that we convince ourselves to be real. A story may be about the past, the present, or the future. It may be about things we should do, what can be, what they could do, or what they are. Stories are untested, uninvestigated theories or assumptions that tell us what things mean. The problem is we don't seem to realize that most of our stories are just assumptions.

I have never experienced a stressful feeling that wasn't caused by attaching to an untrue thought or story.

Rather than understand the original cause, we try to change our stressful feelings by looking outside of ourselves. It is easy to get swept away by some overwhelming feeling, so it is helpful to remember that any stressful feeling is like a compassionate messenger that says, "You are caught up in your story."

Depression, pain, fear, doubt, and worry are gifts that say, "Take a look at what you are thinking right now. You're living in a story that is not true for you." When we get caught in the dream or the illusion, we try to alter and manipulate the stressful feeling rather than deal with the thought behind it. That's why I say that any negative emotion is an alarm clock that is designed to wake you up to the fact that there's a thought that you may want to investigate and get rid of. Inquiry and investigation of any thought that is untrue will always lead you back to happiness and who you really are.

If you put your hand in a fire, does anyone have to tell you to move it? Do you have to decide? No! When your hand starts to burn, it moves. You don't have to direct it. The hand moves itself. In the same way, once you understand through inquiry and investigation of any thought or story that is untrue and realize it is causing you suffering, you will move away from it.

It is simple logic. Before the thought, you were not suffering. With the thought, you are suffering. When you recognize the thought isn't true, you will go back to not suffering and return to happiness.

Self-inquiry is the way to end all suffering and to experience peace, even in a world of apparent chaos. Above all else, self-inquiry is about realizing that all the answers you will ever need are inside of you and are always available to you if you are willing to give up your story. Unless you are living in a great story, of course, then keep up with that story.

Wishing you all life has to offer,
From Ken's desk

KEN GRIFFITH

Stress Thinking

For most people, their life is controlled by their thoughts about money, whether they wish to admit it or not. But if we are in alignment and in the flow (harmony), how could money be a problem? We create a story of success and then chase it, don't we?

Many of us are motivated by the desire for success. What is success? Success is a concept, an illusion. Without a "story," we are always successful wherever we are.

I have never seen a money problem that did not turn out to be a thinking problem. I used to believe I needed money to be happy, even when I had a lot (relative term, I know). I was still stressed out that something terrible would happen, and I would lose all my money, even though I had ridden such rides before. Amazing, eh? I realize now that no amount of money is worth that kind of stress. In fact, I found giving money took away many worries.

If you live with the uninvestigated thought that you need to pile up money to be safe and secure, you are living in a hopeless state of mind. Not only do you believe in scarcity but your version of safety is also sketchy. Banks fail; stock markets crash; companies go under; major home repairs come up; currencies deflate; and people lie, break contracts, and break their promises (or companies fail to enroll).

If you live in this confused state of mind that you need to pile up money to be safe and secure, you can earn millions of dollars and still be insecure and unhappy.

Some people believe that fear of not having enough is what motivates them to make money. But is that really true? Can you be absolutely certain that without fear as a motivator you wouldn't make the same amount of money or even more? Who would you be and what would happen if you never believed that "story" again?

Once I understood and applied the principle of alignment and flow, **I began to notice I always have the perfect amount of money for me right now.**

A clear mind is in the flow. It knows how to live, how to work, what e-mails to send, what phone calls to make, and what to do to create what it wants without fear. When you understand this, you begin to realize you have all the security you wanted money to give you in the first place. And you will also notice it is a lot easier to make more money from this position.

Wishing you all life has to offer,
From Ken's desk

Success—Everybody Wants It, right?

Most people have defined success as "this achievement" or "that thing." Many have actual checklists to determine that they are successful. And I want to be clear. I am all for success. I am all for achieving amazing things and having abundance and cool cars and homes and stuff. But I am here to protect you and help you, and that is what I want to do today.

Too many people check the items off their success lists only to find that they still feel exactly how they felt before. It isn't enough to achieve; you must feel, or else you wind up with empty successes. Need proof? Look at how many professional athletes or Hollywood stars end up in so much trouble after all their "success."

So that is what we are here to do today. We are here to help you make sure your successes are full of joy and happiness and fulfillment. As you know, I believe you have to have a definition of success, mine being "having fun, finding or fulfilling your purpose." To assist you in finding your definition, I want to share with you from a book I am reading some very interesting points on success.

The "Law of Attraction" and "Success"—
What Is "Success" Anyway? by Henk J. M. Schram

Everyone seems to strive to be "successful" in life. We all look to apply the "Law of Attraction" to gain "success."

But what is "success"? What makes you successful, and what makes you a "failure"?

To answer this question, let's first take a look at our world. Our societies are completely focused on our five senses of seeing, hearing, tasting, touching and smelling. Our five senses are constantly stimulated. They are enticed and exploited all the time. It is therefore no surprise that we tend to focus our minds on materialism 24 hours per day. We tend to focus all the time on big cars, big houses, lots of money in the bank, and so on. There is nothing wrong with that in itself, and this does not mean that being "spiritual" equals being poor and living in a dump. That doesn't make sense either. The problem is not with the "material" objects themselves. I'll get back to this later.

First, I'd like to know this . . . So many people want to "attract a new car." But what is it with cars anyway? Somehow the car has become a symbol of status, of "success." I know a number of people (even some well-known ones) who are so obsessed with their cars, they even give names to their car. A friend of mine had a car and was really proud of it. He called this car "Infinity." Another friend of mine doesn't care the least bit about what kind of car he drives.

Still, he needed to buy a car the other day to be able drive to work. But because he didn't really care about it, he simply bought the first set of wheels that he liked even just a bit and of which he thought the price was right for him. "If I can drive to work and back with it, then that's a great car for me," he thought. He bought himself a pretty old car to be honest. It certainly didn't look that fancy. The other friend would have dubbed it a piece of junk. But this guy couldn't care less. In fact, he could see the fun of it. In response to my other friend who called his car "Infinity," this guy decided to give his car a name too. He called it "Finity." I kid you not, this is a true story. What it illustrates is the relativity of "status" and "success." What one person would consider being dignified could be considered by the next person as pathetic.

Like I said, the trap is not with material objects themselves. These are just frequency patterns anyway. The problem comes when we see those objects as the ultimate goals and the very symbols of success that confirm whether we "made it" in life or not. It is for this reason that many people look to others to confirm to themselves if they are "doing well" or if they are "successful." When you don't succeed in terms of big houses, big cars, big money, you are often considered as a "failure," and often consider yourself as such.

The whole system thrives on consumption and the constant expansion of consumption, and the more we consume, the more we are considered to be "successful." This even leads to many people borrowing more of what they don't have and getting in even deeper trouble, simply to provide themselves the very things that should testify to others of their alleged "success."

So is this the kind of "success" you are looking for?

What if I told you that the real success you are looking for is not having all kinds of material stuff, but is actually called "happiness"?

After all, why would you want a lot of money, or a big house, or a big car? Why would you want others to approve of you?

In the end it all comes down to a desire for a sense of security and happiness, and being able to live life on your own terms. The quest ends when you're happy and fulfilled.

But when are you happy and fulfilled? Here's a hint from what a wise man once said: "Money and fame do not happiness make."

Don't get me wrong. There is nothing wrong with having a lot of money, or being well-known, or having big cars and big houses. These are all thought fields and are just experience. The problem is that so many people get absorbed in pursuing the material

"dream" that they forget about why they are doing that in the first place.

I believe it was John Harricharan who said this:

"Most people are so busy trying to make a living; they forget to make a life."

He's right. Most people are "human doings" instead of "human beings."

The funny thing is that the greatest payoff from trying to get what you want through working with the "LOA" or "deliberate creation" comes from a state of being. It is a state of happiness, contentment, and love and gratitude for what IS that gets you what you truly want. Remember, it's **Be-Do-Have**, not Do-Have-Be.

At any rate, the greatest payoff from your attraction efforts does certainly not come from an obsession with even more material stuff in the merry-go-round that gets faster by the day, for the sole reason to seek approval and confirmation of your "success" from others, in order to compensate for a lack of self-esteem, which is the cause of this obsession to begin with.

A sense of security, self-esteem, and **"success" is found within yourself, not outside.**

And the funny thing is that once you give up the obsession with possession and finally acknowledge your true self, the person who you really are deep inside, you seem to manifest what you want much more easily.

When that happens, you can enjoy all kinds of material stuff as much as you like, if that's what you choose. You can choose to have a big car if you like. You can choose to live in a big house if that's what you want.

The difference is that you won't be controlled by the never-ending pursuit of these things. You won't be "on the path to happiness and success" anymore. You would just BE happy instead, and from there, you will *allow* things to manifest instead of chasing them forever. It's a small difference in perception, but with profound effects. It is then that you will start to live life, instead of life living you.

So what is "success"? Success, my friend, is what *you* define it to be; go manifest *your* success, whatever that is for you!

Wishing you all life has to offer,
From Ken's desk

Thoughts … Suffering … Love and Attention

OK, let us dive into the mind. Your world is the densest part of your mind.

Life, the Source, uses your thoughts as the instructions by which to create your reality in the material world. Life expresses your thoughts into physical reality. To express is to make known, to state, to articulate, to communicate, to convey. The force of life makes known your thoughts to yourself and everyone else by forming them into experiences and objects that can be experienced, here in the physical world. You experience your own thoughts firsthand, your images of your mind, so that you may know which ones are suitable and which ones are not. That is how you know yourself, that is how you experience your self, and that is how you grow. This world is designed to enable you to experience your Self. It is designed to enable you to experience an idea and its effects and consequences.

Your state of wealth externally is an extension and testament of your state of wealth internally. How clear and certain you are in thoughts of wealth is evidenced externally.

Life does not select which thoughts to express and which ones not to. How would it choose for you? It therefore expresses all of them to the extent that you have them and believe them. You have true free will. This free will is truly free because of the fact that all of it is acted upon without filtering or favoring. Free will is truly free because of the fact that it actually gets results all the time, not just some of the time, and it gets them exactly.

To the extent that your thoughts are not conscious, deliberate, and focused in any topic of life, you will be affected by the outcome of the thoughts of other people. And to the extent that your thoughts are clear, focused, and noncontradictory, your results will be sped up. A few people are able to perform what many people would call miracles simply by thinking only one way and strongly about a thing. The idea that the outcome of their intention may not happen as they wish it to happen does not even occur to them for a split moment.

Suffering is always the result of an error in thinking. It is an indication of being out of harmony with the laws of the universe. The only purpose behind the existence of suffering is to show a person when a thought is in error and alert them of the existence of a higher thought that would serve them better. Suffering stops as soon as that higher way is found, that higher thought. In the presence of suffering, try not to resist. Instead, examine with an open mind, and the answer will always show itself to you without fail.

When someone is telling you about all their suffering, you might want to help them by saying, "**Walk it off.**" That's what we say to a football player when he is down with a minor injury; why not say it to someone with a minor injury in thinking?

Concentration gives thoughts more power and speed in achieving goals.

Your dreams, thoughts, and visions will build your world. You will rise and fall with the rising and falling of your thoughts.

Remember, what you give attention to, you love. Love = attention. The more attention you give to someone, the more you love them. Don't you give plenty of attention to your loved one, your kids? Unfortunately, some choose to give their ex, or their problems, or their suffering so much more attention, therefore actually loving those things. If you constantly talk of your worries, then you love your worries, and more worries will come your way. If you constantly talk of your opportunities, you then love opportunities, and more will come your way.

You can predict the future by looking at the thoughts, words, and actions of today, and applying the law of cause and effect to them.

You are not necessarily responsible for thoughts that enter you head, but you are responsible for the thoughts you keep there. Choose your thoughts wisely!

Wishing you all life has to offer,
From Ken's desk

Tell the Story the Way You Want It to Be

Life is here to serve you, not put obstacles in your way. Everything you desire will show up or not show up in response to your vibration. And if something else shows itself to you that you prefer, life can give you that too. You're calling your own shots. The key is to feel good no matter what. Tell the story the way you want it to be.

Sometimes we worry because what we want requires so much of our attention or so much is happening in our lives that it is hard to hold a stable position, but you can. Just keep telling yourself, "I am in charge here. I am in charge of my life. I am in charge of what comes. And more importantly, I am in charge of how I FEEL."

When it comes to money, the reason most people want a lot of it is because of fear (which dams up the stream). There is nothing wrong with having money, but the big mistake is asking for the security that comes from promises of others. You want your security to come through your awareness of knowing how the laws of the universe work. You know how to focus on what you desire, and you know how this focus will always bring you the good things in life, including money.

Don't try to see so far down the road. Don't demand that promises be made by others to give you the security you need. This is the thing that makes the difference between someone who can stand in an attitude of belief and trust and someone who cannot.

You have a lot of evidence in your life that supports the power of your focus. Don't try to figure it all out at once. Just feel more appreciation for what you have already, and more will come to you.

Try this affirmation. Use it every time you feel you need to know the outcome of any situation.

"I figure it out as I go. I don't need to know. I figure it out as I go."

With that affirmation, say to yourself, "The universe is yielding to me. Good things are lined up for me. All good things come to me. There is not a reason in the world for me to worry. When I worry, it is nothing more than old patterns of thought that have nothing to do with my ability to create what I desire. I have nothing to worry about. Everything comes to me at the right time in the right way. I figure it out as I go. I don't need to know. I figure it out as I go."

Try it.

Wishing you all life has to offer,
From Ken's desk

The Four Causes of Procrastination

I've talked about procrastination before and some possible solutions but may be the best way to attack it is to find out what causes it first.

Here's the deal about procrastination.

It's not your fault. It is your responsibility to do something about it, BUT if you procrastinate, that doesn't make you a bad person or lazy or a failure. There are just some things you need to know so that you can prevail over procrastination and not the other way around.

Typically, procrastination shows up when your comfort zone is being pushed and change is on the horizon, but it's important for you to know that you can handle it, in fact, the good news is that you can break through and master it.

There Are Four Main Causes for Procrastination Rearing Its Ugly Little Head:

1. **Fear of Change**
2. **Lack of Clarity**
3. **Fear of Failure**
4. **Fear of Success**

Let's go through all four of these now.

1. FEAR of CHANGE

If you are human, you will resist change just because it is change.

Oddly enough, change is the only constant on earth. Bill gates once said, "Change or be changed." In truth, those not willing to change will be beautifully equipped for a world that no longer exists.

Change is hard, but change is essential. All you have to do is be OK with the fact that change is hard. Once you accept that, you can go from there. Even when you are excited about change in concept, when it becomes real, it's scary and that's OK, accept how inevitable and essential change is, and the freedom from procrastination has begun.

2. LACK of CLARITY

When you aren't clear, you get stuck in INACTION and procrastination. Some people can get completely active and proactive for OTHER people, but when it comes to their own lives, they get stuck. This does not mean you need every detail, just some clarity. It is often misstated that knowledge is power: knowledge in action is power. Ignorance on fire will always trump knowledge on ice.

Now, remember, there is a difference between inspired action (moves you forward) and forced action (gives the illusion that you are pushing past procrastination when they are really just doing a bunch of things to make you feel like they are moving forward).

You need to get clear. What do you want? How do you want to FEEL? What kind of person do you want to be? Get clear, and you can always get back on track.

3. FEAR of FAILURE

"I'm going to be so ready soon."

How many times have you thought or said those words or something like that? How long have you been getting everything "just right" so that you would finally be ready?

The truth is that there is a point when preparation becomes procrastination. The fact of the matter is that perfection doesn't exist. And the highest level of anything (a product, your job, you as a person, etc.) is only achieved with a certain level of feedback.

It is the world that gives us the feedback we need (after a certain point) to continue to improve ourselves and everything we bring into the world. So if you want to live your best version of your life, you need to do some preparation, and then you need to get feedback by getting out there.

Action → Knowledge → Action → Confidence

We are like heat-seeking missiles; we achieve greatness through heading down the wrong path and then self-correcting and then heading down the wrong path and self-correcting again. And if you continue along this path, there is no failure; there is just the need for correction.

And I know I said you can't be perfect, but you can be great. You can be extraordinary!

4. FEAR of SUCCESS

Most people can't even fathom why they would ever be scared of success so they write it off.

I think this is the biggest fear most of us have. We all think about success, we imagine it, we get excited by it, but if there is any part of you that is scared that with that success there will be a big sacrifice, then you will continue to procrastinate and place blame and point fingers.

FEAR of what following through and succeeding will cause, what chain of events it will cause—who you will have to be, how you will have to spend your time, how your loved ones will react, how much tax you'll have to pay, Fear of success is the source of so much procrastination!

Fear of success isn't fear of the success itself; it's fear of what sacrifices you will have to make to get and live that success. Sometimes it means letting go of the life you have or the things you own. Listen, you can win out over this fear, and to do so, you have to make your whole life fit what you want. Be honest about what you are scared your success will cause and then get creative about how you can make it work without that being the result. The second you put yourself in a solution mind-set, you are powerful!

It's about designing your whole life, and when you remember that, you will be on track!

Here's an example. If you want a millions of dollars and want to have all of that money come to you without you having to be relegated to a specific area or working at specific times, then DON'T build a business that requires you to hire a bunch of people and have an office.

I promise you, there are so many ways to achieve your goals, more ways than you could ever imagine, but it all has to fit or you will dig in your heels and procrastinate!

Here's a great exercise to help you figure out what you might be scared of.

Look at whatever success you are focused on achieving in your life right now and ask yourself this: If this works, what will the benefits be?

Write down everything GREAT that will come of it.

Then ask yourself this: If this works, what sacrifices will I have to make? Or what might I lose if I have this success?

Once you are armed with the truth of what you are really scared of, then you can shift to a solutions mind-set and finally win the battle with procrastination!

And please don't procrastinate with this exercise. ☺

Wishing you all life has to offer,
From Ken's desk

The Challenges of the Moment

To be successful, we must know when and where to separate what is important. Often we hear people say that home life is the most important thing, but why then do you work? Or we hear the term "workaholic" applied to those more focused on their job.

It is important to note that both family life and work life are vital. They should not be separated as one over the other but one more important at the moment.

The goal should be to leave the problems of home at home. Do not think of your family when on the job for that will cloud your thoughts. So too should it be that you leave the problems of work at work for that will dampen your love. In truth, there is no room at work for your family and no room at home for your work. **To divorce one from the other will allow you to be wedded to both.**

It is a paradox, but without separation one—family life or work—will die. To separate the two will allow the two to flourish.

Too often we are told that we should seek balance. Balance is an unlikely goal. What we should seek is harmony.

Think of a symphony. All the instruments do not have balanced time or balanced tone. The piano may get its solo and backed by others, and the violin will get its time, but in the end, it all creates harmony. It is even said that it is the silence between the notes that makes the music, yet they are not in equal amounts. Your life is to be viewed the same way—not parts divided in equal time or balanced time but as a designed symphony that makes it all come together in beautiful harmony. A balanced life would be a tricky thing, trying to divide everything equally, but a harmonic life keeps the flow of all the parts of your life in sync.

Neither home nor work should be trivialized or one to supersede. You need both, so keep both in their place.

Wishing you all life has to offer,
From Ken's desk

The Cup

What keeps most people stuck? It is the underlying assumption that we don't have what we need. It is the idea that we're missing something. We need more of everything. You name it, we need it: more time, money, energy, information, certainty, resources. Without these, we tell ourselves we can't do what we want to do.

This perception that there is something missing or we don't have what we need to create what we want is the biggest source of unhappiness and dissatisfaction in the world today. It is also the greatest lie we tell ourselves. It causes us to dream about becoming something big, to hold out for doing that one big thing that is so big that we can't see a way to do it, let alone get started.

We have fallen in love with the idea of becoming more than we are, and that very belief keeps us stuck were we are. We are on an endless search for the pot of gold at the end of the rainbow, all the while not realizing that we are standing on the pot of gold.

Many people travel their entire lives on this journey, believing they will find true happiness when they finally get somewhere when, in fact, they are lost right where they are.

The reason people find themselves getting stuck is because they don't think who they are is enough—enough to get that promotion, enough to close that next big account, enough to be financially independent. This causes us to resist the way things are for the way we want them to be in the future.

Before you can create your future, you have to accept the way you are right now. You have everything you need right now.

Here is an analogy:

People living in scarcity and struggle see the cup as half empty.

People who are positive thinkers see the cup as half full.

People who understand their true connection to Source Energy see the cup as overflowing.

But people who are living in the flow and in alignment know they ARE the cup.

What's keeping you from seeing yourself as "the cup"?

Wishing you all life has to offer,
From Ken's desk

The Fork in the Road

We talk a lot about fear, not because I want to always keep it in your mind—I don't—but because it is such a big hurdle to overcome. It is truly amazing how much faith we put in fear. My old mentor Casey once said to me that if I could have as much faith in faith as I have faith in fear, I would be so much more successful.

To cover my first point, we should be careful about spending time on any negative as you are then inviting/attracting the very thing you don't want. More time should be spent on what you do want. In fact, all of your time should be spent on what you do want, but in reality, some cannot get to that place because over the years fear has taken a strangle hold on their way of thinking.

Don't get me wrong. Even with the best possible focus on the positive,. stuff will happen. It is up to you to keep moving in your direction. Wil Rogers put it best when he said, "Even if you are on the right track, if you sit down, eventually you will get run over."

The biggest problem with fear is when we make friends with it. It comforts us in allowing us to be right. If the bad thing happens, then we can say, "See, I told you it would work out that way."

Don't build a house where you should have built a tent. When a bad thing happens, do not let it define you or the way things work for you. Do not let negative outcomes be your circumstances; learn from it quickly and move on. Ask yourself what it is you were to learn from it and be grateful that you were given a lesson to help you grow.

In fact, make it your mission to become a problem solver. Have a definite plan, expand your thinking, and think about what you don't know.

Know that you are qualified to succeed. You have all the talent, all the necessary tools, all resources to become the person you always wanted to be. All you lack is a little direction.

Fear points you in one direction; faith points you in the other. You are at the fork in the road, and all you have to do is decide on which direction. In this metaphor, we can easily say to ourselves, "But how do I decide? The two paths look the same." This is true of two paths in the woods, but when deciding on outcomes, you must realize that each path is made up by you, so really there is only one road.

We become successful when we realize that no matter the outcome of something, we try. It is a success! It either turned out the way we wanted, or we were given another chance to learn something. And hey, maybe, just maybe, it worked out in a way that is better for us than had it worked out the way we wanted it too, truly a win-win situation.

"Do not travel the path well known but carve a new path for others to follow."

Don't forget that we don't know the outcome of a story until we reach the end. Often we think we are at the end, and yet there is so much life ahead of us. The story is nowhere near complete.

Wishing you all life has to offer,
From Ken's desk

The Gatekeeper

I often get questions about the communication between our conscious and subconscious minds that I wanted to clear a bit for all.

Another name you might use for the critical factor between the conscious and subconscious is the gatekeeper (we love gatekeepers in our business ☺). The gatekeeper, as the name implies, is a gatekeeper between what happens in the outside world and what you allow inside.

The function of the gatekeeper is very simple. It's basically to keep things the same. Its primary intention is to make your life easier by rejecting information that doesn't match the subconscious/blueprint you already have inside. In this way, you don't have to keep making new decisions. So the gatekeeper is designed to keep information out, which is tremendously useful when someone tries to persuade you to do something stupid like telling you that you can "jump off a building and you'll fly!"

But it's also very harmful when it keeps you stuck with a belief or habit that you don't want anymore.

The gatekeeper has some very powerful tools at its disposal, which include emotions like fear, doubt, worry, and anger. These are psychological defense mechanisms that automatically reject new information.

So the key is learning how to instantly bypass your inner gatekeeper and get directly to your subconscious mind. When you learn to do that, you can change your inner blueprint in moments.

How? The first thing you will have to come to grips with is that it is very possible that everything you know is not factual. You have to open your mind to the possibility that everything you know is wrong. Not easy and tough on the ego, right?

You must learn to question everything and rule out nothing, to be willing to suspend everything you know, to understand that you cannot discover new things until you stop telling those new things what you think they should be and let them tell you what they really are.

From there, we have to reprogram. That is why I send you these messages daily. Read them, reread them, and challenge you mind. Read many books and go to many seminars. Remember, the old stuff will always stay, but the mind easily expands and never contracts. You need more positive stuff to outweigh the old.

Keep on with the program and keep on track with your vision of success.

Wishing you all life has to offer,
From Ken's desk

The Materialism Paradox

I found this article:

> Researchers have found that there is not just a correlation between low self-esteem and materialism, but also a causal relationship where low self-esteem INCREASES materialism and materialism can CREATE low self-esteem. They also found that as an individual's self-esteem increases, their interest in materialism decreases. In a study primarily focused on how this relationship effects children and adolescents, Lan Nguyen Chaplin (University of Illinois Urbana-Champaign) and Deborah Roedder John (University of Minnesota) found that even a simple gesture to raise self-esteem dramatically decreased materialism.
>
> "By the time children reach early adolescence and experience a decline in self-esteem, the stage is set for the use of material possessions as a coping strategy for feelings of low self-worth." The paradox that findings such as these bring up, is that consumerism is good for the economy in the short run, but bad for the individual in the long run, especially for young people.
>
> Most of us want more income so we can consume more stuff. However, several separate studies show that as societies become richer, they do not become happier. Statistically people have more material possessions and money than they did fifty years ago, but they are actually less happy. In fact, the wealthiest countries have more depression, alcoholism and more crime than they did fifty years ago and yet we have more material goods to purchase than ever before. This paradox is true of Britain, the United States, Australia, continental Europe and Japan.
>
> The real reason people want whatever is currently "hot" or "in style" is because they believe it will contribute towards their satisfaction and happiness in life. The word "believe" is the key here. People believe that buying more and more things, especially name brand clothes and cars, will make them happy, when in fact research has shown time and time again that this simply isn't the case.

The point here is if you believe that when you get enough "stuff" you will be happy, you are setting yourself up to be very disappointed. So instead why not be happy NOW? That's right! Cut out the middleman (all that stuff you think will make you happy when you get it) and just be happy NOW. A radical idea, wouldn't you say? Another paradox: as you see life through abundance, wealth and JOY, money, and stuff will simply come to you, and that is the way to enjoy the stuff AND life.

From Ken's desk

The Mayan Doom

It's 2012, and people are talking about the apocalypse (had a conversation the other day on this).

There have been predictions and indications of the apocalypse from so many different sources. It is hard to keep them all straight. So the buzz is that all these predictions mean that the world is going to end. BUT apocalypse also has another meaning (*a prophetic disclosure; a revelation*).

Here's some news about the apocalypse that many people aren't talking about. The other interpretation for all of these doomsday predictions is not the end of the world, but the end of an era.

So what does this mean to you? It means the following:

You can choose to do one of three things:

1. Ignore all talk of the apocalypse completely.
2. Panic that the world is going to end. Stop all your plans, all your investments, and all your work.

or

3. Look at this as an opportunity to shift into a new era in your own life.

Think about it. If 2012 really is the end of an era, what would that mean to you?

Who do you want to be in the new era?

How do you want to think?

How do you want your life to feel?

Do you want to make your decisions based in empowerment or fear?

What do you want to value?

What will you leave behind in order to move, positively, into the new era?

Who are you ready to become?

Fear will only breed more fear, but if you look at this as an exciting time, a time where everything is shifting, then you are empowered! Opportunities abound!

Wishing you all life has to offer,

From Ken's desk

The Monkey Trap

Are you scared that what you desire will always stay JUST out of reach?

If you answered yes, don't worry. You aren't alone, and I want to help. Here's what I know; that fear is natural. Now, here's something else I know. As long as you are in that fear, you are clutching your dreams so tightly that they stay out of reach.

And this brings us to one of the most difficult things. Are you ready for this? So take what I am about to say and remind yourself of it every day. Here you go. **In order to allow your desires to manifest in your life, you have to let go.**

YIKES! I know the very thought of that strikes fear in most of us. I know how easy it is to think that if you "let it go," then it won't show up. And that is the opposite of true. On so many occasions, I have found that once I put my desire on paper, held it tightly to me, and then watched as nothing happened, I then finally gave up. Not the way you think. Once I gave up holding on and then gave in to letting go, much to my surprise, things started to work out.

To help you really get this and put it into practice in your life, I want to read an excerpt from "The Monkey Trap" by Len Wright:

Are You Caught in This Trap?
Excerpt from "The Monkey Trap" by Len Wright

If you ever feel like you are caught in a trap with your life, you're not far off from the truth! The hamster on the wheel with a big juicy carrot in front of it is a prime example of how most are living these days. That's not a judgment or put-down, I'm only looking honestly at our society in these times.

Just look at how fearful humans have become. How fear of loss is driving, motivating them to run that much faster on the wheel to try to escape the nagging empty feeling inside. People are placing their belief in the illusion that surrounds them and wondering why they feel overwhelmed, confused, frustrated and like their life is passing them by.

If you believe in something that is a mirage, you will always be let down, *disappointed and feeling like once again the answer is to run faster, try harder and accomplish more. Every new experience or plan seems like an oasis that will "save" you from your inner plight. A brand-new start, AGAIN! It's like a dog chasing its own tail, round* *and round it goes, getting absolutely nowhere. Tiring, frustrating and depressing to say the least.*

This condition we are talking about is actually a trap, a self-imposed prison. Read on and you'll learn exactly how you are participating by being both the warden and the prisoner and how to finally set yourself free.

The liberation of your life is what we are talking about here and it's worth your time to find out exactly how you are acting as the puppet in your life rather than the puppet master.

The Monkey Trap and YOU . . .

Deep in the jungles, trappers use a crafty technique to catch monkeys using their own resistance. It shows exactly how you may be doing the same thing in your life and how letting go is always the answer to all of life's questions.

They begin by hollowing out a coconut. Making a small enough hole in the one end, just enough for the monkey to squeeze its flat unclenched hand inside, they then tie a treat to the inside of the coconut and hang it from a tree.

The monkey comes along, notices the treat and squeezes its flat hand inside to grab hold of it.

Once the monkey grabs on tightly to the treat inside, its hand is made into a clenched fist and cannot be pulled back through the narrow hole. As hard as that monkey tries, its hand cannot break loose as a fist, so as long as it is intent on keeping the treat in its grasp, it is trapped.

What's really interesting here is that IF the monkey was to simply Let Go of the treat, it would instantly be free.

In this example, the treat is our attachment to our desires or wants! How we "think" it should be rather than how it is.

The moral of this simple story is that If we hold on to what we think we want we set ourselves up to be trapped but at any moment as soon as we let go, we too instantly gain our freedom from the pain that is self inflicted by our attachment or grasp on our desire.

Let go and watch how love frees you from your pain . . .

So How Can YOU Learn to Let Go?

The next time you feel irritated, frustrated, angry, or depressed, notice what you are paying attention to and focusing on in that moment.

KEN GRIFFITH

Is it a memory that is streaming a movie of thoughts and images? Is it something that caught your eye and then triggered a memory or image that has carried you away into the world of thought? If you are upset with someone, notice how your mind feeds you with images/movies, voices, and feelings that build that emotional energetic state.

The more you focus your attention on what your mind is feeding you, the deeper you sink into that imaginary world. See if you can observe how your mind tries to involve, lure, and catch you in its trap.

The process is as follows.

First, the trigger is set off. This could be anything that brings up a thought or memory of past or future events. You "see" or "hear" the thought and start focusing in on what your mind is portraying to you. Each step into that world of thought will take you further into the abyss of negative states and imagination where no solution can ever be found. So what choice do you have?

Try doubt! Become your own internal skeptic!

That's right I, Ken Griffith, am encouraging you to doubt. It's hard to believe, but stay with me here.

When your mind gives you a command, something to think about or carry out, maybe an experience that you perceive as a "problem," what do YOU do with it? Do you answer it in some way to ease its nagging? Do you try to fix, solve, or find an answer to what is supposedly wrong?

Have you ever considered doubting its authority? Most are not skeptical at all when their mind tells them to do its bidding because they are so used to acting on what they are told inwardly. Basically, we believe that our mind would not deceive us or lead us astray, but this is where we fall down in our understanding. Our minds are exquisite tools, but left to their own devices, they can be harsh task masters.

Question, examine, and investigate the drivers or motivators to all of your actions. Be suspicious as to "WHY" your mind is telling you that you feel the way you do. Ask yourself why you are doing what you are doing. Also ask yourself, "Is this action from love or is my mind trying to run the show here?"

If you find that the action does not serve your **higher self**, let it go and release the need to take any action. Be patient, and the proper forward movement will appear.

Become an observer to these processes, and you'll find yourself being able to drop these negative energies before they take hold. Let go and stop clinging to what your mind tells you will set you free. Be empowered by utilizing your mind as a tool rather than the other way around!

Practice being that silent observer to your mind's movement. Listen and watch as it tries to direct your actions and thoughts, then examine them carefully. Is what you are being told leading you to actions of love, peace, or kindness?

If not, you are being fed lies by an inward conspirator, and you must not answer this state. Letting go doesn't take strength as much as it takes a true understanding of the relationship you currently have with life and that state.

Stop, wait, breathe, and examine BEFORE you take any step; and you'll start to realize how much you've been a follower in your own life. Now you can, by observing the inner workings of YOU, take control and allow for your true potential to blossom.

Wishing you all life has to offer,
From Ken's desk

The Three C's and the Three G's

Right now, most people are flying through their lives feeling the need to attract money fast. There is panic in the air. Many people feel like they are drowning and have nothing to hold onto. In fact, Stats Canada just reported a shrinking middle class.

Are you one of these people? If so, you are certainly not alone, and I want you to know there is a way!

This is important; there are **three unknown forms of resistance** that most people are using without even realizing it. These three forms of resistance are actually pushing money away from the people who feel like they need it most.

Here's the good news! There are actually **three steps to attract money fast**. Now, I want to be clear about this. The three steps I'm going to give you will push your comfort zone, but they work, so **read on with an open mind and a spirit of abundance** as I share with you the three steps to attract money (or anything else) fast.

There really are three steps to attract money fast, and they are probably not what you think. And I'll tell you now; these three steps will probably go against all of the instincts you have.

Let me explain.

When you feel like you need to attract money fast, you are normally in a state of panic. It could be a very small state of panic. It could be overwhelming, but if you feel like you need something fast, there is urgency.

When you feel urgent, the instinct is to push and try to force things to happen. When most people feel like they need to attract money fast, the three steps they try to use are the three C's:

1. Complain
2. Cut Off
3. Constrict and Conserve

1. COMPLAIN:

Imagine this. A guy goes into work and gets laid off from the job he was certain he would have until he retired. Panic sets in and, I guarantee you, the first thing he does is start complaining about his boss, the injustice, the economy, the government, the guy that he thinks pushed him out, etc.

2. CUT OFF:

Then what does he do? He gets angry, his ego is bruised, he needs to figure out how he is going to take care of himself and his family, and he immediately cuts off and closes off and withdraws into himself. If anyone tries to talk to him, he probably shuts them out and cuts off from them.

3. CONSTRICT AND CONSERVE:

The last step is the kicker. He is so focused on his new "*lack of money and need to make money fast*" that he starts to think about all of the ways he can protect himself and cut back. He completely constricts and starts conserving. He literally goes into "starvation mode" for money.

This 3C process seems completely natural, right? He has himself and his family to protect, so he better buckle down, cut his losses, crawl into his cave, and figure out how he can fix this (I know. I did this in my past) and then force it to be better, right? WRONG!

The three C's only make the situation worse! Are the three C's completely natural? Yes, but will they help you out of your situation quickly? **NO!** Nor even long term for that matter because you now have sold yourself that money is scarce. or a scarcity.

The three steps to attract money fast are the opposite of the three C's, and they make you step out of your comfort zone and go against survival instinct.

The Three Steps to Attract Money Fast Are What I Call the Three G's.

These three steps may sound like "pie in the sky," but they work. And I know they work, because I have consistently used them in my life since I learned about them; and they have always resulted in abundance, prosperity, and joy.

So even though they will push your comfort zone, I'm going to give you these three steps and ask you to try them and give them an honest shot the next time you need to attract money or anything fast.

If the three C's have been working for you, by all means, stick with them; but if they haven't, then the three G's are worth a try, don't you think?

The Three Steps to Attract Money Fast or the Three G's Are:
1. Gratitude
2. Give
3. Generate

1. GRATITUDE:

Gratitude is the way to abundance. It's as simple as that. **Right now, I want you to write down at least three things that you can be grateful for** (ten is better).

KEN GRIFFITH

I can hear you kicking and screaming, "Are you crazy, Ken? Nothing in my life is going right, and you want me to be grateful?"

Yes, that's exactly right. I GUARANTEE that you have at least three things you can be grateful for.

Your life might be terrible right now, but when you sit in complaining and self-pity and any of the other awful emotions you may be feeling, you prolong the struggle. (Some just love a good "pity party." Two rules to a pity party are keep them short and invite no one.)

So I ask you this.

What three things can you be grateful for right now?

Part of you is probably yelling at me, "NOTHING. I have NOTHING to be GRATEFUL FOR!"

Here, let me help.

- Are you breathing right now?
- Can you read?
- Can you walk and run and talk and laugh?
- Can you think and imagine?
- Can you hear and smell and eat?
- Do you have someone (anyone) somewhere that loves you?
- Do you have someone (anyone) somewhere that you love?

Even if it doesn't make sense to you, the FIRST STEP in the Three Steps to Attract Money Fast is to be grateful. So what are the three things you are grateful for? It's OK if they are small. Think of each of them, really focus on them individually. Why are you grateful for these things? Focus on them, feel them, breathe into them, and then for each of them say, "'THANK YOU." Just by doing this, you will change your state and shift from an awareness of lack to an awareness of abundance.

Remember, you attract what you focus on!

Now you are ready for the second step in the Three Steps to Attract Money Fast.

The second G is GIVE. To attract money, you have to give money.

Now, be honest. Does that seem crazy? If you answered yes, you aren't alone.

My mentor Don once had to explain this to me. I told him he might think of me as nuts or hard of hearing. I needed the money.

"Yup, I know it's counterintuitive, but when you feel like you NEED something, the fastest way to bring it into your life is to give exactly what it is you feel you need," was his reply. Now contrary to the belief of some, I am not the combative type, but my comfort zone was shot. And I sounded like a crazy person upon hearing this advice, yet he calmly said, "Look, you need to attract money fast, and it's understandable that you think I'm crazy for telling you that when you feel like you need to attract money fast, you should give money. But I want to prove this to you. Are you up for a challenge?"

I never could say no to a challenge (or him really).

He said, "OK, here's your challenge. For one week, you accept that the way you are going to attract money fast is by giving money. You follow through on that with inspired action, and at our session next week, if you don't have more money than you do right now, you don't pay for the session AND I will post a blog post saying that I made a mistake. How does that sound?" Deal.

This is what happened.

The very next day, I am downtown, and a guy who seemed normal came up to me—I suspect he came up to many—asking for $1.50 to add to what he had so that he could but a bus ticket to Belleville.

Now, I still wasn't really in the mood to give away what I barely had, but Don's words rang in my head. I gave him the money and almost immediately felt good and free, and suddenly I realized how much I had been clamping down on my money. Obviously, it wasn't a lot of money, but a day ago, I would have felt like I couldn't give even that and would have avoided the guy at all costs. That's really not like me, but since I felt like I need money, I was clenching onto whatever I had.

The day after, I was feeling much more focused and decided to make that day about doing all of the unfinished things that were hanging over my head. Two days later, one client returned my call, asking for help. He needed to hire a senior underwriter and got permission from the VP to take whoever I felt is best suited for the job without their HR department getting involved. By the end of the week, I got him his guy. And that's $8,400 to me.

I promise you, whatever it is you feel you need more of, go out and give it!

It doesn't have to be a lot. It isn't about the amount. It's about letting go of the constriction you have. When you constrict, you block the flow, but when you give, you open yourself up to receive. It helps you understand and respect that money is not scarce.

- If you need to **attract money fast**, go give it!
- If you want to **attract love**, go give it!
- If you want to **attract positivity**, go give it!

And then let go and trust that you have removed the flow blocks and are now ready to receive.

KEN GRIFFITH

It's time for the third G: Generate.

You MUST commit to generating a positive vibration. Your energy vibration and level attract the same energy vibration and level, so you have to do everything you can to "feel good" in every possible moment.

You're probably saying, "Yeah right, Ken. When I feel like I need to attract money fast, I feel desperate and panicky, so how am I supposed to generate a positive vibration when that isn't how I feel?"

Good question!

If you find yourself in a negative place, I want you to stop and say to yourself, "I'm feeling negative right now. What is something I can think about that I feel great about?" Honestly, all that matters is getting yourself to generate a positive vibration; it doesn't matter what you are positive about.

Here's the deal.

The universe recognizes your vibration pattern—like attracts like. That isn't theory; it's science. What that means is the most important thing in any moment is that you are in a positive place. Smile at people, make sure your body language is open and receptive even if it means going back to the first G, and find one that makes you smile. Just constantly look for things you can appreciate in every moment and give them your full attention.

Give your full focus and attention to generating positive energy, and you will be shocked at the abundance of positivity that starts to flow around you.

You really can attract money (or anything) quickly; it's simple, but it isn't necessarily easy. But now that you know the three C's and the three G's, you have the tools you need to manifest the life you desire—consistently and joyfully!

Let me know if any such stories come about for you.

Wishing you all life has to offer,
From Ken's desk

The Power of Positive Habits

I've got some great advice for you today on creating habits (the positive kind) that can help move you forward along your success journey.

Before you get into this advice below, take a moment to remind yourself that the very fact that you're reading this means you are ahead of the folks who never do a single thing to improve in the areas they want to. The investment of time you're making in your own personal development will pay great dividends for years to come. Therefore, I commend you for taking your professional development seriously.

So here we go:

Did you know that habits are incredibly powerful tools for personal growth and success? Let me ask you a question. When is the last time you made a conscious decision to add a new habit to your life? If you are like most people, you probably answered, "Never!"

The reason for this is that most people only think of habits as something bad. If you ask ten people on the street what the word habit means, nine out of ten will tell you that a habit is a negative action that people do over and over again, like smoking, eating too much, or procrastinating.

But the truth is that positive habits hold the keys to success in virtually everything you do. "What are positive habits?" you ask. A positive habit is simply a habit that produces positive benefits, actions, and attitudes.

Why is there such great power in positive habits to effect change? Because habits, by their very nature, are automatic, and after a period of time, they can also become permanent. This is a very powerful combination.

So how do we go about adding new positive habits to our life? It's really quite easy. You simply begin repeating an action, attitude, or thought process every day for at least twenty-one days. Research has shown that an action that is repeated for a minimum of twenty-one days is likely to become a permanent habit.

Remember that positive habits have positive benefits, and you will reap those benefits for as long as you maintain that habit.

So now that we know what positive habits are and how to acquire them, let's look at some simple positive habits for success.

Positive Habit #1: Make it a habit to set goals.

Did you know that the most successful people all share the common positive habit of goal setting? A study was done to determine the importance of goal setting. Top business execs who had gone on to achieve great success were asked to list their habits. These execs who had made a habit of setting goals were in the top 5 percent of earnings in the population!

It is almost impossible to overestimate the value of goal setting as a positive habit. Goal setting is simple, yet 95 percent of the population never do it. By making goal setting a positive habit, you can start placing yourself in the top 5 percent of the population of successful people, so why not do it.

Here are some simple steps to help you start making goal setting a positive habit:

Step 1: Define your goals, write them down, and be very specific; capture your goals on paper. It is amazing how many people never take the time to write down exactly what it is they want in life. Remember, you can't hit a target if you don't have one.

Step 2: Determine what the time line is for reaching your goals; set specific deadlines for each goal.

Step 3: Identify any obstacles that may stand in your way, list them, and state how you plan to overcome them.

Step 4: Make a list of the people and/or organizations who will help you reach your goals.

Positive Habits #2: Be more productive with the 4D habit.

Many of us are stressed out by the negative effects of work overload in our careers (effort). The 4D habit is a very simple positive habit that will help you to prevent work overload.

Every time you are faced with a new task to perform, apply the four D's as listed below. You will find that your workload will be reduced as you apply this screening and decision-making tool to each task you are confronted with. Decide on the most appropriate choice and take action.

Do It Now: take immediate action, do the task right away, don't procrastinate.

Dump It Now: make a quick decision and dump the task.

Delegate It: give the task to someone else. This is a very critical aspect of time management. Your time is valuable; make it a habit to work on tasks that you do best and delegate the tasks that can be performed by someone else.

Defer the Task: make an immediate decision to postpone the task to a later time. Make sure to schedule a time to complete it.

Positive Habit #3: Create and repeat positive attitude phrases.

A positive attitude is perhaps the most important ingredient to success and a surefire way to maintain a positive attitude is to make it a habit to repeat positive attitude phrases. Choose or create a positive attitude phrase and repeat it aloud many times each day. In a few days, you will notice that your attitude will become more positive. Here are some examples:

"I am reaching my success goals every day."

"I am getting stronger and stronger every day."

"I can overcome any obstacle."

"Every day I am getting closer and closer to my goals in life."

"If I believe it. I can achieve it."

"Every day, my mental attitude is becoming more positive."

Positive habits can truly change your life. I know from personal experience. I am now constantly aware of the habits I have and the new positive habits I am acquiring; I am also aware of the benefits I am receiving. Positive habits are now second nature to me, and soon they will be second nature to you.

Wishing you all life has to offer,

From Ken's desk

The Power of the Mind—Health

The mind is an especially powerful tool when it comes to healing the body, but we so often ignore it and the amazing things it can do for our health. And it goes without saying that without your health, you have nothing. I want this year to be a year of great health for you, a year where you take your body, mind, and spirit to new levels.

Eastern civilizations have long recognized the link between the body and the mind. Buddhists believe that the mind is pure, limitless, and pervasive. It is like the sun shining in a clear sky. The problems or sickness we experience are like clouds in the sky, which block out the sun. Just as clouds that temporarily block out the sun, our problems and sicknesses are only temporary. They can be removed from the mind. Simply put, we have the ability to control the state of our body with our mind!

Ever notice some people with similar problems respond differently to same treatments. Why do some completely recover while others only recover temporarily? And why do the conditions of others worsen? Well, it is the mind that causes these differences! How do we go about achieving ultimate healing?

Here are three ways, a mixture of Buddhist practices and other Eastern practices.

Meditation

In a study published in the journal *Brain Research Bulletin*, researchers found that people trained to meditate over an eight-week period were able to control specific type of brain waves called alpha rhythms.

What are alpha rhythms? Think of radio stations that broadcast at specific frequencies. Our brain works similarly! There are different types of brainwaves that help regulate the flow of information between brain cells. Alpha rhythms flow through cells where sensory information is processed. This information determines and affects the sensations that we feel with our bodies. To put it simply, alpha rhythms impact what we're able to feel!

With regular meditation, we can raise our levels of alpha rhythms and become more aware of our own bodily sensations. For those suffering pain, they can essentially turn down the volume on pain signals.

Visualization

Visualization works hand in hand with meditation. While one has raised alpha rhythms, otherwise known as the alpha state of mind, one must visualize the end result of a goal or desire. And this must be done in the present. Let me illustrate how this is done with an example.

Let's say that you are feeling some sort of pain in your feet, and you would like to get rid of it. So to get rid of that pain, you must visualize yourself free of that pain and experience that moment as if it is happening right this instant. Imagine being able to walk or run without any sort of pain bothering you. Imagine how that feels. Isn't that a wonderful sensation?

Conditioning

There are several elements that affect one's ability to effectively visualize and achieve "ultimate healing." If we consciously integrate these elements into our visualization and meditation exercises, we can achieve that "ultimate healing" that we desire. What are these elements?

- Desire
- Belief
- Expectancy

Do you have an intense desire to recover from your pain or suffering? Do you believe that it is possible to recover from that pain? Also, do you expect it?

Think about it. Have you ever heard someone in pain say, "I know that (belief) if I see the doctor (expectancy), I'll definitely feel better (desire)!" This is because the elements or fundamental energies were present that allow the desired outcome.

So it's important then to be conscious of these forces, that true faith is expectancy. These subjective spiritual energies when combined together can result in something beautiful—your desired outcome. It's interesting to note that this does not apply only to your health but also all aspects of your life. The mind is indeed a powerful thing!

Wishing you all life has to offer,
From Ken's desk

The Two-Word Dream Killer

"I am looking for a lot of men who have an infinite capacity to not know what can't be done."—Henry Ford

"I can believe anything, provided it is incredible."—Oscar Wilde

We have talked often about limiting beliefs and how they hold us back. Much of what we have encouraged you to do is examine and release those limiting beliefs to silence the voice that says **"I can't."**

It's the **"I can't"** voice that, over time, kills your ability and even your desire to dream. Yet many of the marvels of our modern world exist because someone had the audacity to dream, to simply not accept that something could not be done.

Children have vivid imaginations and dream all sorts of fantastic things for themselves. But in our journey to adulthood, we adopt false beliefs about ourselves and our abilities. We often end up not only believing we are limited, but we try to convince others of it as well. You have probably heard the expression, "Argue for your limitations, and they're yours."

Try not to use your personality filters as an excuse for behavior or as an excuse for staying stuck. When you look at your personality and the specific challenges that seem to come up repeatedly for you, be honest, but only in an effort to get you to see and release what blocks you. The focus of your evolution will then be always toward a lighter sense of being, toward a bolder, bigger, and more authentic expression of the unlimited being that you are.

This is an abundant universe of infinite possibilities. If your current circumstances make that difficult to believe, look past them. Imagine a different life, a different world, a different you. Dare to dream. Dream big and crazy and wild. No one has to hear.

It's just you imagining, so go ahead. Give it a try. You've got absolutely nothing to lose and so much to gain.

Wishing you all life has to offer,
From Ken's desk

The Worst Belief You Can Have: "I Believe in Struggle."

Read the title again of this message.

I have to admit this. Although I didn't "realize" it for years, I believed in "struggle" for years. I would have some success, though I always find some way to screw it up, to halt my progress. I would go forward then back four steps, forward a few and keep repeating the cycle. It's like I HAD TO make things more difficult for myself than they needed to be. Do you ever do that?

What I didn't get back then is that I bought into a real bad, real bad, real bad BELIEF. That belief is called STRUGGLE.

It's when we think everything needs to be difficult and a struggle to achieve. It's a belief passed onto us from our environment. It could be the home, schools, culture, jobs we've had, and our environment. It's a belief I see so often in the "employee mind."

One of the reasons the "rich get richer and the poor get poorer" is that the poor have bought the belief called struggle. Struggle is all about negativity. Struggle develops from a self-image that doesn't believe one's even worthy to succeed. Let me say that again. Struggle develops from a self-image that doesn't believe one's even worthy to succeed.

When's the last time you checked in on your self-image? Do you realize there's some ridiculously stupid belief you bought into twenty-five years or more that's holding you back today from your best self? Yes, I believe this is true.

"So, what's the opposite of struggle?" Effort.

Daily effort without all the negative mind-set and emotions that struggle brings. So much of this comes down to our thinking. I had to realize over the years that my thinking was off base, not helpful to my goals, and filled with errors.

Ask yourself this today: What is one negative recurring thought I've had for the last ten years that is still holding me back today? Bring in to your awareness then let it go.

We don't realize so many of the chains that are holding us. After years, decades, they become invisible to the eye.

Today we have a decision, a choice.

We can stay with struggle or move closer to actions that bring us greater fulfillment, greater calm, and better results. Which will you do?

Wishing you all life has to offer,
From Ken's desk

Thought of the Day

Life doesn't come with a money back guarantee, and yet many of us live like it does. People are certain that they will keep their jobs. They are certain of living a long healthy life. Others might be certain that they will lose their jobs or get sick and die young. Certainty comes in many forms, but it rarely corresponds to the truth.

The truth is nothing is certain. The need for certainty is the need for safety. It is the basis of all religion. Since we do not like uncertainty, we choose to believe in something that we feel we can be certain about, even though we have no logical proof that it is true.

Some might argue that if nothing can be counted on, then why bother trying. In order to move forward in life, many people need to have a sense of certainty about the outcome. But this kind of certainty is an illusion.

Certainty is a form of disconnection from the truth and from ourselves. When we feel certain about something, we are disconnected from the natural flow of life.

Certainty is the perpetually elusive dream of most people.

What in life is certain? There is a part of you—your authentic self—that is unchanging. This pure consciousness is certain, while everything else is uncertain, impermanent, and an illusion. But how do you discover or experience this pure, unchanging consciousness?

Through inquiry.

If you are certain about something—anything for that matter—you immediately place a lid on that thing. It cannot change. You won't let it change because if you do, you will be wrong in your certainty. But all things, except one thing, do change.

The only thing that doesn't change is WHO YOU ARE—your authentic self or what is commonly called consciousness. Consciousness is what remains when all concepts, beliefs, values, habits, and ways of thinking are stripped away. In other words, all of your ideas, concepts, beliefs, and so on will change over time. If this is true, then why waste time on trying to be certain?

By inquiring how and why you get certain results in your life, you learn about your beliefs and patterns that create those results. Then through the power of your mind, you can consciously form new patterns. The need for certainty is replaced by a relaxed "learning" pattern.

Can you imagine a world in which nothing changes? It would be absolutely miserable. Inquiry is the habit that leads us out of that misery.

Through uncertainty, you move from being an expert to being a student. All of life, all experiences, everyone, and everything become our teachers.

Wishing you all life has to offer,
From Ken's desk

The Truth about Time

The truth about time is that it does not exist except as you say it does.

The biggest trick time ever played on us was to make us think it was real, that we were under its full control. Yet time is a complete illusion, a strong and persistent illusion.

What wonderful news that is! Time is an illusion created by you. Once you understand how this illusion is created by you, you then begin to recreate it as you wish, consciously and deliberately instead of unconsciously and accidentally as you may have been doing.

The only time that truly exists is now.

> *The distinction between past, present and future is only an illusion, however persistent*—Albert Einstein

> *Whether time is long or short, and whether space is broad or narrow, depend upon the mind. Those whose minds are at leisure can feel one day as a millennium, and those whose thoughts are expansive can perceive a small house to be as spacious as the universe.*—Hung-Tzuch'eng

Time flows in all directions, not forward only as it appears to. The past, present, and future exist simultaneously.

Here is an easy explanation of what time is. This is an extremely simplified explanation, but it will do for now. Imagine a football or soccer field with ten objects spread around it. Now, imagine that a certain object A represents a child being born, and a certain object B represents being a ten–year-old child. If object A was to travel to object B, that travel would take what you now call "ten years of time." That is ten human years of a child growing up. Now, it gets a little complex: What if that football field was to shrink? Object A would reach B and pass through all the experiences of ten years of childhood, but the sensation of time would change. In other words, ten years would feel very different. If that field shrunk enough, ten years could feel like an instant. And you have experienced this often. When you are having a great time, you feel as if time flew by. You did not notice the hours pass, yet your watch said they passed, because your watch is designed to take the same amount of "time" to move from one second marker on the clock face to the next. But you are not designed that way. Time is the moving of your consciousness past preexisting events in the space-time continuum. You will soon see what this is.

The field of life that we live in is not static; it keeps changing its dimensions. That is why we have to keep readjusting our watches worldwide all the time for this crazy thing called time to make sense for us, but only because we think of time as consistent slices of periods. It is not. It is merely our misinterpretation of our consciousness moving by one preexisting event in the field of life to the next event, as you shall soon see. The field of life is not static, nor does our consciousness move at a fixed speed. The field may not change that fast for us, and our consciousness may not change its rate that fast unless we will it to do so, and that is why we do not usually notice these differences that much and see that time is not constant.

But if you were to travel very fast in a spaceship, as you may well have heard from Einstein's Theory of Relativity *(I'm reading a book called* Why Does E=MC2*)*, you can slow down time or even go back in time. Time is more of a sensation of passing events, and the faster or slower you pass these events, the faster or slower the calibration of time changes. It is not the taking of time that changes; it is the calibration of time (one minute no longer takes one minute).

OK, back to the soccer field. Imagine you were one of the objects. You would feel time as you move around the field passing other objects that you see, isn't it? Yes. Now, imagine if you were born moving faster, say three times the speed. Time would seem shorter. Now, imagine you were the soccer field itself! Or even an object large enough to cover the whole field. Now, we are talking! Time would cease to exist for you. Because you are the field and you can feel, touch, and be with all the objects on you at the same time always, there would be no travel from one object to another. It would all be happening Here, now. All of it. All the ten objects would be happening at the same "time" for you, always. This is the eternal moment of now, here. Everything that can possibly happen in the universe, everything that can possibly be created, the past, present, and future, are all running all at the same "time" in one huge field. Your consciousness and awareness are awake to only a small section of this field at any one "time," and as you move them about from one point to another, you experience "time," experiencing a sensation of past, present, and future. The field itself does not experience time; it only experiences an eternal process that is always happening all at one go, now, here, always, all ways. You can think of the whole field as the Source.

As you expend your consciousness and awareness, as you take up more and more of the field, time shrinks for you. Can you see that? Now, the amazing thing is that the mind and the self (or soul or spirit, whichever you are used to referring to) is a lot larger than your physical body. We are used to thinking of the soul or self as a little thing contained inside our body. That is just human thinking—relating things to containers. Have you ever considered that the soul, being far more powerful than the body, actually holds the body together and surrounds it? And the mind holds the brain and nervous system together and surrounds it? If you have considered that the soul and mind are larger than the body and brain, have you ever considered where they end? How many feet away from your body? Or is it how many miles away? Or how many light years away from your body does your soul end? It is not impossible that your soul and mind are a billion times larger than your body (why not?). They are infinite and eternal.

Yet this humongous powerful self is you. Anyway, let us get back to wealth.

Understanding time clearly, how it works and how to take control of it, and understanding your self and your self's composition and relation with everything else physical and nonphysical, is of high importance if you wish to experience massive wealth "fast." It is all a matter of expanded consciousness, right state, and right thought and choice. These lead to your consciousness becoming awake to wealthy parts of the whole and doing so in wider circles.

Now is the only moment that exists. An eternal moment of now is all there is. You can remember the past and dream the future, but you can only be, exist, here, now. Make an irrevocable commitment to yourself to make now the best moment of your life ever!

Do not dwell in the past or live in the future. Your only moment is now. Dwell in the now.

As you will soon see, your outer world mirrors your inner world. You will see in this book how this is so.

Do you feel as if you do not have enough time to do what you wish to do? People short of time on the outside are short of it on the inside. They act, think, and speak, believing they are short of time. Stop thinking and saying you do not have enough time. Do not believe that for a second. The universe has no shortages of anything including time, and neither do you, except for the ones that you build for yourself. Believing in any sort of shortage makes your consciousness smaller and slower so that you may experience what you believe in.

The present moment is the greatest gift you can have. It is perfectly created for you according to your stated designs. You state these designs by the thoughts, states of being, words, and actions that you held most true to yourself earlier. The present is something that you send yourself, a perfectly present moment. It allows you to experience, taste, review, and change your past thoughts, states of being, words, and actions. Be grateful for the present, for you know you can change it, for it allows you to experience your self, for its entire existence is to serve you. Cursing, condemning, and judging the present moment will only keep it as it is longer. What you resist, judge, and condemn persists. What you embrace and bring to the light for nonjudgmental, honest, and clear examination reveals the lessons you are looking for, the key to the next level that you seek.

> *Time is only an illusion produced by the succession of our states of consciousness as we travel through eternal duration, and it does not exist where no consciousness exists in which the illusion can be produced; but "lies asleep."*—H. P. Blavatsky

KEN GRIFFITH

The future influences the present just as much as the past.

—Nietzsche

The first time you do something is a journey of discovery. You take in the details and learn many new things. At this point, there are no labels and memories to enable you to prejudge the new experience. Learning is at its highest. The hundredth time you do it is often very different. For most people, repetition brings about unconsciousness. Most people do and see the things that occur most often in their lives in an unconscious and unaware state. Because they have seen or done something once, they turn to relying on their memories of it and labels about it that they built in their minds the first time. Learning and discovery drops to zero. Memories of the past experiences take over. What good does it serve you to live today based on your memory of it yesterday? You miss the gift of the present moment totally! In your work, do you take an absolutely fresh look at your work and customers each new day, or do you go by how you "know" them in their past?

Everything changes and using memory keeps you from seeing that change, seeing things as they truly are. Try to "forget" everything about what you are looking at, and you will discover a whole new world, and you will grow a whole lot faster, grow your wealth and self a whole lot quicker.

Think about it. It is quite often that a stranger will complement your work mate or spouse over something that you totally miss every day because you do not look at them as if they were totally new to you. Memory has its place, but many people overuse it, often in an unbeneficial way.

Decide right now to face every experience anew by choosing to forget that you have ever faced it before. Decide not to anticipate a specific appearance or behavior, an anticipation based on your memory and emotions. Practice detachment of outcome but have certainty of your choices and intention, and you will find a world that has been hiding from you all along, right in front of your eyes all along.

Wishing you all life has to offer,
From Ken's desk

Self-Esteem

Today I want to address an important topic that doesn't usually get the attention it deserves, particularly in the context of "manifesting your desires" and "cocreating" your reality that we spoke of yesterday.

Still, it's something on which "everything" in your life ultimately depends:

- The quality of your health
- The quality of your relationships
- The quality of your creativity
- Your ability to listen to your intuition and inner guidance
- Your finances
- Actualizing your highest potential
- Etc.

Believe it or not, all these aspects of life completely revolve around and emerge from your understanding and your practice of this one thing.

So what is it? It's SELF-ESTEEM.

Now, that may sound obvious, but listen carefully: There's more to it than you might think! Self-esteem is often presented as having the ability to protect yourself, to assert your feelings, to take charge. And that's certainly a viable definition. But the truth is that's only the beginning.

Self-esteem in its true sense is really the manifestation of your spirit engaged in action in your life. In short: it's your spirit in action. So self-esteem is not just a psychological state. Instead, it's the CORE of your SPIRITUAL state. And as such, when you suffer from low self-esteem (or even the total absence of it), you're really experiencing a "spiritual crisis." And such a deep, inner crisis will be reflected in your life experience, usually as some kind of "crisislike" situation.

So here's the crux:

As you know, you're really cocreating your reality. And from that awareness, your life looks completely different than it did before. That's because you're longing to cocreate it based on your true, authentic desires (i.e., according to an inner map of healthy self-esteem). This explains why there might be so much stress on you on a deep, inner level to come to terms with whether or not you really feel good about yourself. After all, self-esteem is completely related to how well you cocreate your reality! This is absolutely crucial to realize!

But here's the thing:

* We're not born with high quantities of self-esteem in our soul.

KEN GRIFFITH

* And self-esteem doesn't emerge naturally in us either.
* Instead, we have to DEVELOP it.
** But once you do, the authority you have to cocreate your reality increases exponentially!

That's because the dynamics of life won't scare you anymore, and you no longer feel like a victim. As long as you're connected to any fears that make you feel like a victim, YOU are not the authority over your life, and YOU don't create your reality. Instead, OTHER people and circumstances do.

So this is really a crucial, essential, and key aspect to taking back your power to "manifest your true desires" in life: You have to become the authority over your own life and take charge of your own co-creation process. This means you MUST come to terms with yourself: You HAVE TO develop healthy self-esteem.

Here's a great way to go at it;
Now think about it for a moment:

* Picture what your life would look like if you could bring a more empowered "you" into your creativity and into your relationships.
* Imagine how your life would change if you could bring your highest potential to everything you do in life.

How would your health change?
How would your finances change?
How would your life in general change?

Sit in a quiet place this weekend and ask yourself these questions once you have that picture in place: What can I do to move closer to my success life? How does this serve me? Who can help me get to where I want to be?

You'll be amazed at the answers you get.

Wishing you all life has to offer,
From Ken's desk

Top Three Golden Rules of Accumulating Wealth

Whether you are just starting out or even if you are a veteran of wealth building, these three rules will serve you well in your ventures.

Believe that you can be wealthy. This is the most basic rule, which most people refuse to abide by. They may express their desire of money overtly but deep within they do not believe that they deserve to have money. They have doubts. These doubts hamper the process of wealth creation like none other. Read books and participate in recommended seminars. Psychology of affluence plays a huge role in your wealth creation process.

Monitor your earning and expenditure ratio. It is extremely important to keep your expenditure less than your earnings. This is another rule that is so often broken. Before you start with a rebuttal, just look at your credit card statement. In fact, the world is seeing a recessionary phase right now because people chose to spend more than they earned. People chose to buy what they could not afford to pay for, with the money they did not have. This trend is often blamed on excessive consumerism. But if you observe it truthfully, it is just a matter of self-discipline. This created immense disturbance in the world. This could create immense disturbance in your life and in your wealth creation plans. It is not to say though that money is scarce, or you should become some coupon cutting maniac, it is to say manage it properly, and it will come easier to you.

Understand money language. Money needs to be understood. Most people never understand the basics of money, and then they wonder why it never gels well with them. Financial language is different. Even if you are not a student of finance or economics, knowing some simple terms like net worth, assets, liabilities, investment, liquidity, bearish and bullish markets, simple and compound interests, etc., is a good idea. Remember, money is used by all, so it is important to know how it operates. Only when you know the language of money that you can know and understand what it says to you.

Wishing you all life has to offer,
From Ken's desk

Truths about the Truth

The secret of wealth is consciousness of wealth. In order to experience abundance, you have to be abundant. Abundance is your true nature; and when you think, act, and live according to it, you will manifest abundance. The rich in mentality get richer, while the poor in mentality get poorer. The accumulation of material wealth begins with wealth consciousness. Pursuing spiritual development before working on wealth creation is the key to attaining both inner and outer riches. The outer is reflection of inner.

The secret of health is consciousness of health. Disease is a lack of ease psychologically and physically. Conflicting thoughts and feelings in your consciousness is what causes this state of distress. When you notice yourself becoming sick, watch for conflicting thoughts or moods that have arisen within your consciousness and resolve them. Either push them all one way or the other, or find a way to hold them in a harmonious way. External remedies only cure symptoms but dealing with consciousness cures at root.

The secret of secrets is the consciousness of secrets. All the truths about life are not secrets, but they are hidden from us due to our ignorance. By thinking about the discovery of truths as a search for the secrets, we motivate our subconscious mind to go on a treasure hunt. The greatest treasure in this world is wisdom, and life is to be played as a treasure hunting game. Treasures are meant to be appreciated, and so when you think of truths as secrets, your appreciative mind-set will draw them all to you.

Let not your old habits of thinking get in the way here. Give this a lot of thought while suspending everything you know to be true and allow this to tell you what it is. Try this exercise when getting sick. Remember, you do not want to be wealthy. You want to be the person who is wealthy. That person has figured out disease, spiritual development, abundance, getting mentally richer, and the pursuit in the game of life.

Wishing you all life has to offer,
From Ken's desk

Try

One problem with trying anything is the word "try." It allows for the possibility that you might fail.

The reality is that most salespeople are going to miss a sale from time to time, and there's nothing wrong with that.

But when you use words that are disempowering ("try," "maybe," "hopefully," etc.) in your conversation or self-talk, your subconscious mind accepts this programming much the same way as your computer dutifully runs the software you install in it.

Just try to eat dinner tonight. Try to get dressed tomorrow. Only one of two things can happen. You either **do** or you fail. Why not simply DO. How silly will you sound in saying I'm going to try to eat dinner (unless the cook is really bad)? Nike has the right slogan . . . Just Do It.

Don't take my word for it. If you do any amount of research on the subject, you will find countless studies that prove the power of language on the subconscious mind.

Or you can conduct your own experiment. Make the decision to remove all limiting language from your vocabulary. Instead of "giving it a shot," decide to "go all the way" to make the sale.

If you consistently use more confident language, your confidence will increase and so will your life.

Wishing you all life has to offer,
From Ken's desk

What Dreams May Come

Two quotes from the 2011–2012 Stanley Cup winning Los Angeles Kings:

> "I learned that if you don't believe in yourself, no-one else will"—
> Not sure

> "When I was young I would imagine playing in the NHL and at
> the end of each game I played I was voted the 1st star of the game.
> Then I would have my grandmother interview me in English about
> how great I played. I guess I was preparing for this moment all my
> life."—Slovenian born, Anze Kopitar

The first quote says so much toward the attitude you need to succeed as well as the attitude you need in selling your product. You must believe in yourself, and you must believe in your product but remember the first product is you.

As for the second quote, OK, who would have thought there would be a hockey player from Slovenia? Slovenia borders Italy and Croatia. Neither of these countries are known for producing hockey players, soccer yes but hockey? And so here we have a young boy whose family must have thought nuts, playing hockey in his room and imagining being the first star in an NHL game night after night and having his grandmother interview him in English after each of his "games."

What more could you ever want to know about the importance of dreams. What more could you ever want to know about not caring about what others think about you and your crazy dreams. Albert Einstein once said, "Imagination is everything." One of the greatest minds ever in our history said that three-word sentence, and yet societies everywhere keep trying to squash those with great imaginations.

He later went on to say, "If you want intelligent kids, read them fairy tales. If you want really intelligent kids, read them lots of fairy tales."

For the love of your child never discourage them from imagining, but please for the love of yourself, keep dreaming that "impossible dream." The older you get, the more impossible it will seem, but don't tell that to Colonel Sanders who for twenty-five years kept peddling his recipe for chicken, getting no's after no's until at age seventy-six when he started Kentucky Fried Chicken, known to us as KFC now.

Nothing is impossible until you make the impossible.

Wishing you all life has to offer,
From Ken's desk

Most people struggle through life simply reacting to events around them, oblivious to the fact that they help to create those events. Like a ship tossed at sea, they see themselves buffeted by external circumstances, a tiny object subject to the whims of chance.

But here is the reality.

While I agree many were born as victims of circumstances, I don't believe they have to stay that way. Often we do not have a choice about being victimized, but we do have a choice about **staying** that way and using it as our excuse not to live the life we desire.

As I send you more of these e-mails, you will clearly see in which areas of your life you are or have been living in the victim level of awareness. Having that knowledge is the first step to freedom. Unlike most people who believe they are victims and have no choice, you know that you can move up the levels of awareness through conscious choice. This means that no matter what happens to you, you never have to remain a victim.

It is like being locked up in a prison cell, but the key is in the door. All you have to do is turn the key, and you are free. You are only a prisoner if you choose to be a prisoner. You are only a victim if you choose to remain a victim. It's like deciding to be happy. You don't need anything to fall into place, just decide.

Wishing you all life has to offer,
From Ken's desk

Visualize Your Future

I'm a huge football fan, and with the conference championships just finished, with the Superbowl ahead, I thought I would share what I was thinking while watching my Pats barely squeak one out.

Now, whether you are a football fan or not doesn't matter. What does matter is what you can learn from the mental preparation athletes make.

It is strange to me that "visualization" is an expected practice for professional athletes, but when "normal" people talk about visualizing, it is seen as "Pollyanna" and "out there."

So here's the solution. Stop looking at yourself as normal. Start seeing yourself as an athlete in the game of your life.

You won't be able to predict everything that happens any more than football players can predict every play of the game before it happens.

But you can prepare yourself mentally, emotionally, and physically so that you are primed and ready and know that you can handle everything that comes your way. And you can visualize a presentation or a close, or better yet, you living in your dreams!

Back when I played hockey, I often sat in silence before the game started and visualized certain plays happening, and it was amazing how often those plays would come up. And I was ready, ahead of it if you will. In football, I could see the receiver in slow motion while visualizing and again saw it that way when it happened. Again, it's not always perfect to the vision but close enough. The same goes for business and money. I have a visual for money that seems to work. It is not always as I saw it but close enough to be excited and prepared.

Visualize the guy at the other end of the phone seeing a need for an appointment. Visualize the guy in front of you saying yes. Visualize having three prospects per week saying yes. Visualize ten prospects saying yes to appointments.

You see, this isn't about struggle; struggle and hard work aren't the same thing. It is about giving yourself that same level of expectation that a professional athlete has for every single game.

So what can you do to get yourself primed for the best life possible? Whatever your answer is, do it! Visualize that life you knew you were meant to have and in that vision touch and smell what you see. You will feel so empowered and will instantly start to magnetize what you desire into your life!

Visualize!

Wishing you all life has to offer,
From Ken's desk

What Is

The only time we suffer is when we believe a thought that argues with "what is." You know, "it is what it is." When the mind is perfectly clear, "what is" is what we accept in this moment.

If you want your reality to be different than "what is," then you might as well try to teach your cat to bark. You can try and try, and in the end, the cat will look up at you and say, "Meow." Wanting your reality to be different than what it is in this moment is just as stupid. You can spend the rest of your life trying to teach your cat to bark, but you will never succeed.

And yet if you pay attention, you'll notice that you think thoughts like this dozens of times every day. People should be . . . My neighbors should be . . . My husband should . . . My wife should . . . I should . . . These thoughts are ways of wanting reality to be different than it is. Here is my point. All the stress you feel in your life at this moment is caused by arguing with "what is."

People say to me, "But if I simply accept reality, then I will become passive, and nothing will change." I answer them with this question. Which of these statements makes more sense? "I wish I hadn't lost all that money." or "What can I do now to create more income?"

Accepting "what is" doesn't mean you condone or approve of the way things are. It just means you give up all the resistance and inner struggle by wishing it were different. No one wants to lose their money, have their children get sick, or be in a car accident. However, when these things happen, it can be helpful not to mentally argue with them. We know better than to do that, yet we do it because it is a HABITUAL PATTERN.

I am a lover of "what is," not because it is the "right" thing to do, but because it also hurts when I argue with reality, and when I do, I AWLAYS lose. Winning is better, yes?

Wishing you all life has to offer,
From Ken's desk

What would you do if you knew you couldn't fail?

Would you up your game?

Would you live in gratitude?

Would you give freely of yourself?

Would you help others find out they can't fail?

Would you always have a great attitude?

Here's the real question: **Will you do today what others won't so that you can have tomorrow what others can't?**

What separates the knowledge of whether you will or will not fail?

Doubt and faith. Both are decisions you make. Both are created by your conditioning.

Ask yourself this: do you know any success stories where the person said they always doubted the outcome? Isn't it more likely the person talked of their undying faith in what they were doing? In other words, it's their expectation.

With true faith, you know you cannot fail. Put properly, you know you will succeed.

Doubt is a dangerous thing. It brings with it worry, anxiety, and fear. All factors that suggest your ego has gotten out of control, that you believe you run the universe, and more importantly, it means you will forever attract more worry and more fear, and even attract others who carry such traits.

You can only succeed or fail to the extent that you believe you will succeed or fail! You make up the story. Isn't it true that the definition for fear might be "believing that something you cannot see will happen"? But isn't it also true that that same definition would be applied to faith. The good news, by having fear you have shown you have the capacity for faith. All you have to do now is change the expectation. By the way, have you ever heard an intelligent statement (or at least a positive one) after the words "with my luck . . ."? Why is it always followed with a negative? Hmmm.

You have to recondition yourself from doubt to faith, and it doesn't come overnight. Your doubt conditioning didn't come overnight either. It's like filling a cup with grape juice when the cup is already three-fourths full of water. It takes time and a lot of grape juice to finally replace all the water.

It begins in your affirmations.

Most say things like "I will have wealth . . ." or "I want to have wealth . . ." or even "I desire wealth." All those deny or delay. To want is to stay in a state of wanting; therefore, it will never happen. Desire (from the Greek *De-Sire*, of the father) is a much better word than want, but it still delays. You must look into your dreams of success and see what it looks like and then realize it all comes true.

You don't know the gestation period for that, but it will happen. In knowing that it will happen, you can then KNOW that you are indeed wealthy. You cannot fail. Since you know you cannot fail, aren't you then now wealthy? You know it's going to happen, so then act that way now.

Act in the I AM

i.e.,

I own a mansion.

I own a Ferrari.

I have great wealth.

I am a great mentor.

I am strong and powerful.

I am love.

I am beautiful.

I AM wealth . . . I AM abundance . . . I AM joy.

If you make this affirmation every day, you will have no choice but to be the person you always wanted to **be**, you will do the things you will need to **do**, and you WILL **have** all the things you desire.

Wishing you all life has to offer,

From Ken's desk

What's Holding You Back?

You've probably applied "The Secret" or the LOA to improve your life.

Perhaps you've visualized, recited your affirmations, said your prayers, and even performed all the manifestation rituals and routines imaginable.

Well, how did it work out for you? If you're living your dreams as a result, I wish to congratulate you for your success!

But if you're like most people, and you're still unable to move forward, then you absolutely have to see this:

You see, many of the so-called LOA gurus and experts have left out a key component in the manifestation process. Or they only briefly discuss this secret key, but they don't tell you exactly how it works.

So what is this key component? It's BELIEF!

It's belief that has gotten near-death patients to miraculously heal at the last minute, simply by touching a religious object because they believed it would cure them, and their faith did!

How about those "lucky" people who have no special skill or talent but have become extremely rich and successful . . . because they BELIEVE in their own abilities!

But here's the thing. It's easy to say that you believe in something, but the actual process of believing is completely different.

Tell me, have you ever tried to convince yourself to believe in something that is not yet real or something that you've never experienced before? You know how difficult that can be.

You want to believe you're super successful, extremely wealthy, and incredibly famous and more; but your inner voice says otherwise!

That inner critic is always ruining your chances of truly believing in anything you can accomplish.

You must learn to acknowledge and then ignore that inner voice and move on to an emotional attachment to your desires. You must feel them, smell them, taste them.

Only then, and with the right affirmations (I own my own business, I have a Ferrari, I love my dream house, etc.), can you set yourself on a course of full belief.

Wishing you all life has to offer,

From Ken's desk

When

As we reach the half-time point of life, a lot of us begin to reflect on whether or not we are living the lives we want to live. We ask ourselves, "How can I make a difference?" or "Have I done enough?" We ask ourselves these important questions because the biggest regret of all is to reach the end of our lives only to realize that we walked the planet in vain. You don't have to be at that half-time age to think this way, so this is for you too.

I want to share a story with you on this point. It is about a little boy named Peter.

Peter was a child who could never live in the moment. He could never present his gifts to the world; he was always in a rush to get through life. He'd be in class, and he'd want to be on summer vacation. He'd be on summer vacation, and he'd want to be on Christmas holidays.

One day, this little boy was walking in the woods, and he came across a patch of grass. He laid down and fell asleep. Suddenly, he was roused by the sound of his name.

"Peter. Peter. Peter."

He opened up his eyes and could not believe what he saw. In front of him was an ancient woman with snow white hair. In her hands she held a ball. In the center of the ball was a hole out of which dangled a long piece of thread. She looked at him and said, "Peter, this is the thread of your life."

"What?"

She said, "This is the thread of your life. And if you pull on it, days will go by in minutes, and if you pull it a little more, weeks will go by in days. Do you want it?"

Peter said, "Absolutely. I'll be able to fly through the boring parts of life."

The next day, he was sitting in class, not enjoying the moment or experiencing the gifts of the day. Then he remembered the ball, so he pulled it out and tugged on the thread. Tug, tug, tug. The next thing he knows, he's on summer vacation.

He said, "This is fantastic!" He pulled out the ball again. Tug, tug, tug. The next thing he knew, he was a teenager.

He said, "Well, being a teenager is great, but now I think I need a girlfriend." So he grabbed the ball and pulled on the thread again and found himself with a pretty young girlfriend named Elise.

He said, "This is great, but I don't want to be a teenager anymore. I want to be an adult now."

The next thing he knows, he's married to Elise, and the couple has two wonderful children. Then he noticed that his once jet-black hair was slowly turning gray. His once vibrant and vital mother was growing old and frail.

Perturbed, he pulled out the ball and tugged on the string again. The next thing he knew, he was an eighty-five-year-old man. As for his wife Elise, she had passed away years earlier, and the children were grown up and leading lives of their own.

For the first time in his life, he became very sad. He realized that he had not used his time and had not experienced life fully. In his sadness, he walked out to the woods that he had loved as a child and found that patch of grass, and he laid down to take a rest.

All of the sudden, he heard his name being called. "Peter, Peter, Peter."

When he opened his eyes, he couldn't believe what he saw. It was the old woman with snow white hair, and she looked at him and said, "Peter, how have you enjoyed this gift I gave you so many years ago? Have you lived life fully? Have you been your best?"

He looked at her and said, "At first, I loved this gift. I could fly through life quickly. I was always on the move. But now I realize that I didn't live life. I didn't watch the sunrises. I didn't make great friendships. I didn't give my potential to the world. I didn't make a difference. It was all a waste."

The old woman looked at him and said, "Peter, you're a very ungrateful man, but I'm going to give you a second chance to live your life over again."

Confused, Peter went back to sleep. Then he heard his name being called again. But this time, he couldn't believe what he saw. It wasn't the one-hundred-year-old woman. It was his mother. And she was young and vital and laughing.

She shook him awake and said, "Peter, you silly little boy. You've slept in again. It's time to go to school."

Peter realized that it was all just a dream. He stared at his mother, looked out the window at the day, and went off to school grateful for every moment.

The point of wisdom from that story is that every one of us knows that we'll never a chance to live our lives over again, yet so many of us postpone living. Here's the big idea: you will never have a better time to play your best game.

Most of us postpone being better at work until our children grow older. Or we postpone traveling until we have more time. Or we postpone taking better care of our health until we manage our workload better. Yet there will never be a better time to play your best game and shine as brightly as there will be today.

Chinese philosophers once said the best time to plant a tree was twenty years ago; the second best time is today.

Elite performers understand that life is short. There may not be another chance to be great.

When Neil Young was describing Jonny Rotten's life in a song, he said that it is better to burn out than to fade away. Makes sense?

Focus your time and your life on your highest talents and dreams.

Wishing you all life has to offer,
From Ken's desk

Who Is Driving the Bus?

There's great power in that. The bus driver, that is. The bus driver decides where to go and where to stop and when, who gets on the bus and who does not, where to sit and where to stand, what actions are acceptable and what are not.

How our lives are directed is very much like the bus driver. While you may think and believe you are the driver of your own life, you should know that is not necessarily true. The real driver for most of our lives is the subconscious mind. Most actions, decisions, directions, and choices are largely driven by our subconscious mind. Most times, decisions of what to eat and where to go, who to talk to and what is possible, and more importantly what is not are all driven by past imprinting of experience and knowledge into our subconscious mind. This is where behaviors live and breathe. Behaviors are not created by one experience or in one day. They are formed often over decades as a result of thousands of experiences. These behaviors that we don't want seep from the subconscious mind and drive us to eat the ice cream instead of the broccoli. They convince us to sit on the couch rather than get up and go to the gym. They cause us to see failure and challenge where hope and potential and prosperity abound.

With that being the case, there is only one way to change it. Decide upon the activity that you know is the right one and repeat it over and over and over and over again. By doing this you will in effect reprogram the subconscious mind and actually have it take you where you want to go. Do this then. If you don't like the current direction in an area of your life, pull over and ask this question: who is driving the bus?

Wishing you all life has to offer,
From Ken's desk

Why are so many of us struggling? Because we have forgotten WHO WE ARE.

Who we are is our true and authentic self that is always connected and one with Source Energy. On the other hand, who we THINK we are is how we show up in life. If we are struggling, we will never be who we are. Let that sink in for a moment.

Who we THINK we are comes from listening to other people rather than listening to ourselves. For a large portion of my life, I believed what others told me to believe. I learned early that what other people think of me is more important that what I think of myself. At least this is what I thought.

Living in the flow and living in abundance is about focusing on WHO YOU ARE and what you can do in this moment congruent to your visions and dreams. It is not about who you are not, what you cannot do, and what you don't have.

WHO YOU ARE is everything. It is the ONLY thing that really matters because everything hinges on your ability to be yourself, and to do that, you must become intimately aware of the false beliefs you have about yourself and about the way life works.

When you live in the "flow" and in alignment with Source Energy, you know you already have what you need. People who live in the flow and in alignment are more than just positive thinkers. They are attraction in action.

They accept life is not always easy and doesn't always follow a straight and convenient path. They let life unfold through them instead of putting their life into a box of expectations. Let's face it though. Does anyone have or has anyone had your mind, your heart, your eyes, your ears, your hands, and your mouth? No one else can produce your child, or has the exact abilities you do. You are a unique creature of nature, and nature knows no defeat. No wind, no rain, no rock, no lake had the same beginning as you. You were conceived in love and brought forth with a purpose.

You are not to let the miracle that produced you to end at your birth. Why not extend that miracle to the deeds of today?

Your greatness is not dependent upon anything you accomplish. You don't need to prove anything to anyone—even yourself. I am here to tell you one thing. You and everyone that comes in contact with you are already great. To live your greatness, you must know WHO YOU ARE, and you must do what you can do in THIS MOMENT. Nothing else is required.

Wishing you all life has to offer,
From Ken's desk

Who Are You?

You are here on this planet to manifest your greatness. The problem is that WHO YOU ARE—your authentic nonphysical self—is already great, but you don't know that yet if you are experiencing struggle.

Another way to look at this is to imagine the seed of the oak tree. Everything that defines the oak tree is already in the acorn. Unlike us, the acorn does not live under the illusion that it needs to be something else or needs to strive toward an accomplishment that is not in its nature.

Your inherent greatness is your soul, your authentic nonphysical self, stripped of all the conditioning, excuses, and contingencies that have created your LIMITED SELF.

OK, if everyone is born great, then why are so many people still struggling? Why do so many relationships and businesses fail?

The answer is actually quite simple. We are as great as we ALLOW ourselves to be.

The problem is most of us don't allow ourselves to live our greatness. Instead, we are quick to place huge limits on what we can do before we have even begun to do it.

The only limits you have are the ones you are placing on yourself. Do me a favor. Put them aside for now. You can always go back to them later if you need to, but I promise you, you will not need them any longer if you practice living in the "flow" and living in "alignment." Remember, we are as great as we allow ourselves to be. ALLOW yourself to be great for the next few months and see what happens.

Wishing you all life has to offer,
From Ken's desk

Your Purpose

Are you where you are supposed to be?

The esoteric question of the ages (other than chicken or the egg) is why are we here?

In other words, what is your purpose? To dig, you must first look at how you view the world. It is how you view the world that shapes how you see how you fit in it. Too oft we view life from the rear-view mirror—our past—and we try to apply the past to our future, especially a bad idea if your past sucked (remember, while you may think you were wrong in the past, it was your past that was wrong for you). At further glance, we find out that we view the world through the conditioning we have had. Your parents' thinking, your teachers' thinking, your church's thinking, and your peers' thinking have created your vision of what the world looks like.

Lore, "wisdom" of the ages, even TV has shaped our thought to conform to the thoughts of others. We all see a tree, and we all say it is a tree. But do we all see that tree exactly the same? Not likely. It's just that we have all identified the thing that we see is a tree. Isn't it true that five people can look at one person, and two say that one person is beautiful, while two say that person is average, and the fifth says that person is ugly?

It is based upon your conditioning that you know the person is even there, but your uniqueness gives you a special perspective.

Upon recognizing that the way you have viewed all in front of you is based on past beliefs and false, you start to see possibilities not thought of, stuff that is "way out there." Like understanding that the car you drive doesn't exist except in your head. That should send you spinning for a while (or thinking you should stop reading anything I write).

The point being recognizing who you are and where you come from (your true DNA) —the Source—will allow you to see where your greatness will come from and how it is measured. It will allow you to properly write the next chapters of your life. Chapters based on who you think you are as opposed to chapters of the past, based on who "they" believed you to be. It will allow you see your uniqueness and give you hints as to the purpose of your being here.

Let's try a hypothesis. Let's say you are in your version of heaven (even if you don't believe such things). And you can do anything you want because all it takes is though for it to come true. What would you do for the day? And what would you do the next day and the next day? See, this is true wealth, the ability to do whatever you want. And let's say you have now done all the things you wanted to do for a thousand years. At this point, you might actually be bored of this wealth, so as a spirit, you figure out that you no longer appreciate this wealth and decide that you must learn to appreciate it again.

What would you do? You might decide to give true poverty a try so you set out some goals to create this poverty. You decide to put yourself on the planet earth in a situation where you would have to work your way back, but then you recognize that all you would have to do is use your thought and it is all back to where you were. So you then realize that you must cut yourself off from this ability. Step 1: Cut off from the source. It then comes to you that you knowledge would send you back so you have to change the way you think. Step 2: Set goals to be poor. Come to believe in fear, doubt, anxiety, and in the beliefs of others.

There you go. EGO—the separation, gives way to you believing that you are on control of the universe, and your lack of proper knowledge makes you wonder why things don't work out the way you want, which leads to more fear and doubt and anxiety and further separation. Bam, you have now mastered poverty.

Well, if you really want to work your way out, wouldn't you first examine step 1? And wouldn't step 1 allow you to realize all you created in step 2 to be untrue? Now, you are on your way back.

And that way back will once again allow you to appreciate you wealth again. As it happens, some went deeper in this poverty plan to the point where the way back might be a little longer than others, but it does still take you back. The only way to stop this process is to quit. Remember the law of gender? Everything has a gestation period.

Even if it doesn't seem like it, this is true. YOU are the master of your life!

What one thing can you do today to remind yourself that despite all appearances YOU are in charge of your life? It can be small, but do something to remind yourself.

Wishing you all life has to offer,
From Ken's desk

We Live in a "Give-and-Receive" World, not a "Give-and-Take" World

How many times have we heard, "Once I have enough money, I will invest" or … "I will tithe (give to charity) when I have money."

Sorry, kids, it doesn't work that way. And as for taking, just see how many areas of your life grow with that attitude.

One of the true secrets to creating wealth is by giving freely, and by freely, I mean without the angst of thinking you are losing—money or time. Give time, and the time you give will be the most rewarding time you'll have. Give money, and more will find its way to you.

With Christmas coming soon, please consider giving, not just in how you buy gifts for your friends and family but perhaps giving a bit more to that Salvation Army stand you see entering the mall, or to that charity that's been on your mind, or that nice but homeless guy you pass by. Give thanks!

Think about working the kitchen at a shelter. They are always looking for volunteers. I've done this on a number of occasions, not actually work the kitchen. My job was to talk to those who came in. Unbelievably rewarding!

Amazing thing how simply asking someone who lives on the streets questions like "What's your name?" "Where did you grow up?" and "What was that like?" reminds them of their youth, gives them a smile, and by such a little act they for the first time in years, they feel a little respect.

Let's face it; **money is not a measure of human worth. But we all do want more.**

We all want more wealth – which includes money, time, energy, relationships, and health.

Give a little more of yourself and watch all those areas grow.

From Ken's desk

Your Authentic Self

Life doesn't come with a money back guarantee, and yet many of us live like it does. People are certain that they will keep their jobs. They are certain of living a long healthy life. Others might be certain that they will lose their jobs or get sick and die young. Certainty comes in many forms, but it rarely corresponds to the truth.

The truth is nothing is certain. The need for certainty is the need for safety. Since we do not like uncertainty, we choose to believe in something that we feel we can be certain about, even though we have no logical proof that it is true.

Some might argue that if nothing can be counted on, then why bother trying. Conversely, what if everything always worked out the way you thought? What if you knew each prospect you wanted to sell to always took the order? Certainly, your value diminishes (you become and get paid as an order taker), and where would the challenge you crave come from? In order to move forward in life, many people need to have a sense of certainty about the outcome. But this kind of certainty is an illusion. Certainty is a form of disconnection from the truth and from ourselves. When we feel certain about something, we are disconnected from the natural flow of life.

Certainty is the perpetual elusive dream of most people.

What in life is certain? There is a part of you—your authentic self—that is unchanging. This pure consciousness is certain while everything else is uncertain, impermanent, and an illusion. But how do you discover or experience this pure unchanging consciousness? Through inquiry.

If you are certain about something—anything for that matter—you immediately place a lid on that thing. It cannot change. You won't let it change because if you do, you will be wrong in your certainty. But all things, except one thing, do change.

The only thing that doesn't change is WHO YOU ARE—your authentic self or what is commonly called consciousness. Consciousness is what remains when all concepts, beliefs, values, habits, and ways of thinking are stripped away. In other words, all of your ideas, concepts, beliefs, and so on will change over time. No? The obstinate man does not hold opinions, opinions hold him. While facts remain the same, our knowledge of the facts do change, and if this is true, then why waste time on trying to be certain?

By inquiring how and why you get certain results in your life, you learn about your beliefs and patterns that create those results. Then through the power of your mind, you can consciously form new patterns. The need for certainty is replaced by a relaxed "learning" pattern.

Can you imagine a world in which nothing changes? It would be absolutely miserable. Inquiry is the habit that leads us out of that misery.

Through uncertainty, you move from being an expert to being a student. All of life, all experiences, everyone, and everything become our teachers. Stay in the question, and that question is What are the possibilities?

Wishing you all life has to offer,
From Ken's desk

KEN GRIFFITH

Your Core Concern

We all have a core concern that is at the basis of most of our fear, doubt, and worry. We all spend a lot of time and energy trying to avoid feeling our core concern. Much of this is done unconsciously.

Becoming aware of your habitual focus of attention and coping strategy helps shine a light on that core concern, and the simple act of awareness begins to loosen the hold the core concern has on you. I know I've talked of this before, but it deserves repeating.

I am trying to get you to be more aware of your core concern. I am NOT telling you to get rid of it. Much of the nonproductive behavior that you engage in is due to trying to rid yourself of that core concern, trying not *feel* it, and especially trying not let anyone see that you feel it.

What I am suggesting is that you accept it with no judgment, just a statement of what is and a release. This is very powerful. Try it. "Oh, that's just my fear/anger/avarice/etc. talking."

We spend so much energy trying NOT to feel, but the trick is to just let the feeling in—acknowledge it, thank it for its wisdom, and let it move on. Like a thought passing through your mind, a feeling passes through your body. It's all right. Let it in, let it out. Trying to repress or rid yourself of it only increases its hold on you.

Anytime you accept "what is," you release resistance, and then you have much more energy available to you. Is there anything about yourself that you don't accept? What if you just dropped all resistance to it? What if you said, "This is what I am, and that's OK"? Wouldn't that feel good? No judgment, no guilt, no shame. Those are very low vibration emotions, and they never help or effect change. They keep you stuck. In acceptance, there is healing and movement. And isn't that what you are looking for?

Wishing you all life has to offer,
From Ken's desk

Define Your Life's Purpose

Remember your first days of training here when I talked about your dreams being defined by your vision, you values, and you purpose? Most like to skip over the purpose part; it seems like a lot to think on, but such a mistake can be far too costly to your happiness.

It doesn't matter how you think you arrived here on this planet or under whose direction. The fact remains that each of us has specific talents and gifts that are uniquely coded within our own DNA.

As you go through life, you don't just pick up things you like doing by chance. You discover what you're good at because you were meant to discover it, just as you were meant to figure out what your fingers do and how your elbows work.

Your unique gifts are hardwired into your system just as surely as your lungs are given their blueprint to breathe.

And it's from these specific talents and gifts that you're able to define and determine your definite purpose, the reason why you're here.

What's in you cannot be found in another living human being. In fact, it's quite possible that what you bring to the table hasn't been duplicated—ever—since time began.

That's right! This "purpose" is serious business.

If you fail to determine your definite purpose, everything else is wrong. It's like working with a broken compass. You may think you're going north, but you're not. You're not sure which direction you're heading, so you're just wandering aimlessly.

Without your purpose identified firmly in your mind, you will wander through life, never quite feeling that you're "in the flow." I say, then, that it's imperative you recognize what it is you're good at. What it is you really love to do.

Your purpose in this lifetime is to do the thing that you love.

People will tell you they already know what they're good at, and what they love to do most, but they'll never earn money doing it. Whoever gave you that idea?

When you're sorting out your purpose, I don't want you thinking about that nonissue at all. You can earn money at anything. Once you determine your purpose, you won't even have to think hard on how to earn money. It's as if you're being guided by an unseen hand, heading in the right direction, and everything falls into place.

The key to your life is not that you settle for the "safe" thing that will bring in the money. The key is to turn and do what you really love. Fall in love with an idea. That's your life! That's your purpose.

Wishing you all life has to offer,
From Ken's desk

Your State of Mind

I thought you would enjoy this metaphor.

This man gets up every morning, takes his shower, shaves, eats breakfast, and climbs down the stairs and boards the bus for a forty-five-minute ride. He steps off the bus and feels the beach under his feet.

He walks the beach up and down every day, all day long, looking for the Statue of Liberty. Lo and behold, there is no Statue of Liberty.

As night falls, he stretches and looks out over the water to see the Santa Monica pier and turns and spins around to see the Hollywood sign. He boards the bus, disappointed again because he did not find the Statue of Liberty. He has been doing this for years. Every day he does the same thing.

Once again, he goes to the Santa Monica pier, much more disappointed than the day before, sits in his chair, crying tears of sadness, dismay, frustration. Finally, a woman walks up to him and asks him why he is so distraught. The man tells her every day he comes to the Santa Monica pier to see the Statue of Liberty but he can never find it. The woman says to him, "No wonder you cannot find it. You are in the wrong state."

The lesson here is even if you are a well-meaning person, if you are in the wrong STATE OF MIND, you will not find what you are looking for. You must be in the right STATE to achieve anything in life.

It starts with being aware of your surroundings and how they suite your goals. It must be accompanied by a positive attitude and a willingness to change, while still being ever so present to each moment of your day. Clues will appear to guide you to the course of your destination.

Today will bring you a new awareness, a lesson, or a manifestation that you are making progress—IF YOU LOOK FOR IT! No matter how large or small.

Wishing you all life has to offer.

From Ken's desk

Part II
Today's Sales Tip

Two Mistakes Marketers often Make—Try to Avoid!

Aiming at everyone. No company can be all things to all people; as much of a cliché as that is, it's true. Companies paint themselves into a corner because of a misplaced fear that by targeting one group they'll be turning away others. But **aiming at everyone** is an oxymoron; the best marketers understand that by narrowing their target audience they can increase the intensity of their brand's appeal, piquing interest and driving margins. You're better off being the first choice of 10 percent of the population than being one of ten options for everyone.

Remember that when a customer is asking for something you don't have. Let's do what we do best, the best we can. More often than you think, you can turn them around from their preconceived notion of what they want to what they really need. The people who built the Titanic wanted more silverware and chandeliers. What they needed were more life boats. What should you be selling them?

Betting on rationality. This mistake is subtle but dangerous. Marketing planning is often a left-brain effort, where rational exercises like determining budgets and plotting strategy take place. But consumers don't make decisions where logic and argument reside; research suggests that emotion not only influences most purchase decisions, it also tends to trump reason along the way. Don't try to convince your prospects; connect with them. They're depending on their gut more than you realize.

*I know, I know, too repetitive, but **facts tell, stories sell**. Presenting too much in the numbers gives too much pause to think, rethink, and rethink again. It's called* **analyzing**.

From Ken's desk

A Little Tip(s)

When opportunity presents itself, **the opportunity of a lifetime,** understand this: **to take advantage of an opportunity of a lifetime, you must act within the lifetime of the opportunity.** Take it and run!

So

If you start with the right attitude, plan with aptitude, execute with servitude, and act in gratitude, you will **separate yourself from the multitudes.**

The more you know about anything, the more creative you can be with new information. **Keep learning.**

When you dare to be powerful, to use your strength in the service of your vision, then it becomes less and less important whether you are afraid. **Be powerful!**

Arthur Schopenhauer said, "Every man takes the limits of his own field of vision, for the limits of the world." **Expand your vision.**

George "Papa Bear" Hallas once said, "Nobody who gave it their best ever regretted it." **Give it your best shot.**

Fear of loss and **hating to lose** are two different things. Whatever you fear will be on your mind and therefore attracting the same; hating to lose is situational. **Hate to lose.**

In sales, 50 percent is guts, drive, discipline, and heart. The other 50 percent is intelligence. Doesn't that sound like good news? **Keep driving toward your goals.**

In direct sales, you will sometimes come up against CAVE men—citizens against virtually everything. So what? Move on. Next! Remember, your motto in business and life should be **want everyone, need no one.**

Aristotle said, "We are what we repeatedly do, excellence then is not an act, but a habit." **Create good success habits.**

Remember, when you miss a sale, the customer misses an opportunity. **Serve with passion.**

From Ken's desk S2

A Selling Attitude

Good selling requires that you understand the product well and work to appreciate the customer's requirement. But before and beyond all that, the secret of a good salesperson is about what goes on inside their head.

Above all, selling is an attitude. It's how you think and feel. It's about your whole approach to yourself, your company, your products, and, of course, your customers. All of this can be condensed to three words: confidence, pride, and care.

Confidence. The basis of all successful selling is confidence. This does not mean blind hope. It is more about how you think about yourself and the future.

A confident person believes in themselves and their abilities to sell. In order to create *trust*, the first thing that you sell is yourself. While self-belief does not guarantee a sale, it always increases the probability of success.

If you go into a selling situation and you do not even believe in yourself, then you are doomed to failure. If you do not believe in yourself, then the customer will not believe in you either, nor will they believe what you say. Your doubt will become their doubt, and doubt does not lead to the sale.

Blind belief is not always a good thing. Being positive because you have studied your product and the markets, it is a greater reason to be confident. Belief and optimism provide powerful support, but they do not replace factual knowledge.

If you are ready to sell, with good information at your fingertips, then you have good reason to be optimistic. Even if you do not have complete information (and who does), a tendency to optimism also helps create a positive attitude. Remember, ignorance on fire does beat out knowledge on ice, so fear not if you are not fully informed.

Finally, self-belief and an optimistic approach lead to a "can-do" attitude, which means you will get out there and create the sale through your thoughts and actions. Belief is not enough: you've got to put in the work too.

Pride. There are two forms of pride. As one of the *seven deadly sins*, it can be a very selfish thing. But pride placed outside yourself is an important attitude that communicates and transmits itself to your customers.

First, you should be proud to work at your company. Associating yourself with the *brand* and the brand values should make you feel good. You should be happy to tell others where you work.

Second, you should be proud of what you are selling. Just thinking that you have the privilege of selling such a fine product should make you very happy indeed.

As with pride in the company, an intrinsic pride in the product is a powerful motivator, both for you and for your customer. And why not? Don't we serve our customers?

Care. Finally, a selling attitude is a caring attitude. Rather hit-and-run on customers, if you want them to ever renew, you should care about them and their problems, and hence be proud of how your products will help.

Care for customers can include taking time out from the normal selling context to check up on them, that our service is working OK, and that they are happy with it. It can even include sending them Christmas and birthday cards.

When others know that you care about them, personally, then they will be far more willing to trust you. And trust is the first doorway. And isn't it true that **people won't care how much you know until they know how much you care?**

From Ken's desk

Are You a Peddler or a Seller?

Being allowed on the customer's premise can come down to whether you are selling or merely peddling. Know the difference.

There's a huge difference between peddling and selling. And if you don't know the difference, you may not be doing as good a job as you'd like.

Peddling is the kind of business transaction that takes place on street corners, carnivals, and telephone boiler rooms (or every JE transaction). Selling is the kind of business transaction that's the heart and soul of the capitalist system.

Here's how to tell the difference:

Peddlers:
- Try to close a deal as quickly as possible
- Brag about how their product is the best
- Try to push hot buttons to make the customer buy
- Offer discounts to close the deal

Sellers:
- Discover if there's a good match and withdraw if there isn't
- Focus on how to best solve a specific customer problem
- Help the customer make the best decision possible
- Stand firm on an offer that makes sense for both buyer and seller

This doesn't mean you won't try to close the deal that day as you are still helping the customer make the best decision for him and may only have the one shot, but it is about your mind-set.

You'd be amazed at how many people think they're selling, when actually they're peddling. In fact, there are plenty of "sales training" programs out there that actually teach people how to peddle rather than how to sell.

That's ironic, and unfortunate, because nothing annoys and irritates customers more than a peddler. By contrast, sellers who are well-informed, well-spoken, and knowledgeable are almost always welcome.

Make sure you know which you are and which you should be.

From Ken's desk

Big Dogs

Rather than hang out and discuss ideas with others in the company who are at or below your production level, interact and learn from the top producers. The only thing others at your level can teach you is how to stay at the production level you are currently at or worse, those below can only teach you how to fail. Learn from those who are where you want to be. Look at them as mentors and teachers and as colleagues. Listen to them on the phone, hitch a ride as they make sales calls if possible, find out what they read and who they value as teachers and mentors. Emulate success, not mediocrity.

A great many companies—probably the vast majority—neglect sales training in favor of product training. Many companies mistakenly believe they are the same thing. Not only are they not the same thing, neither is also very effective without the other. Sales is 50 percent sizzle and 50 percent steak. At first, you won't be particularly enthusiastic about spending your money attending seminars and workshops. After all, you'll argue, your company should be paying since your skills are going to be used to sell their products. True. Except your skills are going to be with you for life, not just while selling for the company you currently works for. Your product knowledge is to a large extent company specific; your sales skills will be universal and benefiting you for life. Make the investment in yourself.

Stop comparing your production and progress only against those with the same amount of experience but to compare yourself against the best in the company and the industry. If you want to be a top dog, you have to compare yourself against the top dogs, even if at the moment that comparison isn't comfortable (or seemingly comparable). If you are only competing against others at your level, you are giving yourself a false trophy. Your goal shouldn't be one of the best mediocre producers but rather to be one of the top producers. Keep your eye on the ultimate goal and only compare yourself against that goal. Like a long-distance runner, you might click off the landmarks as you pass them, but you must know how you stack up with where you want to be and keep your eye on the ultimate goal.

If you're looking to take the next big step in your career, start eating with the big dogs and leave the other average ones behind, take control of your own sales training, and compare yourself with the big producers, not just the ones you think you can compete with easily. It will make a difference, and you might find the difference comes pretty quickly.

From Ken's desk

Bridging

Sometimes we come across a customer who is unwilling to share his thoughts and seems guarded when you are asking your opening questions.

Here you are trying to build rapport, and the guy is giving you one word answers. It seems like his chair might more personality than him. What do you do?

You have asked things like, How did you get into the widget business and all he says is I've always worked with widgets, and how is the widget business and he says, "Good."

You need to use a bridge to keep the conversation going and get him more involved.

Bridging closes the gap from short answers to what is really in their head. Practice using bridging lines like;

Meaning . . . ?
For example . . . ?
So then . . . ?
Therefore . . . ?
Then you . . . ?
Which means . . . ?

You do this by leaning forward. Stretch the last letter of the bridge (meaninnnnnggggggggg? Then youuuuuuu?).And then lean back and shut up. It is best when you do the old hand on the chin with the finger up (a sign that you are listening intently). This conditions them to continue talking for as long as you lean back.

This may feel strange at first but once mastered it is as effective as nodding – which is one of the most powerful persuasion tools in sales. Remember, them talking is them closing themselves. You just have to build the bridge.

From Ken's desk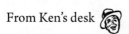

Call Your Paycheck

Whenever I work with salespeople to fine-tune their selling strategy (or help them create one), there is usually some one-on-one training with people who are "call adverse."

They make excuses for not making calls, setting appointments, or meeting with prospects. Sometimes it's because they haven't been trained sufficiently (my fault). Sometimes it's because they've recently missed a sale and taken it personally (their fault). And sometimes they just aren't in the mood to do the work.

If you ever feel the same way, you might try this exercise: start visualizing your paycheck on the other end of the phone, and you will find it much easier to reach out.

Let's face it. All of us have days when we aren't "in the mood" to prospect.

But our job as professional salespeople is to get in the mood, because our paycheck is waiting for us to call.

From Ken's desk

Consumers versus Business Owners

Successful business owners think and act like business owners not consumers. They make it their business to understand their business. Yes, part of understanding your business means understanding consumers but successful business owners rely on business strategies, as opposed to consumer strategies, to produce profit and gain market share.

Consumers are conditioned to believe the "cheaper is better." Big mistake!

Consumers sit or lie on the *consumer couch* accepting messages from the media at face value—dangerous. Over time, consumers hear certain messages so routinely that they begin to accept them as irrefutable fact;

"Buy on sale and save"

"Deep discount stores are the best places to 'save' money"

"The lower the prices the better the store"

"The bigger the store, the better the shopping"

They go off to This Mart or That Mart or Costco (note the word—cost) to save $100 on a $200 item that is 50 percent off. Question is did they save money? Isn't saving $100 putting the money in a savings account?

Has anyone, ever, saved their way to wealth?

Countless hours on the consumer couch has conditioned to spend wealth, not create it. Can you see the difference of thinking like a consumer and thinking like a business owner?

Business owner thinking is about creating wealth, fair prices, added value, investing in assets, and building a bigger business and a better person.

Our job is to ensure that our prospects are thinking like business owners when in front of us and not like consumers. They can't do that if you are thinking like a consumer.

If you are constantly driving around looking for the cheapest gas station, clipping coupons, or just constantly looking to "save" money, then you have become a *consumer couch potato*. You have lost the ability to think like a business owner.

We live in a world where we know the price of everything but the value of nothing And that is hurting sales, both for you and our prospect.

We must not only educate our prospects on what we can do for them but first on **attaching value to their problems** and to look at things through the eyes of the business owner, not as a consumer.

From Ken's desk

Curiosity

When they declare that they do not want to buy from you, act curious.

Do not just ask "Why?", but express a curious interest that says "how interesting—I wonder why."

Getting the objection out before you go gives you one, last shot to keep them at the table. Even if they still *invite you to leave*, it also lets you know why you failed to sell to them today and so improve your sales skills.

Examples questions might be:

I was just wondering what led to your decision not to buy this today?

Most people really go for this. I am a little curious as to how you decided otherwise.

Did I not explain it clearly enough?

Was I a bit too enthusiastic? Sorry, but I just love what I do for people.

Being curious appeals in part to their child-self, whereby you say, "Wow, isn't that interesting!" (fascinating) and invite them to a game of exploration and discovery.

When you are non-threatening and not in "closing mode" they may well relent and give you the information you need.

And remember **"The price of success is much lower than the price of failure."**

"Success seems to be connected with action. Successful people keep moving. They make mistakes, but they don't quit."

Go get 'em

From Ken's desk

Customers Don't Have Needs. They Have Problems

We've all heard that you have to build rapport. Truth is, you won't sell anything until you get rapport with the other person. Rapport is a state of emotional bonding, where they are aligned with you and vice versa. If you move, then if you are in rapport, then they will move too. Then we can get to **the problem.**

A lot of sales training and books tell you about the importance of selling to customer needs. Although this is basically true, customers don't sit down and think "I've got a need." Instead, they experience problems and hence seek solutions to these.

The customer has to perceive the problem, of course. You may perceive the problem, but if the customer doesn't, then there's no way they can bite the solution line.

So the sales job is about finding, eliciting, and solving these problems. Where understanding of needs does come in useful, here is that problems appear when needs are not met. But when you talk to customers, it usually works best if the subject is problems.

Urgency is proportional to pain. Problems are like health. The more a problem hurts now, the more the need for a solution now. And the more it hurts, the more they'll be prepared to pay for a speedy solution.

It's got to hurt enough. The operation of resolving the pain is itself a painful process, so if the pain is below this threshold, the patient will prefer to continue to suffer than accept any treatment.

It is sometimes your job to get them to feel the pain. Come up with examples of those who felt the effects of not budgeting. Remind them of how past increases dug into their profits. Ask how they budget when they never know the cost of things such as their energy commodities. Ask how they feel about the government adding all their mistakes to his/her electricity bills.

You've heard the line—"No pain, no gain." His pain is your gain. Better yet, **your gain alleviates his pain.**

From Ken's desk

Driven by Your Customer

Great salespeople give so much apparent control to customers that the customer seems to sell the product to themselves.

They do this by being incredibly sensitive to the customer's situation and **state of mind**, then nudging gently with the right questions such that the customer realizes their need and ends up asking for the product. OK, that might be a little over the top, but you get the idea.

Great salespeople turn casual conversation into an art, persuading by subtle **inference and influence** rather than more overt presentation and persuasive talk. They can smell commission breath on you.

They love their customer. Love is a funny word that is much misunderstood. Loving the customer doesn't mean hugs and kisses, but it does mean caring about them both before *and* after the sale.

When salespeople truly care about the success of their customers, it shows all over their faces and all over their actions too. A loving salesperson will never dupe their customers and will always give them a fair deal. Note the emphasis on fair. That means the salesperson gets something out of it too.

It's difficult not to trust someone who loves you. In fact, it's difficult not to love them back, and loved customers often love their salespeople. Now there's a relationship to kill for.

Oh and by the way, be paranoid. Paranoia is a normal and healthy state. This is as compared with the enormous dangers of complacency. The sale is never in the bag until the ink is dry. Metro Goldwin Meyer said, "A verbal agreement is worth the paper it is written on."

Always assume the customer has not fallen in love with you or your products. Never assume that a sale will fall into your lap without due and continuous effort on your part.

Once the energy is in flow, to the bank money will go.

From Ken's desk

Everyone Is Selling Something.

Teachers sell their students on making good grades, preachers sell their congregations on attending church and receiving salvation, and parents sell their children on being good citizens. And kids always sell their parents on something they want. To see this in action, just tell a kid "no" and watch the sales campaign begin!

If you want to achieve your full potential in life, you gotta sell. Your entire life is a continuous process of communicating, persuading, and influencing other people.

The average person makes hundreds of presentations a day. Anytime you communicate with someone—whether it's in business or at home, via e-mail, or face-to-face—you're making a presentation. And each of these presentations can have an impact on your life and future.

Anytime you make a presentation, you're trying to sell someone on something, even if it's as simple as selling someone on your idea or opinion.

Even athletes sell—star athletes sell style, skills, and showmanship. Through their performances, they sell people on the idea that they're the best, and because of this, they create great excitement. Because people recognize them as winners, they want to buy the products they endorse and tickets to watch them play.

But a star athlete must also continually sell himself to himself to consistently perform at the highest level. If superstar athletes' confidence slips, they lose their edge and their performance suffers.

Selling yourself is a critical factor that determines the level of success you will ultimately achieve and how quickly you will achieve it. You should network, market yourself, and get your name out there. When you promote yourself to others (in an appropriate way), more opportunities will come your way. Good things will happen to you because people will recognize you and your abilities.

When companies downsize, who typically stays? The people who have marketed themselves, their results, and their value to the company. Selling yourself is a universal need.

Selling yourself involves two steps. First, it means selling others on you and your products or services. But it also means selling you to you. You've got to believe 100 percent in yourself, your abilities, and whatever it is you represent. How can you sell others on you if you're not first sold on yourself?

I'm not talking about having a big ego. I'm talking about totally convincing yourself that you are the best person for the job or that the person you're exchanging with is getting a good deal. To sell to others, you gotta be sold on yourself and believe that you have the knowledge, skills, and abilities to achieve success.

To do this best, keep reading, keep trying new ideas, keep a keen eye out for

KEN GRIFFITH

what is going on around you, listen for great lines in movies you watch, learn to model those who sell well, keep an open mind for what might be, be fully present in each moment, and know that you were created perfect.

From Ken's desk

Facts Do Not Move Commodities

My business is in the world of commodities, but the sales approach for your business may have the same approach.

In the great argument of where commodities such as natural gas will go, either flat, up or down, we see so-called experts on either side debating several factors.

The truth is facts do not determine the rise or fall of such commodities. Fear, emotions, and **the unknown** are what make them move.

To base your argument solely on facts, you can only use the facts you have and the facts of the future are not in yet. As an example, in 1986, we were told that we had one hundred years of natural gas in the ground, and all was good. For the next three years, we saw natural gas pricing rise and fall, and then from 1997 to 2007, we saw a steady rise of 486 percent. Why?

Doesn't that counter the "facts" of having one hundred years of supply? And what of the major spikes of 2001 and 2005? What factors created those?

The spike of 2001 was created by 9/11, not by the fact of what happened that day but by the fear of the unknown generated. In 2005, we saw both Katrina and the fall of Enron, again facts on the own right, but the rising prices were created by the unknown.

And while these disasters were indeed facts, they could not be predicted and are therefore not facts. So here we are today with half the experts saying natural gas will remain flat for at least three years and half the experts saying the rates will rise back to the norms of pre 2008 steadily and within a couple of years.

The big thing to remember is that as soon as a forecast is made, it is wrong. That is why it is so important to focus on risk management when protecting your stocks, your company, and your life. You cannot predict the future with 100 percent accuracy, but a little insurance can go a long way to peace of mind, yes?

*Note: The "facts" of how much supply we have today has changed in one year from 108 years to 39 years . . . hmmm.

From Ken's desk

Facts Tell, Stories Sell

Would you like to build more profit into our product or service (in other words, into your pocket)? If so, you're probably wondering how it can be done.

Build in more features and capabilities than our competition, some might say. Or drive costs out by cutting back—such as no internal customer service department. Nothing wrong with either of those answers provided you make customers happy. But neither of these strategies is the real secret to building an amazingly profitable business.

The real secret to doubling, tripling, or even quadrupling your profits actually has nothing to do with your product at all. It's not about the product. As pointed out, gas is gas, oil is oil. It's not what our product does that makes people value it. It's how they **feel** about our product or service. It is their perceive value for what we offer.

Question: **Does a Rolex watch tell time, 150 times better than a Timex?** So why buy a Rolex? It is the perceived value, isn't it?

So the real question is this: What are YOU doing to help your customers increase **their perceived value** of what you're selling?

Are you telling the stories of your satisfied customers? Are you talking of how they now own a crystal ball on their commodities? Of how they hit their budget targets each year? How they do not have to tap into external budgeting to recoup losses due to spikes? Or how successful many companies have been by hedging? Encana for example.

How about the success stories of SouthWest Airlines or WestJet? Both Herb Kelleher and Clive Beddow were thought to be nuts when they hedged their fuel costs (as it seem to cost so much more at the time), but in the end, it was American Airlines who almost landed (no pun intended) in insolvency, and Air Canada who did . . . twice!

WestJet CEO Clive Beddow said it best, "As long as I know what I have to budget around, I can budget around anything."

You might add something like, "In truth, if you hedge and you are wrong at least you already budgeted for it. If you hedged and are right then you may have saved your commodities from crippling all your profits, yes."

How about my favorite, "Every ship at the bottom of the ocean has a chart room. So the question is; what happened to make it sink? Was it the course or was it that it couldn't weather a storm?"

You see, it's the stories that products or services help people to tell that determines their value.

Remember, **facts tell, stories sell.**

Not sure about that. What sells more, documentaries or movies? Take "Nixon" for example. Documentaries have been done on Richard Nixon, but the movie (full of inaccuracies) became the compelling truth and became watched by so many more than any of the documentaries.

Your stories will determine the value the customers will see.

From Ken's desk

Five Ways to Close a Deal

Everybody who sells should be able to master these five classic ways to ask for the business.

Many sellers are afraid to ask potential customers whether they're going to buy. The reason is simple: They're secretly worried the answer will be no, and that all their hard work developing the opportunity will turn out to be wasted.

After all, if you don't close the deal, you can continue to enjoy the pleasant fantasy of winning the business.

As a result, some sellers shilly-shally about, hoping that the customer will volunteer something like, "Here's my money. Give me the product!" (Which almost never happens.)

Because closing is so important, everybody who sells should know the five classic closes and when to use them. Here they are:

1. The Assumptive Close

Concept: You ask a question that, when the customer answers it, implicitly commits the customer to the sale.

Example: "Help me understand your process and how your company will purchase this product."

Best Usage: When you're not certain that the customer is convinced. Talking about the details will either confirm the customer's decision to buy or allow for further discussion. Be careful with this one, though: If your delivery is too ham-handed, this close can seem manipulative.

2. The Reverse Close

Concept: You ask a question that elicits a *no* response but which is actually a *yes* to the close.

Example: "Is there any reason, if we gave you the product at this price, that you wouldn't do business with our company?"

Best Usage: When the customer has a pessimistic personality that enjoys nit-picking and finding fault. Remember to have a backup plan if the answer is "Yes, which is why I'm not going to buy."

3. The Time-Sensitive Close

Concept: You attach the purchase to a time line that the customer has already communicated.

Example: "You said you want to get this done by [a certain time]; let's look at our calendars and figure out what we need to do today."

Best Usage: When the customer has committed to achieving a specific goal within a specific time. This is also useful as an intermediate close on the next step—thereby laying the groundwork for a final close.

4. The Direct-Question Close

Concept: You summarize the conversation (or series of conversations) and simply ask for the business.

Example: "It looks like we've answered all the questions. Shall we move forward with this?"

Best Usage: This is the general purpose close and can be applied in almost any sales situation. It never seems manipulative and seldom backfires. Should the answer be no, however, start a conversation that investigates why the customer isn't yet ready to buy.

5. The Direct-Statement Close

Concept: You communicate your confidence that the purchase is going to happen by simply stating that it is going to happen.

Example: "Let's move forward on this."

Best Usage: Use this when you've received multiple green lights signaling that the customer is ready to buy. This close has an added benefit, by the way, by positioning the purchase as an agreement between equals, rather than a supplication from the seller to the buyer.

From Ken's desk

Follow Up

Consider this: You've established contact, of whatever kind (online, in person, on the phone, etc.) with an individual who has a need for our service. And upon presenting, you've determined that he or she is willing and able to make the investment.

You provide all the information about you, your company, your product, and pricing to demonstrate your ability to provide value and help in a timely and professional manner. Then they ask that you follow up in a couple of days.

You follow up and then . . . nothing . . . no sale. = ☹

What happened? Now what?

Well, believe it or not, it may be as simple as this: Not enough follow-up. So the sales tip I have for you today is "follow-up, follow-up, follow-up." And when you're done with that, "follow-up again."

Look at these stats I found about the most successful sales strategies: Now they may differ a bit for us from product/customer (i.e., RPP to Spot), but this market research is valid.

SALES STATISTICS

48% OF SALES NEVER FOLLOW UP WITH A PROSPECT
25% OF SALES PEOPLE MAKE A SECOND CONTACT AND STOP
12% OF SALES PEOPLE ONLY MAKE THREE CONTACTS AND STOP
ONLY 10% OF SALES PEOPLE MAKE MORE THAN THREE CONTACTS
2% OF SALES ARE MADE ON THE FIRST CONTACT
3% OF SALES ARE MADE ON THE SECOND CONTACT
5% OF SALES ARE MADE ON THE THIRD CONTACT
10% OF SALES ARE MADE ON THE FOURTH CONTACT
80% OF SALES ARE MADE ON THE FIFTH TO TWELFTH CONTACT

pretty surprising, isn't it? Most will not follow-up five to twelve times, but with these sales stats, just think of the money you're leaving on the table, especially for those calling to set appointments.

Just think of the money you're wasting on creating and cultivating prospects who are qualified to buy, and would, IF you followed up one, two, or three more times.

Consider your sales strategies and the process you use to engage and follow-up with the most valuable qualified prospects you've connected with.

Imagine the possibilities if you design in to your sales strategy a way to effectively follow-up and increase your sales by 80 percent or more.

From Ken's desk 🙂

Getting from No to Yes on the Phone

Bob: "No"

You: "Bob, have you ever heard of a business decision, where the decision was NO, that actually grew a business? Has never happened has it?

Bob: "No but a NO can save a company thousands of dollars"

You: "Right. But even a NO can only be a good decision when made with all the possible information, yes?

And Bob what really is the cost of getting all the information vs. the cost of a wrong decision?

From Ken's desk

Handle with Care

Virtually every salesperson is facing tremendous pressure right now to bring in new business.

While it is important to find and sign new customers, it is even more important to keep the ones you already have. You can't afford to let prospecting activity completely replace client maintenance activity.

So schedule time every week to check in with existing accounts and make sure they are still happy or, if they are not, take steps to make them so. Find out what other challenges they face, or even just make sure you commemorate the important dates in their life. You never know, it could get you some referrals.

Now more than ever, it is essential to minimize customer churn.

If you need to remind yourself to take care of what you got, get a big, bold rubber stamp and mark every client folder with the words: HANDLE WITH CARE!

From Ken's desk

How Do I Get My Energy Closer to 100 Percent?

Safe to say sales is a "high-energy" field, yes?

Unfortunately, we are surrounded by a lot of negative energy. Yet if we can raise our energy, we will start to feel ourselves pulling out of the negative energy surrounding us. The energy in our environment is often pulling us down so we have to protect ourselves by aligning ourselves with people and situations that do not deplete our energy.

How can we build up our energy? By only focusing on things that make us feel good. I have also found associating with like-minded people raises my energy faster than anything else because I am surrounded by the groups combined energy. The problem is, when I leave that uplifting energetic environment and go back to my normal daily routine, that higher energy level is often dissipated.

I soon realized that I had to learn to condition my energy to maintain or vibrate at a consistently high level. Once I learned how to maintain my energy, I could also use that energy to uplift other people. The easiest way to do this is to make the decision that you will feel "good." That's all it takes. If you feel "bad" in any moment, reach for a thought that makes you feel just a little bit better and see what happens.

One of the fastest ways to open the flow of riches into your life is to help other people raise their energy. In fact, it has become a major part of my purpose to raise the energy of every person I meet. This is not easy to do, but the rewards are far beyond the effort it takes to do this on a daily basis.

I practice it every day. Even when I meet a total stranger, I make the effort to uplift their energy, even if it is as simple as giving them a smile or being warm and friendly.

Since energy is transferable without having to say a word, you can raise the energy level of the people around you just by sending them your thoughts. Try this experiment. As you come into contact with other people, especially the ones that seem unhappy or stressed, take a moment and project a good feeling toward them. Say something like. "I wish the best for you." Or better yet, say "I love you." Now I know this is not easy, but the rewards will be well worth your time and effort if you do it consistently, moment by moment and day by day. It has an accumulative affect that will simply amaze you.

If you are like most people you will read this and say, "I cannot see how this is going to help my money situation. I bought this program to increase the flow of money into my life. Just show me how to do that!" That's EXACTLY what I am showing you right now. The money you desire will flow into your life in direct proportion to the energy level or consciousness you are willing to maintain.

Now, you have two choices. You can read this and forget about it, agreeing that it is a good idea but do nothing about it, OR you can DO something about it. Just try it for a week, and see what a difference it makes in your life.

From Ken's desk

How Do You persuade?

If "sales" is the art and science of persuasion, then the question is; How do you persuade?

As the story goes; Many, many years ago, Aristotle said that if you took two weights of the same material, the one that was larger of the two would fall faster. For years this was taught but many years later Galileo came along and said that this was simply not true. When challenged by his students, he went to the top of the Leaning Tower of Pisa and dropped two weights dramatically different in size but of the same material, and they hit the ground at precisely the same time. Galileo had proved his point. And yet at the University of Pisa, they kept teaching that the heavier weight would fall faster.

Here is why; he had *convinced* the students he was right, but he had not *persuaded* them.

So how do you persuade? You don't persuade by telling them, you persuade by asking and listening to them!

That is why we spend so much focus in training on the art of questions and how to ask the questions. Remember, the one who is in control of every conversation, is the one asking questions.

Too often we want to delve right in and impart with all our great knowledge only to later on find out the needs of the company don't fit what we sell or what they want.

Master the art of opening questions and listening to their answers. The answers will give you the direction to go and lead you to their emotional attachment to the problem that you are trying to help them with.

Come up with five standard questions to ask at each presentation (prior to your spiel) and be prepared to ask more. Then be prepared to close a lot more ☺

Remember, questions are the answers.

From Ken's desk

How to Boost Your Productivity

Do you have a lot on your plate? Do your projects tend to get backed up and forgotten about? Or do you just never seem to get to the things you need to do (procrastination)? If so then this is for you. If not, read it anyway. It might help

The 12 tips below will help to boost your productivity and help you get more done. If you apply the following steps you will be on your way to accomplishing more and having more free time.

1. Daily Goals. To be more productive, start using a to-do list. It's a little tool that will be a big help. Just grab a pad and pen. Every day write down your daily list of things to do. As you accomplish them, cross them off the list. Simple, right?

2. Worst First. Do the things you don't want to do first. When you create a list do you ever notice there is usually one task that you keep putting off? It's on your to do list for days and then weeks. It's usually a challenging task that requires effort and often involves doing something out of your comfort zone. Do this one first and get it out of the way. The rest of you day will be so much lighter.

3. Drop It! Drop the unnecessary things that are cluttering up your to do list. Be sure to check your list frequently and prune when necessary. Things have a way of staying on your list for a long time without getting done. If that's the case, consider if it belongs on your list or not. If it does then see step #2 ☺.

4. Milestones. Chop a big task into minitargets. When you have big task to do, try cutting it down into manageable size chunks. Start with one chunk and continue without stopping till you reach the first target. Mission complete! When you're ready, review your project and make any necessary changes to your approach. Then continue with a new chunk and start moving toward the next target.

5. Doing Time. Pick a time frame, something reasonable, and commit to working non-stop for that amount of time. This isn't about reaching a certain target or goal, but working continuously for a set amount of time. For example write or read every day for thirty minutes.

6. Easy Things Last. Put your easiest things to do . . . last. Saving the fun or easy things for last will allow you to finish the day with a strong sense of accomplishment. Most likely at the end of the day you're tired, so why save a big time and energy

KEN GRIFFITH

consuming task when you're not at 100 percent%? Knock that off early in the day and breeze through easier tasks that don't require much attention later in the day.

7. Improve Your Work Space. If you have a work space then use it to your benefit. Make it creative, fun, and stimulating. I like to have quote cards on my home office wall . . . you know, besides the picture of The Duke reminding us men to be real men.

8. Downtime. Use down-time to dream/visualize about your goals. Spend some time seeing your goals as accomplished. Feel what it's like when your work is done, and you're enjoying the spoils.

9. Before Bed. At the end of your workday, identify the first task you'll work on the next day, and set out any needed materials in advance. The next day begin working on that task immediately.

10. Reenergize. Find a relaxation technique or meditation to relax and refresh your mind and body for at least fifteen minutes per day (thirty minutes is better). You will experience better productivity when you're relaxed and energized.

11. Paper. Keep paper and pen around. When you're working on a project, lots of ideas make their way into your mind. Some are keepers, and some are just distractions. Don't spend time on them now. Just write them down and get to them later. The good ones will still sound good later, and the distractions won't.

12. Cross-Pollination. Be active in a variety of new things. Take an exercise class, take a cooking class (my next plan), learn martial arts, take an improvisation class, whatever. You'll often find ideas in one field can boost your performance in another.

There you go: twelve tips to boost your productivity. Take it slow. Pick a few that you feel drawn to and start implementing them right away. Reading about the tips is great, but putting them to work is what will make a difference in your life and help you to get more done.

Truly caring for your success.
From Ken's desk

How to Make the Most Impressive Elevator Speech / Phone Speech

An effective elevator pitch can be crucial for entrepreneurs trying to secure funding from angel investors. The goal of the pitch—written or delivered face-to-face—is to briefly share the "who, what, where, when, why, and how" of your business, while piquing an investor's interest. The tricky part is cramming all of that into one explanation that, hypothetically, should be delivered in the time span of an elevator ride.

The pitch has to grab them quickly. For instance, with written pitch applications, we read the first few sentences and then toss half to two thirds of them away.

The best pitches describe the market the business is in, explain what problem it solves and demonstrate a track record. The worst ones fail for countless reasons.

Mistake no. 1: You don't explain what problem your business solves.

Some entrepreneurs spend too much time talking about how his or her product or service works and not enough time explaining what problem it solves. People buy solutions to problems, don't tell them about how your lawn fertilizer works. Tell me about my lawn.

In our business, we might want to ask how the customer feels about fluctuating rates and how that affects his/her business.

The Fix: Share why customers will buy your product or service.

"If you don't understand or can't explain what problem you're solving and why customers want to give you money, then we're probably never going to want to buy from you. Three questions to startups that you should be able to answer in your business:

Who's your best customer? What benefit do they gain from having the product? And, why should others do the same?

Mistake No. 2: You offer too many facts and numbers.

Entrepreneurs often use statistics to help explain their business. While some figures—such as your sales and revenue—are important to establish a track record, don't go overboard.

Leave out the "step-by-step numerical proof of your market size," he says. "Be compelling. Save the reams of facts for later."

The Fix: Tell a story.

To capture an investor's full attention, explain your business by telling a story *(Remember . . . facts tell; stories sell)*. If you were selling a product for people who are blind, don't start off talking about the difficulties blind people face. Instead, say something like, "Imagine if you or a loved one were to go blind tomorrow."

We might say, "Imagine commodities rising as they did just a few short years ago . . .
"

Mistake No. 3: You're too attached to your business plan.

Say for instance you have a device that monitors electricity; and, according to your business plan, you sell that device to customers for a fixed price. But when a customer wants to lease the device instead of owning it, and you tell them you can't do that, that might be a problem for a customer.

i.e. We only sell a fixed rate for five years . . .

The Fix: Embrace new revenue opportunities.

Being flexible and willing to accommodate customers when they want your service in a slightly different way than you already offer is good. The goal should be to make your product as sellable as possible.

Often we will pass up on a one year deal not realizing it means a renewal in one year

Mistake No. 4: You discuss ownership stakes.

While it might seem natural to explain how much the cost is, don't do it in the initial pitch.

"It is like the sticker price on a car. If it's too high, you don't even talk to the salesman. You just walk off the lot."

The Fix: Save it for the follow-up.

Remember, your goal in the pitch is to build a relationship with the prospect. Get their interest peaked and not sell the whole plan.

See it as you having the best tasting cookie there is, and you want to share it so that others find out just how good it is; and then just before handing it to them you lick it. They may not be so interested in taking it from you now, right?

From Ken's desk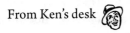

How to Sell against a Competitor?

We live in a competitive world, and that means that you'll frequently be drawn into situations where you need to sell "against" a competitor, rather than simply selling what you've got.

There's an art to doing this effectively once you understand that there are two important aspects to selling against a competitor.

The first aspect is very basic: Know how your offering is different from that of the competition. This is mostly a matter of doing your homework, researching your industry, and figuring why a customer might find your product more attractive than a similar offering from your competitors.

If you don't do your homework, you might as well forget it, because you're probably going to lose the sale. However, if you *do* know how to position your product, you can address the second aspect: guiding your conversation with the customer so that the superiority of your offering becomes clear in the customer's mind.

There are two ground rules for these conversations:

- **Never bad-mouth a competitor.** Bad-mouthing tells the prospect that you're bitter and petty. It makes the competitor look good by comparison.
- **Be honest with the customer.** If you truly believe that buying from a competitor would be bad for the customer, you *must* communicate that belief.

At first glance, it seems that the two ground rules are mutually exclusive, but they're not. In order to satisfy both, you need to ask questions that raise questions.

Ask the Right Questions
(this is a very important technique, so read closely)

Suppose you're selling for a start-up, and your competitor is a large established firm. And let's suppose you know from your research that the competitor's customer service department is often high-handed and annoying. By contrast, your firm is famously easy to work with, which is your competitive advantage.

Your challenge is to point out your competitive advantage without rubbishing the competition.

Now, you could simply claim to have "great customer service," but the competitor probably claims the same thing. You could also say something like "Why would you want to work with those guys? They're a bunch of arrogant SOBs!" But directly

KEN GRIFFITH

criticizing the competition only makes you look as though you're afraid that the competition is going to steal your sale.

Instead, you should ask a question that gets the prospect thinking in a way that's advantageous to your marketing position. For example:

- PROSPECT: "We had a meeting with MegaCorp about this problem."
- YOU: "Well, they're certainly an established company. Have you talked to some of their customers about their service?"
- PROSPECT: "No. Why?"
- YOU: "I've heard that they have their own way of doing things. You might want to ensure they have a service culture that matches your expectations."

Note that you've said nothing negative about the competitor, but you've planted a seed that there's something wrong that warrants the prospect's attention.

Plant a Seed

Here's another example. Suppose you're selling for a well-established, publicly held company against a small firm that's funded primarily through venture capital.

You could, of course, blurt out something like "They'll probably run out of money, so I wouldn't buy from them if I were you." Unfortunately, that kind of blunt approach makes you sound like a tattletale and a know-it-all.

It's much more effective to raise the issue with a well-considered question:

- YOU: "Just so I can be sure to provide value, who else are you talking to about this opportunity?"
- PROSPECT: "We've had a meeting with TeenyCorp."
- YOU: "I've heard some good things about their product. Just out of curiosity, how does your company protect itself against risk when purchasing this type of product?"

Once again, you've said nothing negative, but you've asked a question that plants the seed that buying from the competitor could be risky. In addition, your question is likely to start a conversation that allows you to talk about the stability of your own firm.

These questions are of the type of mind-set you need. From experience, create a list of scenarios and have prepared responses. That is what professionals do. They practice off the field, not while in the game.

From Ken's desk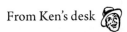

I Want the Lowest Price

You don't have to use all the following to deflect this objection, but know all of it and you'll gain the advantage.

"It's not always wise to guide our buying decisions by price alone. It is never recommended to invest too much for anything; however, investing too little has its drawbacks as well. By spending too much, you lose a little money. By spending too little, you risk more because the service or product you bought will not give you the satisfaction you were expecting. It is an economic truth that you rarely get the most by spending the least, right?"

Zig Ziglar put it best when he said, "It is better to have paid a little more that you expected, than to have paid a little less than you should have." Do you see what I mean here?

"In truth, there is no business, in any industry, that can claim to have the highest quality, the best service . . . and . . . the lowest price. Isn't that true? To have the lowest price would surely mean cutting some corners or having hidden costs. Most don't even recognize that the cheapest toilet paper actually cost more than the expensive ones. They don't realize the larger inside roll, the looseness of the wrapping, and the noticeable reduction of actual sheets."

"Let me ask you a question. If in looking for our service—or anything for that matter—there are three things we look at before buying, which is quality, service, and lowest price . . . which of these would be willing to most willing to give up? Quality, service, or the lowest price."

"Perhaps better put, would you agree with me when I say that we live in a 'you-get-what-you-paid-for-world'? So it's not always about price, is it?"

"If it were always about getting the lowest price, we would all be driving $500 cars and living in mobile-homes, wouldn't we?"

From Ken's desk

KEN GRIFFITH

Iceberg Insurance

The people who built the *Titanic* were positive it wouldn't sink so the idea of more life boats was thought to be of no value.

Today people think the price of natural gas will never rise so they don't see the value in locking long term with a premium.

Imagine trying to sell life boats to the makers/owners of the *Titanic*. What would they say when you try to explain the benefits and urgency they had by not having enough life boats. How would they react?

First off, they had no history of such a ship—invincible. They had sold themselves; therefore, it couldn't sink. There are no ships like it before, even though many a ship had sunk in the past. Do we see a metaphor here? I think so.

Today many would claim we have never seen such a glut of natural gas like today so why would we insure ourselves against it.

The *Titanic* did not want for life boats; the want was for more silverware and more chandeliers, more gold trimmings and fine champagne.

Not too different than when the Canadian dollar was well below the U.S. dollar, manufacturers here were counting profits instead of investing in new machinery.

And then what happened. Now they complain that the government is to blame for their problems. Like the *Titanic*, no need to insure against the unthinkable and then the complaint was where are the other ships to come and help.

The forecast for the Titanic was that it would never sink. The forecast for next week's weather may give you skepticism. Earlier this year it was forecasted by many that the world was to come to its end. It was also forecasted that Katrina was to spell Armageddon for Louisiana, and yet today the state is very much alive. In 1971, the greatest scientists in the world told us that we had twenty years of oil left, and that life as we know it would end. What have we learned? That we should never really believe in forecasts. Well, maybe not if the forecast looks the way you want it to like, right?

Think of this. Isn't it amazing how much money people of California saved by not buying earthquake insurance? You know, until it happened. Have you ever felt like you were burned by buying car insurance? So why protect yourself today from *what only might happen* in natural gas?

In the end, the *Titanic* **did** sink, and it **did** need more life boats. And yet we look at forecasts in NG and believe them, yet we look at examples like the Titanic and ignore them.

Iceberg insurance works better than hoping in forecasts, yes?

Zig Ziglar said it best: **"It is always better to have paid a little more than you had expected, than to have paid a little less than you should have."**

From Ken's desk

Tips for Closing the Appointment

While these were specifically design for my business, you can adjust toward yours very easily

The "I Don't Want to Sign Anything" Close

I understand, Bob. I wouldn't sign anything either unless it made sense, right? What I am suggesting to you is spend a little time to investigate if what we can do for you makes sense . . . and at no obligation to you. Let's face it, Bob, we are in the business of gaining customers, not repelling them. Fair?

The "I am looking for the lowest rate," Close

It's amazing you say that. I was just talking to someone else who said the same thing. They were talking about rate shopping, and I would have thought that the memories of Enron would still be in the minds of business owners. Enron actually coined the phrase "rate suckers" where they preyed on those so focused on rates knowing they would never read the back of the contracts and got screwed later on.

It's really not all about rates, is it?

In fact, if we always shopped for the cheapest things we'd all have $200 cars and live in Mobile homes, right? What we are really looking for is value, isn't it?

Let me ask you a question: have you ever been in a convenience store? Sure, right? And isn't everything in a convenience store also found in a grocery store but much cheaper? So again, it's not always about price or rate sometimes it's about the value of convenience.

What we offer as a value to you is the convenience of not having to worry about rising energy costs. Now isn't that worth a small amount of your time?

Assuming this area of concern is satisfied, would you be able to go ahead?

The "I got burned before" close

Bob, the one thing you and both know is that from 1997 to 2007, natural gas rates went up 486%, which means that anyone who rode the market for those years did get burned. It's funny but often argued that locking in doesn't work. Truth is we are all entitled to our own opinions, but we are not entitled to our own facts.

If what you meant was that you were with a retailer and lost then I guess you signed either in 2001, 2005 or 2008. Those were the only years where someone was likely to buy on a peak ... of course now with rates being as low as they were in 2002 people can lock rates based on logic instead of the emotional decisions made in those years.

One way to look at it Bob is one bad date back in high school didn't stop you from dating, right? You simply learned and moved on. Same as when you get upset with a bank, you don't move your money to under the mattress; you move it to another bank, right?

From Ken's desk

Negotiating in the Eleventh Hour.

It is common with large business sales to end up in some sort of negotiation. What you don't want is eleventh hour negotiations.

Done right, negotiating centers on clear and precise communication and collaboration—a continual series of "mutual agreements and understanding."

Let's take a deeper look at this quality decision process. The first decision element revolves around the customer recognizing that they are experiencing some consequences due to the absence of the value your product/service provides. Ask yourself, "What would the customer be experiencing without your product?

Now think of yourself as a doctor. You are looking for the symptoms of the absence of business health in your patient. Relative to negotiations, the symptom either exists or it doesn't. You and your customer will reach agreement on that quickly, and if the symptoms exist, you move on to the next decision, "What are the consequences of the symptoms?" or "How bad is it?"

The next decision revolves around determining the financial impact of the problem. It is important to bring your customer a process that will guide them through measuring the financial impact of their problem, just as a doctor brings the capability of running tests to determine the extent of the symptoms. If you don't have a cost of the problem, there isn't a problem. In other words, if you can't help your customer measure the financial impact of the problem your solution, they will be unable to measure the value of your solution, likely not want to buy your solution at all or at least not want to pay the price you will ask.

When the cost of the problem is agreed on, the next decision for the customer is, "Is this bad enough to take action?"

When these decisions are mutually agreed upon, we have "negotiated" away a high percentage of the objections we would traditionally hear and those that might lead to a "no."

Think about it – how many times have we given a customer a proposal before they decided they really had a problem? They were only "interested" in the solution we had.

A collaborative approach eliminates the dependency on traditional closing and objection handling skills. With this approach, you and your customer have come to common conclusions and understanding of all the key elements that would otherwise be subject to objection or negotiation when there are surprises in the eleventh hour. You will have agreed on the nature and financial impact of their problems and the financial value of that solution. In short, the customer has agreed to each element of a quality decision process and is not seeing any new "terms" in the proposal with which to have a reason to object.

From Ken's desk

"NO" Goal Setting

The best answer is sales is often thought to be YES. It is not. The best answer is NO. Order takers get yeses, salespeople get yeses, and continue working for a no, or get a NO and go find another NO.

Not quite where a customer invites you to leave or encourages you to never come back? But a simple NO

Let's examine;

So you want to retire at sixty-five
Here are some stats you need to know
5% of people will retire without assistance
36% will have died before retirement
6% will continue working (not by choice)
53% will depend on family or charity or the government

It's the 5 percent% that are the lucky ones, right? They are the ones who failed the most. Remember, the more you fail, the more success you have! It is to the degree that you are willing to fail that sets your degree of success.

So we must learn to fail; we must set goals to fail.

Here Are the Five Steps to Failure

1. Recognize the ability to fail—100% of people can do this
2. Have the willingness to fail—20% will sustain this level
3. Create a wantingness to fail—beyond willing; beyond tolerance and acceptance; 5% will have faith in failure
4. Fail bigger and faster – have BIG "impossible" goals; if failing is good, failing faster is better
5. Fail exponentially – surround yourself with others who want to fail

What do most do?

Average sales reps reach their quota (their inside the head quota) and then avoid pain.

Extra effort = unnecessary pain. Ben Franklin said, "Success has ruined many a man."

If you reach your YES goals early in the week or day, what happens? Time to slack off for the average rep, right?

Let's use some round numbers to explain;

If your goal is to close ten deals in one day, and you know it normally takes 100 tries to get 10 then your closing ratio is 10%. (Actually if you were to set NO goals then the ratio would have been 90% . . . not bad, eh). So what happens if you get your 10 in the first 20 attempts. You walk away feeling proud of your 50% closing ratio but with no extra cash in your pocket.

Now what if your goal was to get 90 NOs? You'd have to keep going wouldn't you. Why would you take yourself out of the game when you are on a hot streak? Just imagine Tony LaRussa pulling Albert Pujols after he had just gone 3 for 3 at the plate. You would think he has lost it, right? Then why do it to yourself?

Never quit on a customer until you get a NO

So how do we set NO goals; First off understand that when setting goals you must have 3 levels of goal setting.

Minimum;
If, 100 calls = 10 deals, then you need 90 NOs

Stretch; or, Play it safe
Just go for 100 NOs to give you a buffer

Optimum; to increase by 30%
90 NOs + 30% = 90 x 1.3 = 117
117 NOs or better yet round up and make it an even 120
The **minimum** keeps you from having a bad week.
The **stretch** builds a 10% buffer
The **optimum** will create an explosion or "your'" level of desire.

So how many times are you willing to fail before you succeed?

Accepting NO and setting NO goals does not work for average people. (If you accept NO goals you will no longer be average). Average people quit or accept what must be done.

Think of it this way: **When mining for gold, you don't look for gold . . . you remove dirt.** He who removes the most dirt finds the most gold.

CREDO: I like to fail . . . I fail big and I fail often (repeat x 2)
Sticks and stones may break my bones, but NO will never hurt me

From Ken's desk

No One Told You

What do you REALLY believe is possible?

Do you talk about believing that you can be, do, and have anything you desire, but you secretly think you are stuck and this is all there is for you?

We've all been there. And it's time that you hear the truth.

You REALLY can be, do, and have anything you desire, once you get your beliefs in alignment with those desires. Why have you doubted or disbelieved (truly)? Because no one told you.

No one told you. How could they? They didn't know themselves. And many of those you love and care about still don't know. So they never told you. And they still can't tell you.

Instead, they told you that you can't succeed. That life is difficult. That you have to work hard to make money. That relationships are difficult. That life is a struggle. That you're not good enough. That some people are lucky, and you're not one of them.

How could they know? How could they possibly know what you can or cannot do? They didn't know.

They don't know but you believed them.

And so life got difficult. You don't think you can succeed. It gets harder to make money. Your relationships don't always work out the way you want them to. You don't feel like you're good enough. You don't believe you're lucky and you doubt that things will ever get better.

That's not the way it has to be.

You shouldn't believe any of that! **Because you are good enough.**

Life can be fun and easy. You can take that trip you've always wanted to take. You can buy that home you want. You can own the car you want. You can meet your soul mate and live the life you really want to live. You can make as much money as you want.

All of it is possible when you believe.

But you don't believe.

And the only reason that you don't believe is because no one ever told you that you can believe. That you should believe. They didn't give you reasons to believe. They gave you reasons not to believe.

No one ever told you that you can achieve your goals. No one ever told you that you have an incredible power within you. That once you direct that power you'll be able to have more, be more, achieve more, and live more with passion while doing what you really love—no matter what that is.

You see, the only reason you're not where you want to be in life, why you don't have what you want, and why you're not enjoying the success you want is because you've been conditioned to accept the limiting beliefs and thoughts of the people around you.

Sure you can change the people around you, but those limiting thoughts and beliefs are in your head; they're planted on your subconscious, and so you'll keep creating the same old life, the same old pain, and the same old struggles. It's what your subconscious thinks you want.

But you don't want that. You want more, you want better, and where you are just isn't good enough anymore.

So what do you do?

Change the thoughts, change the beliefs, and you change your life.

Direct your subconscious to create what you really want. You start directing the subconscious by creating new beliefs, new thoughts, and getting rid of the limiting beliefs and limiting thoughts. That means you no longer accept what they told you when you were growing up. Don't believe those who don't support you. When somebody says, "You can't," you respond with, "Of course, I can."

You see, you can do anything you want.

You can achieve whatever goal you set out to achieve—when you believe you can.

But for too long you've believed that you can't, and this belief system is what destroys your life. And it gets worse. Because the longer you believe that you can't, the worse things get and the harder it becomes to change those beliefs.

So start today.

Change those beliefs.

No longer accept that you can't. Believe that you can, and you will. Yes, you can achieve anything you want. Yes, you can be with the right person. Yes, you can make more money and live the life you want to live. Start directing your subconscious to create more of what you want.

Everyone believes that their child will walk and talk. Your parents believed you would too, and they were right. That's the kind of belief that you need to have in yourself. You need to believe, beyond any possible doubt that you can and will achieve any and all of your goals.

When you have this powerful belief in place, you really will achieve all your goals.

You see, when you firmly believe that you can and will do something, your subconscious and your higher powers all work together to help you achieve that goal. It's like a thousand hands show up to help you. You'll get numerous opportunities, and people of all sorts will show up to help you. That's when you know you're on the right track. That's when you know that things are going your way.

So how do you do this?

You get rid of the negative thinking. You get rid of the self-doubt. You stop worrying and start trusting. You start believing.

KEN GRIFFITH

To do that, you need to redirect your mind and redirect your subconscious to help you achieve the goals you want to achieve. When you start filling your mind with positive thoughts, you begin to attract more positive situations and people. When you get rid of the negative thinking, you get rid of the self-doubt and worry. You then start to discover new opportunities to help you get more of what you want.

If anyone ever says, "You can't," don't believe them. Yes, you can achieve any goal you set. **Yes, you can live the life you want to live.**

You've already achieved so much—just believe in yourself, and the rest will follow.

The greatest success starts with a single step and a simple belief that you can. Believe that you can and you will. Remember, believe in yourself. Never give up! Finish the race, fight the good fight, and keep the faith. Remember, faith means to expect.

Follow your dreams.

Yes, you can when you believe.

So no one told you? **Well, I'm telling you now. You can and will, do and have anything you desire.**

From Ken's desk

Overclosing

It is not unknown for salespeople to talk their customers into closure then carry right on and talk them out again. You can overdo closing, and it requires a close sensitivity to avoid this trap.

It is often the fear of the other person saying no that often causes a salesperson to keep on talking. You must have faith and also accept that when they say no, it is no real comment about you. If you take rejection personally, then you are probably in the wrong job.

Watch out for the other person not only in what they say but also in the *emotions* behind the words.

Never try closing when they are in a negative emotional state. You will only cause further objection and possibly anger that means they will never buy from you again.

In all of these methods, remember that all closing techniques are appropriate only in particular circumstances. This can include the emotional state and readiness of the customer.

It also depends on the sophistication of the customer. A professional buyer in a big company has been on all the sales courses themselves and can see a closing technique coming from several miles away. Using simple methods with sophisticated buyers will only serve to annoy them, so rather than treating the situation like *transactional selling*, use more *relationship selling* methods, seeking to understand them and meet their needs, both professional and human. Everyone, even buyers, like to be treated with respect, and if they do catch you being a bit crass, then apologize and be more careful where you tread!

From Ken's desk

KEN GRIFFITH

Potential

"Potential is a French word; it means you're worth s**t so far."—Willie Wilson (ex-center-fielder, KC Royals)

Do you know the difference between your potential and your capacity? I am sure you have read and heard a lot about potential, but there is a major difference between our potential and our capacity. The major difference is that potential is based on the future. When someone has the potential to do something, it is about becoming something other than who they are in the present moment.

Capacity is based on the present moment. Your capacity already exists. Capacity is defined by doing what you can do today, in this moment.

At one time I thought I could help everyone. I wanted to spread my message everywhere so that people could be free of their limitations, but then I realize something that changed my whole approach. I finally realized this wasn't realistic or even possible. But what I could do was make a difference to those people, such as you, who come into my path. Although I have the potential to help many people, I only have the capacity to help those who want my help in this moment.

So for now, forget about your potential and focus on your capacity in this moment. Do what you can do right now. Even the smallest step will bring you closer to your desire. Don't wait. Take that small step now! Do it today! Your potential will be realized by your willingness to focus on your capacity.

Remember, *you are not in charge of your success. Your habits are in charge of your success. The good news is that you are in charge of your habits.*

From Ken's desk

Procrastination

One of the most respected people of our time, General Colin Powell, once said, "Indecision has cost Americans, the Government, and business, billions more than wrong decisions."

Procrastination is a killer. We forget that a nondecision is a decision. We all know this is a pay-me-now or pay-me later world, right? And we all know what pay-me-later means, yes?

Whether you say yes or no, right now, the only concern would be if it were a wrong decision, but if you hold off, **you will still make a yes or no decision** so what really can change in a week? Certainly, we know prices of things tend to rise over decreasing but the real process is in what Warren Buffett said, "that people **avoid wealth** by passing up on a good deal in the hopes that one day it will become a great deal." Isn't that right?

So what we have now is a decision right? Yes means we go forward and protect you from the unknown; and no. well, have you ever heard of a business decision where the decision was no that actually grew a business?

From Ken's desk

Questions Are the Answers

To be successful in sales, we must not only ask a lot of questions, but we also have to carefully craft those questions. There are "leading" questions and "nonleading questions."

Nonleading questions, while offering no pressure, are open to any response.

E.g., "What are your thoughts about . . . ?" or "Are you open to switching?" They are open to get either a no or to an answer you may not be prepared for.

Leading questions suggest an answer or are designed to influence the answer, if not even just to confirm.

One of my favorites is, "Would you agree that we live in a 'pay me now' or 'pay me later' world?" or "If I came to you five years ago and had evidence of a 58% rate increase over the next five years and you could protect against it, would you have?"

The point being, if sales is the art and science of persuasion (and it is), and closing is helping people make decisions that are good for them, that if left alone they wouldn't make themselves (and it is), then it is our job to persuade or influence our prospect to that win-win decision, right?

So let's work on how we open and close with the questions we ask. One of the best, if not the best, question to ask for the close is, "Does that make sense?"

What answer does that allow for? Yes simply means you can proceed with the authorization, and no simply means you either didn't do an effective job of explaining or the prospect didn't do an effective job of listening—.Let's go with the latter but take credit for the former. Either way, you get to go through it again until he gets it.

As for opening questions, you know the standard questions; i.e., How long have you been in business? Who is your competition? Where do you sit in the market place? etc. But how about your lead-in questions, the ones that allow you to present and that sets up for closing, the ones that deal with all the possible objections, so that you don't have to deal with them after words.

Look back to the objections you normally get and create "leading" questions that address those. Practice asking those questions hundreds of times, and odds are you'll never hear those objections again.

From Ken's desk

Rational Close

Use logic and reason to persuade. Show them evidence that the budgeting works well, and that other customers were satisfied.

With care, you can construct a powerful *argument* that uses a traditional and proven structure for persuasion. That is why you do not skip over your presentation. They need visuals and evidence.

As we are brought up in a social and educational system that defines science and reason to be correct, such an approach is powerfully persuasive.

Some people decide by *thinking* and other more by feeling. This approach works well with many people, though it is most effective with the thinking decision makers a.k.a. controllers and CFOs.

That's why I like dealing with numbers people. They make logical decisions over emotional decisions. Those who make emotional decisions tend to wait for increases to do anything, and then their decisions become those of panic.

"Well, now, we've gone through all your needs and this meets these well, right? And the rate we have is good, true? Now, is there anything else that would stop you deciding to go ahead today? No? So let's do the paperwork."

From Ken's desk

Rejection

Whether in the sales game or in the entrepreneurship game (both for us) you better get used to hearing the word "no." If starting a business was easy, everyone would want in. (too many already do). If sales were easy, nobody would pay high commissions. Rejection helps knock out the weak. In my case, those early rejections forced me to really listen to my potential customers and find out what I needed to do to change "no, thanks" to "where do I sign?"

You can't escape rejection, I learned. But you can let it go. Here are some exercises that paid big dividends for me:

- **Dissect thoughts under the microscope.** When faced with a challenge, what do you tell yourself? "I'm no good. This is too hard. I'll never make it.?" Don't let negative self-talk sabotage your attitude.
- **Identify realistic fears.** Whom do you fear? What might go wrong? Who has the power to reject you? Why would that person say no? The answers will help you prepare your best offer and facing them will help you keep your composure.
- **Focus on the moment.** Keep your perspective. Rejection lasts only a moment, and once it's over, you'll be able to move on to the next opportunity.
- **Be more assertive.** Most fears of rejection rest on the desire for approval from other people. Don't base your self-esteem on their opinions. Learn to express your own needs (appropriately) and say no to requests when you genuinely can't help.
- **Analyze every failure, but never wallow in one.** Harry Truman once said, "As soon as I realize I've made one damned fool mistake, I rush out and make another one." Failure is a condition all of us experience. It's our reaction to our failures that distinguishes winners from losers.
- **Don't rationalize away the hurt.** Turned down for funding? Didn't get the contract? Turned down for funding? Lost a top employee to a big competitor? Don't let your worth be defined by others. Get back in the game. It's not a permanent condition; it's a short-term setback.

Ten setbacks are the going price for any worthwhile win. Look at the major league baseball standings at the end of any season: Out of thirty teams, only eight make the playoffs, and only one winds up winning the World Series. Are those annual standings the end of the world for the twenty-nine losers? Hardly.

Cary Grant, Marilyn Monroe, Alfred Hitchcock, and Richard Burton never won an Oscar. Babe Ruth was never named most valuable player. Thomas Jefferson, John Quincy Adams, and Andrew Jackson all lost elections for the presidency before they won one. Losers? No, legends.

Don't get dejected if you've been rejected. Just get your skills perfected!

In the end, it is about one word:

Commitment!

You have to be committed to you and the life you want to design. If you are going to jump ship and recoil and lick your wounds every time a challenge shows up, the message you are giving yourself is that you aren't committed to your vision. The message you are giving yourself is that you have to settle.

Well here's the truth.

You DON'T have to settle!

Once you decide to go "all in" on your vision, then you need to commit to it, 100 percent.

Challenges will show up, and resistance will show up, but challenges and resistance are only what you decide they are. Every challenge presents an opportunity for you to grow beyond where you are right now.

Remember, we have all heard success stories of people who rise above seemingly insurmountable circumstances to live the life of their dreams . . .

Use those people as your reminder of the infinite possibilities that surround you in each and every moment rejection comes your way.

From Ken's desk

Sales Homework

Ever been called by some telemarketer wanting you to buy insurance or a newspaper subscription? Do you hang up on these annoying people? You probably should hang up on them, **unless you are in sales!**

Wouldn't you want to hear how they are selling? What they are doing right and what they are doing wrong. How you might say things differently than them or what you might learn as a good "'trick."

How about when shopping for clothes or furniture, do you hate it the salesman approaches and pressures you? Or do you try to learn how to approach and guide as they have been taught.

Better yet, how about car salesmen, come on, who doesn't want to avoid these guys? Unless you want to master sales.

I think you see my point here. When not at work, you can enjoy a shopping experience and call it homework. "But I can't afford a car (or anything ☺) right now, Ken." So nobody said you had to buy. In fact, you can practice all your objections on these guys. See how they handle it and tell them how they should have handled it if you want. And besides, you could be spending valuable dream building time and learning to hone your skills at the same time. Can you say win-win?

So listen to that annoying caller, give that pestering sales rep some time, understand that there are not many professions out there where so many others are willing to teach you for free.

From Ken's desk

Sales Is the Art and Science of Persuasion

For you to be as successful as you possibly can, you need to embrace the concept of persuasion. The challenge for many people when it comes to doing this is that persuasion gets a bad rap. So many people hear the word persuasion and instantly attach negative and immoral meaning to it.

Listen, I'm not going to pretend that there isn't negative persuasion out there. But on the flip side, there are tons of positive persuasion, and that is what we are going to focus on. You can actually harness the power of persuasion to increase the quality of your life and the lives of the people around you.

The fact of the matter is, if you desire success in any area of your life—whether it's in your relationships, career, health. You will need to effectively and positively use the power of persuasion.

The best part about this skill is that you will actually significantly increase the value and positive energy that surrounds all of your interactions, for everyone involved! Some of this may seem simple, but trust me, when you overlook it (as so many do) you are holding yourself and other people back.

Whether it is business or personal relationships, persuasion should not be something you turn on and off. To be authentic, this is not something you simply turn on from nine to five. It should become a part you. These tips will help you start with those around you. Eventually, they become a part of you in the field of business.

Tips to Make Anyone Like You (come on, you want to be liked, don't you?)

Tip # 1: Keep On Smiling.

One simple way to get people to like you is by smiling.

People tend to shy away from those who seem unfriendly. For a stranger, a blank expression is almost as good as a "stay away from me" kind of signal.

However, your smile should not be forced. When you smile but deep inside you have bad feelings toward someone, it would show in your body language, and they can actually read it.

What you could do is focus on the positive traits about that person and think about those qualities when you smile to them. That way, your positive thoughts would allow you to create a genuinely likeable smile.

Tip # 2: Be Sincere.

Nobody wants to deal with fake people. If you can't give a person a sincere comment, then don't bother giving one at all.

It's easy to spot a fake a mile away. The way you smile, or the way you carry yourself, more or less tells other people whether you're real or not.

Tip # 3: Be the Bearer of Good News.

Everybody wants to hear good news. One remarkable way to make people like you is by giving them positive news as often as possible.

In time, you'll be associated with good news and good luck. (This also works vice-versa. If you're usually the bearer of bad news, then people will unconsciously see you as a dark cloud.)

Tip # 4: Be a Positive Person.

If you want to know how to make people like you, start by being a positive person. Nobody wants to be around a grumpy person.

When things suddenly turn for the worse, try to find the silver lining. Always look at the brighter side. People can't help but be attracted to those who aren't drowning in angst.

Tip # 5: Make People Happy.

Making people happy is the easiest route to getting someone to like you and getting that same person to listen to you. Become a "happy pill." Be pleasant company.

If you really want to learn how to get someone to like you, you have to cultivate your relationship with that person over time.

Tip # 6: Use Proper Body Language.

Making people know you're interested in them is one key to getting liked. There are nonverbal cues you can use to indicate your interest.

One of them would be maintaining eye contact. By keeping your eyes on the person talking, you are telling them that they have your complete attention.

Another way to communicate effectively is by nodding your head at some of the points you agree with. I also recommend leaning a bit forward to show that you're interested in the topic of conversation.

Tip # 7: Expose Yourself More.

The more someone sees you or communicates with you, the more they will grow to like you. So get out there, show yourself, and make yourself heard, as often as you can!

Tip # 8: Share Your Secrets.

Share your emotions or feelings with others. Better yet, share your "secrets" if possible.

People tend to trust you if you make them perceive that you're sharing a secret with them.

When you tell a secret, they tend to open up in response and drop their defenses. They will feel like you are treating them as close friends. They will also feel valued and important.

And when you divulge something that is normally not being shared, they will feel special; hence, defenses are lowered and your likeability rate goes higher.

Say something like, "I'd like to share a secret with you, but please don't tell anyone." or "I should have kept this for myself, but I'm going to tell you anyway because you're a good friend."

They might even feel the need to return the favor and share their own secrets and confidential experiences with you, a.k.a. close themselves.

From Ken's desk

Sales is: Everyone lives by selling something.

Sales is more contingent upon the attitude of the salesman, not the attitude of the prospect. To succeed in sales, simply talk to lots of people every day. And here's what's exciting. There are lots of people! In sales, if you work just for money, you'll never make it. But if you love what you are doing and always put the customer first, success will be yours. A smart salesperson listens to emotions not facts.

Sales is a series of failures to create a huge success. The Japanese proverb says, "Fall down seven times. Stand up eight." Two sure ways to fail—think and never do or do and never think. Sales is an attitude. If you were to sell life insurance, don't sell life insurance. Sell what life insurance can do. If you sell a fixed commodity, don't sell the fixed commodity. Sell what that fixed commodity can do. Remember, you don't get paid for the hour. You get paid for the value you bring to the hour.

Sales is perseverance. I do not think there is any other quality so essential to success of any kind as the quality of perseverance. It overcomes almost everything, even nature. Forget about the business outlook; be on the outlook for business.

Sales is more about what you think than what the customer thinks. In sales, there are going to be times when you can't make everyone happy. Don't expect to, and you won't be disappointed. Just do your best for each client in each situation as it arises. Then, learn from each situation how to do it better the next time, and remember, it is not your customer's job to remember you. It is your obligation and responsibility to make sure they don't have the chance to forget you.

Sales is energy. Confidence and enthusiasm are the greatest sales producers in any kind of economy. A salesman, like the storage battery in your car, is constantly discharging energy. Unless he is recharged at frequent intervals he soon runs dry. This is one of the greatest responsibilities of sales leadership. Timid salesmen have skinny kids. The sale begins when the customer says yes.

Sales is mastering the skills, correcting some thinking, and going to work. Every sale has five basic obstacles: no need, no money, no hurry, no desire, no trust, eliminating these obstacles is the goal. Always be closing doesn't mean you're always closing the deal, but it does mean that you need to be always closing on the next step in the process. For every sale you miss because you're too enthusiastic, you will miss a hundred because you're not enthusiastic enough. A sale is not something you pursue; it's what happens to you while you are immersed in serving your customer. What separates those who achieve from those who do not, is in direct proportion to one's ability to ask for help (i.e., drop the ego).

From Ken's desk

Sales Professionals

How's this for a motto? *You will have everything in life that you want if you will just help enough other people get what they want.*

Sales professionals know that happiness is not pleasure; it is victory.

It is in having the ability to confidently ask your customer, "Bob, if your best friend were to walk in right now, would you introduce him to me?"

A lot of what stops people from becoming great is in their thinking. That is why I push the three steps to making it big; Master the skill, correct some thinking, and go to work. It's all about mastering the skills, but to do so, you have to correct some thinking first.

Most of us have been taught to follow the crowd. We subscribe to "tribal" thinking, which is the thinking of the masses. It is not easy to break from this type of thinking, or nonthinking. A lot of people find this a huge stumbling block because they believe what social, political, religious, and other authority figures have told them is "true."

There is a lot of fear tied up in leaving the tribe. However, you will never experience true freedom or riches unless you learn to think for yourself. But to do this, you must be capable of critical thought, which is something the members of the tribe cannot do.

Put another way. Most people don't know how to think. They have been told WHAT to think for so long, they no longer know HOW to think. What's the lesson for you?

I'm convinced that true freedom and riches requires you to think contrary to what the tribe is thinking. And it ALWAYS requires you to question the beliefs you hold. On everything. This is not easy because we are addicted to certainty.

We would rather be certain about our beliefs than face the fact that what we believe may not be "true." But the more you question what the tribe believes, the more you will realize that they are hypnotized. You don't have to wait for them to wake up from the trance. You can do it right now!

Also, "tribal" thinking leads people to fear followed by procrastination. Until the salesperson learns to "look up to" or "look down upon" no person, fear will prevail. This thought that people have different levels, and that we should treat them as such is formed from old beliefs.

Remember, regarding your product or service, you are the expert. You have more experience, knowledge, and more expertise in your field than the prospect will ever have. Treat everybody the same, and your strengths will shine; treat each situation with a new perspective and it will shine, and you become the consummate professional.

It then becomes your job to teach others.

From Ken's desk

Seven Dumb Sales Tactics to Avoid

These big mistakes seem to be shockingly common. Make sure you're not guilty of any of them. Here are my top 7 dumb mistakes we are guilty of:

1. Answering Objections the Customer Hasn't Surfaced: Though it's a good idea to anticipate objections that the customer might have and prepare reasonable answers to them, it's a horrible idea to surface those objections yourself, because you've just created an issue that probably didn't exist. Explaining away something preemptively can also make you seem defensive and unsure of the real value of your offering.

Fix: Never start any sentence with "You may be wondering . . . " or "Perhaps you're asking yourself . . . "

2. Leaving the "Next Step" to the Customer: I've read dozens of sales e-mails that end with a suggestion that the customer should call or contact the seller "if you're interested" or "in order to learn more." The people who send these letters always complain that they don't get any responses.

No kidding—you're asking the customer to do your work for you.

Fix: Keep the ball in your court. Try substituting a closer like this: "I will call you next week to discuss whether it makes sense to go ahead."

3. Selling Features Rather Than Results: Incredibly, some people (usually marketing folks) believe that customers buy a product because it has desirable features. They therefore rattle off a list of those features, hoping that at least one will pique the customer's interest.

In fact, customers care only about the results of purchasing a product and the ways it will affect their lives and their businesses.

Fix: Figure out why a customer buys your product rather than somebody else's. Then sell *that* result, using the features to buttress your ability to deliver that result.

4. Faking Intimacy: Like it or not, the minute you're positioned in somebody's mind as "a person who is trying to sell me something," you're fighting an uphill battle to win trust. Under those circumstances, the absolute worst thing you can do is to try to "suck up" by acting smarmy.

The most common manifestation: brightly asking, "How are you doing today?" at the beginning of a cold call. It makes people want to puke.

Fix: Remain personable and professional—but no more—until such time as you actually forge a friendship, which typically takes weeks.

5. Talking More Than Listening: I've written about this problem repeatedly in the past, but the error is so common that it bears repeating. When you're selling, it's all too easy to get excited and nervous and then try to "drive the sale" forward by talking or giving a sales pitch. Customers find this extraordinarily irritating.

Fix: In your mind, redefine *selling* as a passive activity that consists mostly of listening, considering, and reacting to what the customer does and says.

6. Wasting Time on Dead-End "Opportunities": What with voice mail, gatekeepers, and a challenging economy, it sometimes seems like a miracle when you actually get into a sales conversation with a live human being. When that happens, the possibility of making a sale can become so seductive that you don't want to spoil the dream by asking questions that might reveal this as a false opportunity.

Fix: Within the first five minutes of your first conversation, ask questions that will reveal whether the customer has a real need, as well as the money to satisfy it.

7. Treating a "Close" as the End of the Process: Maybe it's the result of unfortunate terminology, but a lot of companies and individuals take "closing the deal" to mean that the sales activity has ended. Nothing could be further from the truth.

The real work happens *after* you've closed the deal, because that's when you can start building the kind of relationship that will eventually generate follow-on business and referral sales, both of which are far easier and profitable than winning new business.

Fix: Always aim for long-term relationships rather than short-term revenue. That way, a "close" is the beginning, not the end, of the process.

From Ken's desk

Slide Uphill

The reason so few people are successful is no one has yet found a way for someone to lie down and slide uphill.—**W. Clement Stone**

Yup, success is an uphill ride. Upon learning that it is now up to you as to whether you want to take that ride, you have a decision to make. No different than when you hear, "The rich get richer while the poor get poorer." When people hear that statement, some lament over it and some get to the realization that if this is a fact, then I better pick a team or someone will pick my team for me, and it won't be the one I want.

We've all heard the cliché, life is a journey. Well not necessarily so for some and for those brave enough to embark on a journey there will be days when you would rather be at home sitting on the couch, but that is so much better than being home sitting on the couch wishing to be on a journey.

Look , a simple motto for life is **Eat well, stay fit, die anyway.** You can't really escape the last one, can you? So why not take great chances, go beyond what you thought capable or acceptable, say things no one would expect, and reach for the top. This life bit is just an experience anyways, so why not go all out? Look and act silly once in a while. Question the obvious.

Most of all, don't be afraid to use what seem like "harsh" closing lines. Don't be afraid to challenge some customers and DON'T BE AFRAID OF SUCCESS.

The view from the top is an awesome one, but you can't get there lying down.

From Ken's desk

Listening

"Talking is sharing, listening is caring."—Unknown

When we are carefully listening to our prospects interests, desire, hobbies, and other thoughts; we are putting them in debt to us. Then they have a feeling they "owe" us something, and consequently, they are more willing to listen to our story.

No one has missed a sale because they listened to the prospects needs, wants, and desires. Listening is just not as difficult as we make it. When we are not talking or preparing to talk, we can listen. Interestingly enough, the more we know about our prospects needs, the better position we are in to meet those needs, but not only that. The trust factor also goes up when the prospect sees we care. And the one thing that customers have always rated highest in the sales world is trust.

Work on becoming a good listener. When asking your opening questions, don't just ask for the sake of "the setup." Ask to learn of their experience. They will tell you more than you think to help you close the deal. Once you have asked a question, clear your head so that you may truly hear what is being said. Don't worry about not being prepared to ask the next question; the right question will appear to you.

It takes practice, but that practice (like all other practices) will pay off very nicely.

Remember:

People will never care how much you know, until they know how much you care.

From Ken's desk

The "Hard Times" Close

It's funny. My job should be really easy during times such as these when rates are low, and yet my job is actually easy when rates are high. Imagine, customers prefer to buy from me when my rates are at their highest. Doesn't make sense, does it?

Everyone knows "buy low, sell high," and yet 80 percent of people do exactly the opposite.

Why? Because they forget the past and are blinded to the future. They use emotions when buying instead of logic. They *wish* for everything to stay the same.

Remember, every valley is surrounded by two peaks. We just came down from a peak and are in the valley. Did you want to sign while climbing the next peak?

Roosevelt once said, "The time to repair the leak in the roof, is when the sun is shining."

From Ken's desk

The 1-2-3 Close

The 1-2-3 close works through the principle of triples, a curious pattern where three things given together act as a coherent set of three hammer blows that give a compelling message.

Example: *This product is **less expensive, faster,** and **more reliable** than the competition.*

We might use this as "Our ramp product easier to absorb, easier to budget with, and takes all risk away from your business." Or "It is less expensive than our competition, more in-tune to the market place, and is the best commodity budget-plan out there."

If on the phone; twenty minutes with our consultant will give you the best information, the latest updates, and the best program offers.

It's a time tested and all-encompassing close. Great speakers use the time honored. "Tell them what you are going to tell them … tell them … tell them what you told them." Politicians use the three tenses: "I did do it," "I am doing it," and "I will continue to do it." Great closers do the same.

It sinks the message in. If done well nodding yes, you have virtually trained your customer on saying yes.

Same goes for the contract (registration form, right?). As you present the form, ask if the information you wrote and know if it is true, accurate, i.e. "is this your correct phone number? Is this your correct mailing address? And is this the best e-mail to get you?

Once you have gotten them to say yes three times, the fourth is easy for them. "Just need you to authorize right here."

e.g., "This Ramp product **easier to absorb, easier to budget** with, and **takes all risk away** from your business. Once on this program, please understand that while I am here for you now. I'll be here for you through the term, and I will be here to guide you once the term is complete"

Easy as 1-2-3.

From Ken's desk

The ABCs

ABC is a common term that stands for "always be closing," which is both good and bad advice.

ABC is good advice when it is used to keep in mind that you are always aiming toward a close. It is bad when you just use it to mean battering the customer to death with a barrage of unsubtle closing techniques.

Selling can be a lot like fishing. If you tug hard on the line, it will snap, and the fish will get away. The best method is a gentle coaxing that gradually brings the fish in to shore, although sometimes when they are spooked you have to let them out again and calm them down further away.

Silence After

When you have used a closing technique, be quiet afterward and let them respond. If you just keep talking, then you may miss what they have to say, like yes for example.

Silence also builds <u>tension</u> and will encourage them to respond, and a response to a well-put closing question will more likely be positive.

Does that make sense?

"Does that make sense" is a great closing line upon completing your presentation. Again, the key here is to "shut up." He who speaks first loses!

If you get a yes, then you can add, "Then all we have to do is complete this registration form, and I can get your preferred rate approved."

Should you get a no, start with an apology. "I am sorry, sometimes I get a little passionate and go too fast, what part did I not cover?" And go over all till we can go back to "Now, does this all make sense?"

Remember, practice, practice, practice. Professional athletes practice before they go on the field, not just on the days with no game.

From Ken's desk

Tips on making a phone call

It is important to realize that you are communicating with a live person on the other end of the phone and to treat them with all of the courtesy that you would if they were standing in front of you. Also, outstanding phone manners can be a marketing tool for your personal brand and give you a leg up in your career moves. Here's how.

When you are the caller:

- Get yourself organized and know what you are going to say to the person or their voice mail. You only have one chance to make a first impression. Sound professional and confident by **using a strong voice** that rises and falls throughout the sentence, **emphasizing certain words** for effect.
- Use the receiver's name and then immediately identify yourself and your company. Say your name articulately and slowly, especially if it is a difficult name. Don't run your last name into your first name.
- **In the same breath,** explain the purpose of your call and then ask, "Is this a good time?" Suggest a positive, not a negative, response, such as, "Did I get you at a bad time?" With a possible, "Well, not that you mention it . . ." If the person is busy, suggest or ask for a telephone appointment.

Leaving a Message

- When you leave a message, be upbeat, succinct, and articulate and repeat your phone number at the beginning and end of the message. Speak slowly. You might want to leave the time of your call and whether there is a sense of urgency in returning the call.
- Once you leave a message with your phone number, wait a few days before calling back.

Your Voice Mail

"Your call is very important to me, and I will try my best to get back to you within two hours (or a certain time frame)." His tone was always genuine, and you knew without a doubt he would get back to you.

Taking a Call

- "When you pick up the phone, SMILE!" You can actually hear a smile in the tone of someone's voice.
- Do not say, "Bob speaking," since saying that you are speaking is redundant because the caller knows you are speaking. Many business professionals merely say their first and last name, with the proper upbeat inflection.

Remember, the goal is to **get to the end of the script.** From there, the appointment is made.

From Ken's desk

The Conditional Close

When the other person offers an objection, make it a condition of resolving their objection that they make the purchase.

You can also use this approach to make any trade. For example, if you want them to watch a promotional video, offer a cup of coffee.

Always, by the way, phrase it in the form "If I . . . will you . . ." rather than "Will you . . . if I . . ." This is because our brains work very quickly, and starting with "will you" causes them to begin thinking immediately about objections, and they may miss the exchange. On the other hand, starting with "If I . . ." will cause psychological closure on what you are offering, thus drawing them in to the close.

Examples

You say you want a red one. If I can phone up and get you one, will you take it today?

If we can figure out the finances for you, will you choose this one?

If I get you a cup of coffee, would you like to sit down and look through the brochure?

How it works

The conditional close uses the *exchange principle* to build a social agreement that if I solve your problem, you will buy the product in return.

The one I like to use is "If I can satisfy this area of concern, would you be willing to go ahead with the program?"

In using the exchange principle, it allows them to offer other "areas of concern" (otherwise known as objections), and it gives you the go ahead to close them.

From Ken's desk

The Old Ways

Where did the old ways and techniques come from? Remember the industrial revolution? Inexpensive products were turned out quickly, and they needed buyers. Remember the various wars? Populations were "liberated" and needed products. Yep. It is possible that the sales training you got (or are getting) is based on eighteenth century thinking. Why else would it be so number driven?

Problems come when the same approach used for selling a tea kettle is also used to sell energy solutions. The two worlds do not coexist in comfort.

What is the better way? *Harvard Business Review* suggests the better way to sell is a process based on effective psychology.

The sales agents who are most successful tend to be the most sophisticated sellers. They study their craft and improve their skills. They understand this:

1. It's not about closing. It's about helping.
2. It's not just a number game. If anything, it's a game of relevance and connection.
3. It's based on the prospect's values.

Selling is NOT simple. Hitting a golf ball, so it goes where you want it to go, is far more difficult than it looks. Trust me on this one. Again, you have to master motor skills. Then apply them under complete control. Selling is similar. To orchestrate a sales conversation, and especially one on a complex financial or energy budget, requires the mastery of many different skills. Then you have to apply them in a process, while paying attention to what someone else is saying. It is an art. And it is not simple. So why would anyone step into the sales arena unprepared?

Two reasons:

First, it's in hopes that mere luck or innate talent will win out. Is it any wonder that the attrition rate in this industry is embarrassing?

Second, many rookie sellers get terrible advice, evidenced by the three points listed above. Selling is hard enough without bad advice. When that bad advice comes to you, it is a recipe for failure. Over the last decade, I've observed what I think of as "truths" or points of wisdom. Here are five that might provide you with better advice:

1. Sales techniques that worked for one person will not necessarily work for someone else who has different skills and talents. For example, a transactional salesperson will sell in a very different way from a consultative

seller. Take what you can from whom ever has the best advice then adapt it to your own style.

2. Unless you can read your prospect, you stand a 75 percent chance of failure with him/her. Unless you can read your prospect, you deliver the same logic to everyone. How could that be successful? Learn to read people.

3. Prospects generally are highly resistant to replacing their current provider. Relationships are like big, powerful magnets. Even when their current provider is providing a substandard service or performance, the prospect is still reluctant to replace them. So offer a second opinion or a comparison as to a push.

4. Prospects typically do not understand the benefits of budgeting beyond a very rudimentary level. So a reference to a technical term is totally lost on them, worse, it confuses them, and a confused mind always says no. Give clear examples of those who have gained a competitive advantage.

5. People have preexisting opinions about our industry, our company, our products, and you. They might not be positive opinions. So do not make the mistake of assuming your prospects really want to hear from you. Give them a reason to like you or that you have their best interests in mind very quickly

In conclusion, the old ways sometimes work. But is that the kind of odds you want? Do you want to gamble your career on "sometimes?" Selling is not a job. It's a career. Like any career, it demands continual learning. If you are selling in the same way you did ten years ago, you're probably long overdue for a review and adjustment. My advice is to find someone who can help you sell in your own natural style, rather than someone else's.

From Ken's desk

The Opportunity Cost Close

Technique:

Highlight the cost of not buying and hence show that the actual cost is not as high as it appears from the price.

Use "cost" in its broadest sense, including hassle, dissatisfaction, and problems. Time, in particular, always costs. Each visit to help decide is costing time. It is better to decide now.

Examples:

If you keep your existing fire system and it fails, what would that cost you? What would it do to your reputation? The cost of not upgrading looks much higher than getting the latest system installed now, right?

How do you feel about having to pay for something every month and yet not know what that cost is going to be?

I know it looks expensive now, but I would hate for you to look back in a year's time and realize how much you have spent in energy costs by staying with the open market and how much you could have saved by budgeting at the right time.

How it works:

There is always cost, whether you do or do not do something. In business and finance, the "opportunity cost" is the name given to the cost of not doing something.

Price is not the same as cost. Price is what the customer pays. Cost is a whole range of problems that may or may not be translatable into money. Cost is the salesperson's friend.

Again, what is the cost of not doing something now?

From Ken's desk

The Optimist's Creed

The **Optimist's Creed** was authored by C. D. Larson in 1912. He was an early advocate of positive thought.

Use the optimist's creed below as a part of your daily practice to keep your mind-set focused on the positive. It is recommended to read the creed out loud once in the morning and again in the evening before bed. Give it a try for thirty days and watch how much your life will improve.

I Promise Myself:
To be so strong that nothing can disturb my peace of mind.
To talk health, happiness, and prosperity to every person I meet.
To make all my friends feel that there is something worthwhile in them.
To look at the sunny side of everything and make my optimism come true.
To think only of the best, to work only for the best, and to expect only the best.
To be just as enthusiastic about the success of others as I am about my own.
To forget the mistakes of the past and press on to the greater achievements of the future.
To wear a cheerful expression at all times and give a smile to every living creature I meet.
To give so much time to improving myself that I have no time to criticize others.
To be too large for worry, too noble for anger, too strong for fear, and too happy to permit the presence of trouble.
To think well of myself and to proclaim this fact to the world, not in loud words, but in great deeds.
To live in the faith that the whole world is on my side, so long as I am true to the best that is in Me.

From Ken's desk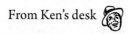

The Partner Close

"Bob, this all sounds good but I will have to pass this through my partner before we sign anything."

This is a killer of most sales. How can someone agree to something they have not seen? I think you'll agree that 99 percent of these turn into NOs, right?

It is imperative you learn, no master, the partner close.

"Bob, I've always had a great deal of respect for business that have partners in starting it up and continuing to run the business. Successful partnerships tend to have the same mind-sets but also important they want to protect each other."

When a decision is to made, the first objective of any partner is to protect the other partner. It is much the case with lawyers. When you hear a no from a lawyer, you feel protected, whereas a yes sometimes feels like they didn't do their job.

In the case of your partner, no doubt his first instinct would be to say no, but let me ask you a real question: "When I asked you if this made sense after seeing what I had shown you, you said yes. Do you think that if you partner had been here and saw what you saw, it would have made sense to him too? Great, then why don't we just give him the good news."

"You can authorize here, give him the good news, but what I will do is hold onto it for a day (I don't want to risk losing this rate). If I don't hear from you tomorrow, I'll then put it through, fair?"

Mastering this close—or any close—doesn't mean you'll get them all, but if you increased your closing by even 10 percent, it could make all the difference of putting you in with the pros and getting paid like the pros.

From Ken's desk

The Price Promise Close

This one can be a bit tricky, so only use it if you believe it is the last hurdle in closing the deal.

Promise to match any rate that they may find lower than ours.

Sometimes you come across a customer that cannot get it out of his head that he should "shop" for the best deal. By offering to match any they find, the first thought is that your rate likely is the best rate so they won't even bother "shopping," whereas in the worst case he does, and as you may lose some commission, you still get the deal.

The real trick here is to be sure the customer likes you enough that he won't just sign with that other guy with the lower rate. For them to like you, you must be likable, right?

Be sure to put boundaries on the offer: ten days or ten business days.

Again, in practice, extremely few people take up on this type of offer, because either they know the difference would be too small or the confidence you gave them actually stops them from looking at other prices!

From Ken's desk

The Recession and the Big Bargain

This is still a good time to talk of the advantages of investing in a budgeting tool such as ours. People often look at recessions the wrong way so let's have this talk.

"There are many people talking about the negative impact of today's recessionary economy, but I've decided not to let it bother me, you know why? I recognize that many business owners see the long-term opportunity when prices/rates/costs are low. People who actually understand buy low, sell high tend to make great fortunes. People who only look at the short term challenges tend to fall off and struggle even when times get good again: read, costs are high again."

Michael Bloomberg actually stated that it is only the businesses that invest in tough times who you will see in business in the long term.

Now, we are talking of the same type of opportunity here, aren't we?

Here is another truth. During inflation, everything is a bargain. Do you know why? During inflation, knowledgeable people trade money for things. During deflation, people trade things for money. Whatever you acquire today will be more expensive tomorrow, won't it?

Our service is actually a bargain today because inflation will hit pricing tomorrow, and you do want a bargain, don't you?"

From Ken's desk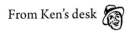

The Soft Sell "Think About It"

Not everyone decides quickly and many, and if pressed, many will back away or react against the sales methods being used.

Decision making is often a complex thought process. Pros and cons are weighed, and the person may not decide until they have gone through this process. This is particularly common in sales, which involves significant money or other commitments like the ones our customers make.

Sometimes it just takes a little time to sink in. You have given them a lot of information that they need to process it and fit it in with their current models of the world.

Of course, there is a danger when the person thinks about it that they will say no. On the other hand, this final "soft sell" stage may well convince them that it is they who are in control and so will make the decision to buy.

After you've said what you can, you've given the person a little time to think about what you have told and shown them, but their body language tells you they want to "think about it." Offer them an option to do just that.

Examples:

I can see you're carefully thinking about. I'm going to step outside for a couple of minutes so you can decide in your own time.

or

How long would you like to think about it? Can I get you a cup of coffee while you decide?

When you return, watch their *body language* to see if they are showing signs of being *ready* to buy. If necessary, use an *assumptive* method to nudge them over the edge, such as "I'm hoping that time allowed you to see the advantages of going forward."

From Ken's desk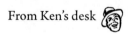

The Thermometer Close

This is what I would call an upfront (between the eyes) closing technique, by using the technique the salesperson is not trying to close the sale out but merely attempting to move the conversation and the opportunity forward. In other words, you realize your prospect will not make a decision today. But you still leave the door open to change his mind.

It goes like so:

YOU: *"So does this make sense to you?"*

Next, the stall. BOB: *"Unfortunately I can't (won't) make this decision today, so perhaps if you could leave it till next week, that would be great.*

Here comes the upfront closing technique, which allows you to test where the sale is relative to a successful close.

YOU: *"*No problem, Bob. I will put you down to come back on Tuesday. Obviously, I would like it be a yes on Tuesday, but if was to ask you say on a scale of one to ten, one meaning you never want to see my face again and ten meaning you want to get this started right away, where would you say you are right now . . . four or five?*"*

By giving him a low number, you are showing there is no pressure and more importantly allowing him to raise it. Odds are he will come back with "seven or eight." Now, it is your chance to see where he really is.

YOU: *"So we are not too far off here, Bob? What would I have to do to close the gap? What is the missing piece here?"*

Bob really has no choice but to spill the beans here. You may even find out that he really means no but was afraid to say it to your face, which can save you enough time to close another prospect (remember, want everyone, need no one). The better you get though, the better chance you have of turning them around right on the spot.

"Bob, if we can resolve your concerns, in other words close that gap, would you be willing to go ahead with the program?"

It sometimes just means they missed some details you thought you covered.

"If this is your only area of concern . . . and you seem satisfied now . . . why don't we just put this to bed now so you can go back to concentrating on the business you do."

Nothing to lose, right?

From Ken's desk

The Yes, Yes, Yes Close

Using the ABCs of closing, during your presentation, ask them several questions where the answer is easy to answer and is a yes. The minimum set is usually three questions. You also do not want to overdo this, so either space out the questions or limit the number (although one research showed that eight yeses were needed overall before closure).

Encourage them to say yes by nodding your head gently as you talk with them.

If you need to hide the question, you can bury it among other questions.

Examples are:

You can see how we have hit all-time lows in commodity rates now, yes?

One thing we know for sure is that guys like Bill Gates and Warren Buffett know how to buy low and sell high, yes? And if they are investing in energy now, they must see it going up, yes?

Logical decisions are always better than emotional decisions, yes?

How it works:

This works by setting up a repetitive pattern of yes answers that gets the other person into a habitual response. When the pattern is established, and they are automatically answering yes, then the question that you really want yes to is slipped in.

Once inviting them to authorize the registration form, ask for another series of yesses.

Is this the proper mailing address for you?

Is this the best phone number to get you if needed?

Did I get your e-mail address correct?

Yes, yes, yes is now in their heads so with a little guidance. "I just need you to authorize where indicated so we can get this going for you." They are hooked on yes and are simply following.

From Ken's desk

The "I Have to Think about This" Close

What a nice polite way of saying no. "I have to think about" this pertains to procrastination or a flat out fib. How many of these anchors have you had that actually closed?

There are a couple of ways of filtering this statement out and turning it into a deal.

(Remember, whenever dealing with difficult objections, always use a low, empathetic tone.)

1. "Bob, in my experience, what I have found is that when someone wants to 'think about it,' the tendency is for this to go into a giant inbox that ever increases until it is completely forgotten. If what you are really saying is you don't want to do this, if somehow this does not make sense for your business, then it is really best for both of us to simply say no right now. This will save us both from me calling you every two days and then you avoiding my calls and both of us being frustrated."

Or

2. "Bob, that makes sense. I prefer it when people take their time in making decisions. It means the final decision will be binding because they have exhausted all logic. Let me ask, how much time do you need, two or three days? While I'm at it, tell me, if we were to use a scale of one to ten, one meaning you never want to see my face again and ten meaning you want to get this rolling right now, where do you see yourself? A four or a five?" *(Caution here. Always keep your number on the low side. It gives them a good comfort level, and it is always better when they are higher than you.)*

Or

3. "Bob, one of the most respected people of our time, General Colin Powell, once said that procrastination has cost the American government and American business billions more than wrong decisions. Are we just procrastinating here? Earlier, you said this makes sense. What do you think will change in making your decision over the next couple of days?"

In the first case, by pressing for a no, you get one of two possibilities. Either you get a no, which releases a possible anchor from you, or you have now turned it into a yes. Either way, you win.

In the second case, you have let him know that by making a decision to delay, he has authorized you to pester him to no end. He won't like that, and you have now allowed yourself to present to show your expertise when you follow up, and he gives you the big, "Oh I haven't had time to review it yet" and you say, "That's exactly what I told you would happen before I left" and now swing it into the first case.

In the third case, you have pressed him to divulge his true thoughts or he has given you the opportunity to use the first two lines to which he'll cave one way or another. Again, you either lose an anchor or get the deal.

As a reminder, if you only get 10 percent of these to turn into a deal on the spot, YOU WIN!

Welcome to the PROS, and remember, pros always beat amateurs.

From Ken's desk

The Best "Closers"

Are you a top closer? The best "closers" do share certain traits:

They fully engage their prospects before closing; they communicate a superior (needs related) solution; they **never** push or pressure, but gently guide; they use lots of trial closes; they make appear incidental or matter-of-fact when presenting a close; AND, they are assumptive, confident, and convicted.

Through the presentation, they gauge the prospect by asking for reactions, **feelings**, opinions, and ideas, then use those indicators to either go slower or faster to the close. They ask a lot of questions and attach emotions to the answers to those questions. They place value quickly to solutions and have mastered how to communicate that value.

Top "closers" **expect the deal.** They are never toppled by rejection and do not accept "maybes." They know the most important word in sales is "NEXT," and they are guided by courage, faith, and enthusiasm.

"Courage is not the absence of fear, it is saddling up anyways."—John Wayne

"Faith is the expectation of something great."—unknown

"Enthusiasm is the gap between opportunity and success."

So are you a top "closer"?

From Ken's desk

Trial Closing

Always be closing means that you should always be heading toward a close, although you must also be careful about overdoing this. If people are nowhere near ready to buy, this will just annoy them.

Trial closing is not a normal "closing technique" but a test to determine whether the person is ready to close. Use it after you have made a strong selling point or use it when you have answered objections.

Trial closing may use other closing techniques or may be a more tentative question.

Examples:

Ask "If..." questions.
If I could offer long-term solutions on commodities, would you be interested?

Ask questions that *assume* they have already bought the product.
It looks like you really like budgeting is important to you, is that true?

You may not even need to see more if you've been watching the markets, and I don't want to waste your time. Just so I understand fully, am I here to register your business now or did you need more info?

Do you prefer long-term solutions?

Are you already aware of the benefits of budgeting on commodities?

When you have asked a trial close question, as with most other closes, be quiet, watch, and listen carefully for their response.

From Ken's desk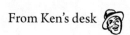

Value versus Cost

Do you believe there are companies out there that will be better off when you share your expertise with them?

But does **something feel "off" when you try to "sell" your services?** You even fear that they will perceive a cost and back off.

The reason is that **you are thinking about yourself rather than the person you are here to serve.** If you are committed to helping others make a difference in their lives, then you have a responsibility to ask those others to pay for your services because that's the most likely way they will actually receive the value you have to give them. Hence, commission.

Why is this true?

In our society, the cost of something has universally been associated with its value. When your clients pay you for your services, they are making a commitment to follow through. No different than on the phone booking an appointment. What is the value of a twenty-minute appointment versus a forty-five-minute appointment.

The fact that the money people pay you will help you pay your bills is secondary. The key importance of charging for what you provide is that **those who pay you are much more likely to gain benefit and be helped.**

If you know what you have is valuable, then it should be your clear intention that as many people as possible will benefit from what you have to share. Remember, everyone knows the cost of everything and the value of nothing.

Fear not, oh brave soldier, what you have is the cookie. They don't know they want/need. Just sell it, and they will be happy to pay for it. It must first come from your belief of the cookie.

From Ken's desk

What's the Best Day of the Week?

Here's a sales tip. The best day of the week is TODAY, of course. Yesterdays are lost forever, and we know only too well that tomorrow isn't promised to anyone. If you're reading the morning newspaper and don't see your name in the obituary, declare it a great day.

Some salespeople squander time, and some people squander money, and even more salespeople squander both. That's just plain stupid. Start treating every day as a gift, and you'll spend your time more productively. You begin every day with a blank canvas. You're an artist, and you have complete control over how you spend the day. Grab your brush and start painting.

To make the most of every day, do the following:

Know your numbers. Know your statistics. Identify your selling weaknesses and work diligently to transform them into strengths. Every day ask this question, "How can I do it better?" Then do it better.

Adjust your *attitude*. Tough people always figure out a way to deal with tough times. Be tough. You can achieve anything you can imagine. The key is to be imagining good things happening to you. To be on the safe side though, make sure you convert your *dreams* into written goals with specific action steps.

Keep *learning*. Don't let a single day go by without *learning* something new about your selling profession. Read a good sales book or listen to sales CD's as you drive from account to account. The more you study, the more you'll sell. Remember, you have to learn more to earn more.

Enjoy the ride. Face it. Life's too short. Customers and sales prospects are people. Enjoy the time you spend with them. Take an active interest in their business and learn about their personal interests. You probably have more in common than you think.

When not at work, don't put your family on hold. Don't hit the mute button when it comes to outside interests and hobbies. Nothing is more dreadful than facing *retirement* with zero hobbies and no favorite pastimes. Waking up and falling asleep with CNN or TSN is no way to usher in your golden years. Usher them in with all your dreams.

From Ken's desk

How Decisions Are Made

Why do people not make decisions? **Fear of failure.** Or at least fear of a mistake, which is failure to most.

"Mr. Customer, if you make the 'yes' decision and prices remain flat, the margin for error in making a purchasing decision is very small. The best part is you already budgeted for the premium so you didn't lose any money. You get budget certainty. In running a business, forecasts are vital to success! Does anyone think that prices are going to fall substantively from here? No. What else do we know about forecasts? They are usually wrong. Thirdly, if markets are not volatile there is a very low risk premium built into the fixed price. Once volatile again, not only do you have risk in the market but you have no risk in the premium."

Our job is to take that fear away, to make a logical argument against that fear. Use this argument.

Remember how upset customers are who signed three or four years ago buying stocks. They became upset with their deal because they chose to sign when rates were high and rising, the exact opposite of today, an emotional decision versus a logical decision.

Tell yourself and your customers of this and then ask the questions:

For example, in five years, do you think you'll be upset with yourself or me if you were to sign at a fixed rate equal to the open market rates of 2003? Would it be better to wait until rates start to climb and then sign, just so you can yell at me in five years? What would you rather make now, an emotional decision or a logical one?

From Ken's desk

What Do They Want?

Do you know what your prospects really want? Do you know how to help your potential customers to buy from you and do this with confidence? Do you know how to really listen to your potential clients in order to close the deal?

I know so many of us dislike the idea of "selling" to people, but that is what having a business is. It is providing a service or product and providing it to them in order to grow our business and make their life better.

So why is it so hard for some? Because they don't know the reasons why people buy and don't buy. Let's face it. You need their business or you'll have to close yours! It's that simple, but it's not so easy. There are factors/reasons why people don't buy our service.

These are the top three reasons why people don't buy from you:

1. **They don't KNOW, LIKE, or trust you yet.**
2. **They don't BELIEVE our service can help them.**
3. **They don't BELIEVE in themselves. (This is one they usually will NEVER admit to . . . but it's true. They fear making a mistake.)**

What do you have to do in your presentations? You have to fill the gap between where your client wants to be and where they are now.

You do that with assurance and by communicating your knowledge **but most importantly by listening to your potential clients' fears, frustrations, pain, and convincing them you know their pain** (remember Bill Clinton's "America, I feel your pain"). And you should because if you don't, you really have no business being in business.

You NEED to know your clients' issues in order to solve their problems. It's not about "selling" to them something they don't want or tricking them into buying something they don't need. **It's about filling the gap between pain and comfort. Get to know their pain.** Ask about how they felt when gas rates were above 30 cents and 40 cents. Ask how they cope with their other supplies that have no set prices from month to month (I know, I know). Ask him/her how they measure profits when some underlying cost keeps changing. Ask how they feel about these problems.

Remember that when you decide to have a presentation with a potential client. It will mean **the difference between enrolling that business you could really help or NOT.**

From Ken's desk

You Don't Sell Products, Benefits, or Solutions—You Sell Feelings

Sales used to be about selling products, but a sole focus on products leads to objections, so sales moved to selling benefits. Better again, the focus turned to understanding the underlying problem to be solved, but this is still not the whole story.

When we make any decision, including the "buy" decision, we do so by an emotional process. It may not seem that way, and there may be much logical processing, but the point of decision is always emotional and usually subconscious.

Here's a trick. **Ask for honesty.**

Ask them for honesty, and you will get it. Ask, "Can you be honest about this?" They will say, "Yes, of course." Then you can ask them for critical information, and you will get the truth.

By asking for honesty, when they say yes, then they must then maintain *consistency* with that statement and *be* honest.

Then ask for the sale. A lot of salespeople are so paranoid about the customer saying no. The trick is to swallow your fear and ask. When the time comes, ask for the sale. In our business, "Does that make sense?" is our first close. If you have to go over it all again, "Can I have your business?" works as well.

From Ken's desk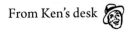

Are You Giving Your Best Effort or Your Best Excuse?

I know what prevents most people from achieving the success they want. But before I tell you, I want you to do one thing right now. Don't worry. Nobody around you knows that you're reading this. You don't have to worry about "measuring up" to someone's expectations. This is just between you and your mind.

All I want you to do is be honest with yourself—truly honest—and answer this question: "Am I giving my *best* effort?"

Your best. Not good. Not even great. But the absolute best that you can do. I'll be honest with you. Most days, I don't give my best effort. I try very hard, but there is usually a situation I could have managed better, time I could have used more effectively, or a task I could have done that was more important than something I did do.

Why does this happen? Why don't we do what is best for us?

The danger of our best excuse:

We make excuses all the time.

Usually, our excuses don't change things too much. (Your life will move on just fine if you make up an excuse and don't go out to dinner with some friends tonight.) But in some cases, we avoid important actions or choices that could literally alter the course of our lives. And when these important decisions come up, we often resort to our best excuses rather than making tough decisions.

The "best excuse" is the excuse that we truly believe. It's the excuse that we convince ourselves is right. It's the excuse that holds us back from taking action and makes it easy for us to play it safe. In other words, the best excuses are the most dangerous ones.

There are an infinite number of ways to come up with an excuse, but our best excuses often reveal themselves in a few ways.

1. The best excuses are actions on a loop.

Sometimes our best excuses don't seem like excuses at all. They look like action to us, but really it's just the same action in an endless loop. "I want to start a business, so I'm going to read more about this." "I need to find a new diet to follow." "I want to boost my social media presence. I'll find some good people to follow on Twitter or Facebook or LinkedIn."

Each of the above actions can be useful if you do it once and move on to the next step, but when you start to do it over and over again, they become an excuse. The hardest part is that this excuse looks like action. "No, really, I'm trying to lose

KEN GRIFFITH

weight. I've put ten hours into finding the best diet plan." In the beginning, we feel like we're making progress, but after one time around the track, this repeated action just becomes an excuse.

2. The best excuses are great reasons for not doing something.

Before you think that making excuses is merely the problem of the lazy or uneducated, let me assure you that it's not. Smart and successful people (like you and I) are great at creating excuses.

Ask a smart person why they aren't doing X or Y, and they will come back with a confident answer. "Well, that works for some people, but that's not really my style. At this point, I have a pretty good feel for what works for me." "It's best to be prepared. I'm very deliberate about my decisions. I'll do the proper research on this and then make a call." "Yeah, I've done some reading on that. It seems like it's very difficult to do successfully."

Lame. Lame. Lame.

Here's the problem: Smart people can come up with legitimate reasons for not doing something all day long. It doesn't matter what the task is; you can usually find a good reason to avoid it. The real question is, "Is this something you shouldn't do, or are you simply coming up with a good reason to avoid a tough decision?"

3. The best excuses make useless comparisons.

Comparisons are the ultimate excuse generator.

It's so easy to look at someone successful, determine why they "made it," and then conclude that you can't achieve the same level of success because your situation is different. "They had X and Y, and I don't, so I shouldn't bother with doing this." "They went to school A and got degree B, and I didn't." "Their parents are friends with person Z, and mine aren't, so I can't make this happen."

Here's the tricky thing about comparisons, though; they can actually be useful. In the short term, it can be good to compare yourself with high performers because you can see if you're taking the right actions. For example, I'm always comparing myself with what other entrepreneurs are doing. I want to be taking similar actions as successful entrepreneurs, and comparing my actions with them helps me determine if I'm on the right track.

But in the grand scheme of things, comparisons are useless. Everyone runs their own race. You are where you are. The question is, "Where will you go from here?"

It's about much more than money.

There is more to this than just earning money.

Yes, excuses prevent you from getting more done, building a business, and earning more money. But they also block you from something more valuable. This quote from English teacher and revered basketball coach John Wooden hints at what I'm talking about:

"I wanted to give the youngsters under my supervision—whether it be in athletics or in the English classroom—something to which to aspire, other than just a higher mark in the classroom, or more points in some athletic contest."—Coach John Wooden, on doing your personal best

It's not just about a "higher mark" or a bigger bank account. It's about the satisfaction that comes with reaching your full potential.

Ever heard the term overachieved? It is often given to sports teams or specific athletes who seemed to do better than expected. I never bought into that. You know why?

Because overachieving is impossible. You can't do more than you're capable of doing.

The problem is, most people never find out what they're capable of doing. Most people don't realize how much potential they are leaving on the table. And that's why giving your best effort is about more than earning an extra $1,000 or $10,000 or $10,000,000. Giving your best effort is about achieving what you're really capable of doing.

It's about the peace of mind that comes with knowing that you did your absolute best. It's about closing your eyes at night and knowing that today—even if it was just for one day—you gave your best effort and that so few people can say they did the same.

What have you actually tried?

It doesn't matter whether it's dieting or dating or earning more money, we love to whine about how we "have tried everything and nothing works."

Here's why most people don't earn more money: because they try and fail and forget to try again. They don't give their *best effort* when it comes to earning more money. It's not that they don't *want* to earn more. They definitely want it. But they don't put in the repeated effort to get it. It's easier to complain about a lack of success and go back to browsing the Web than it is to struggle through ten failures before you figure out what works for your situation.

And just to be clear about this, I'm not saying you should work all day.

There is nothing wrong with watching TV or going to the movies or sitting around and doing nothing at all. In fact, if you don't take time to relax, then you're going to have trouble giving your best effort on a consistent basis.

But there is definitely something wrong with claiming that you have "tried everything" and "nothing seems to work" when you have chosen to sit and watch

KEN GRIFFITH

TV each night. There is nothing wrong with choosing to relax, but it's your own choice, and don't make it an excuse for not taking action.

Usually, when I dish out some tough love like this, the immediate response is "I'll do whatever I need to do. I have no problem giving up TV. But I just don't know what to do."

Fair enough . . . sort of. I know what it's like to not know the next step. I have exactly zero entrepreneurs in my family. I had no one to talk to about how to start. I had to figure it all out on my own.

So I get that you want to know what to do. I wanted that too.

But here's the thing. Knowledge isn't enough. It never will be. Even if you learn everything you can and have brilliant ideas, so what? Anyone can have an idea. Action is what makes an idea worth having.

You don't need to be perfect to earn more money. You don't need to find the best system. You just need to pick a system, take action, and stick with it. In fact, most of the time, the only way to win is to try things and fail because you can't beat failure if you've never dealt with it in the first place.

Why do you think so many new entrepreneurs repeat the mistakes of old ones? It's not because they don't know about the mistakes. It's because some things have to be experienced to be learned.

So don't send me an e-mail and tell me that you can't make money because you don't know what to do.

Don't know how to promote yourself?

Don't know how to take a small step forward?

Don't know the best way to start earning more money?

Don't know how to be creative?

Don't know how to get over fear and get started?

Don't know how to start a side job while you have a family?

Don't know how to negotiate for a higher salary?

Don't know how to get people talking about your business?

Don't know how to find your passion?

Don't know how to negotiate?

Don't know how most people make money online?

But whatever you do, don't send me an e-mail and tell me that you don't know what to do. What you are doing here is plenty to get you going.

Go out and try something. Try a new way to sell. Try a new way to prospect. Try a new way product within. Just try something. Then send me an e-mail and tell me what didn't work, and we'll figure out what you should do next.

You don't need to do it all at once, but you do need to do it more than once. Steps, remember?

Do you want something more? Do you want something better? Do you want something to change?

Don't give up on a dream after one failure. It's time to own up, take responsibility, and make it happen.

How can you achieve the success that you want and deserve? Stop giving your best excuse and start giving **your best effort.** ☺

From Ken's desk

Your Energy Level

One of the fastest ways to increase the flow into your life is to raise your energy to have more life force and more power. But how do you go about raising your energy?

In the graph below, 0 percent represents no energy, and 100 percent represents maximum energy.

0%————25%————50%————100%

If someone is at 0 percent energy, then they are dead. Unfortunately, many people are living just above 0 percent energy.

At the other end of the graph, 100 percent represents the highest positive energy available. As you move up the scale, you will have more of the good things in life because you are vibrating and evolving at a higher level.

The higher up you move on the scale, the more easily you will be able to use the LOA. All you have to do is think a thought, attach emotion to that thought, and then it manifests rapidly because your life force is flowing freely and is not blocked.

Your energy level not only attracts money into your life but also attracts everything else, including other people. If you have a very dense or low level of energy, you are going to manifest that same energy you are projecting. In other words, you will attract people and relationships into your life that have the same low-level, dense energy. This is explained in the levels of awareness that you are studying.

What most people really want in their life is energy without even being aware of it. People think they want money, but from what you are learning, you realize that money is just another form of energy.

Stop right here and think about this because it is a key point to opening the flow of money into your life. When you fully understand this, you will see the whole world differently. We can sum it up this way. If you raise your energy level, you will raise your income. It is that simple.

So how do you raise your energy level?

Ever notice on certain occasions that you simply want to lie on the couch and do nothing, then someone calls with exciting news ("got tickets to the game" or "big sale on shoes") and your energy level goes off the charts?

It's your emotions taking over, and your energy skyrockets. Likewise, your emotions can take you down upon hearing some bad news.

Now, imagine constantly being excited about life, your future. You see, the key to attaining all you want is to get emotional about those things. Once you have figured out the dreams you want to live—be they travel, that big home, the fast cars, or living in Africa helping the needy—you have to get emotional about it. You have to constantly research your desires, touch them, smell them, close your eyes, and put yourself in them.

It is not good enough to say you want a Ferrari. You have to get specific and add emotion to it (i.e., a Ferrari 550 Maranello, silver with black interior, 465 horsepower, 440ft/lb torque, now going 0–100 kmph in 4.3 seconds on a perfect sunny day, on a perfect country highway, with your favorite person in the world beside you). YUM! Smell it? ☺

To know that your future is so much bigger than your past, you'll feel like you just threw away those old, worn-out running shoes for jet-powered racing shoes and you are racing toward your amazing future.

Know what you want; get excited about it, knowing you are going to get it; and breathe it in every day!

Now instead of a Ferrari going from 0 to 100 in 4 seconds, it is you going from 0 to 100 in 4 seconds on the energy scale. LIVE LIFE. LOVE LIFE. It's up to you!

From Ken's desk

Sales Tools

The world is inundated with sales tools: worksheets, playbooks, sales scripts, software, brochures, and so forth. But all of those sales tools put together are insignificant if you don't have the intellectual and emotional tools that truly create success.

Here are seven sales "tools" you need to develop:

1. Patience

If you're patient, you let customers decide at their own speed. You realize that nobody ever got a plant to grow faster by pulling at the leaves of a seedling. If you lack patience, you'll be frustrated whenever things take longer than you'd like. Customers will sense your frustration and hesitate to buy.

2. Commitment

If you're truly committed to both your customer's success and your own success, you'll do whatever it takes (within legal and ethical bounds) to get the job done. You'll banish all thoughts of ever giving up. If you lack commitment, you'll consistently fail to follow through and will often drop the ball at the worst possible moment.

3. Enthusiasm

Enthusiasm is contagious: If you're enthusiastic about yourself, your firm, and your product, your customers will "pick up" your enthusiasm and believe in your ability to improve their lives. If you lack enthusiasm, however, you'll always find yourself surrounded by naysayers and endless "objections."

4. Curiosity

Curiosity is essential to growth, and if you're growing as an individual and a professional, you'll spend time each day learning something new to better serve your customers. You'll read books, listen to audio training, take courses, and network with peers. If you're not growing, your ideas will become stale, your career will languish, and your ability to compete will slowly drain away.

5. Courage

If you've got courage, you take the necessary risks to expand yourself and your business into new areas, even when you're facing enormous odds. You'll see setbacks as learning opportunities rather than failures. But if you lack courage, you'll freeze up when things get weird, turning small failures into big ones.

6. Integrity

If you've got integrity, there's no disconnect between your stated purpose and your real motivations. Because there's no hidden agenda, customers sense the honesty and feel comfortable working with you. If you lack integrity, however, customers will have a nagging feeling that something is "not quite right" and tend to balk rather than buy.

7. Flexibility

Life is all about change; nothing stays the same. If you've got flexibility, you can observe what's working and what's not and change your approach to match changing circumstances. If you lack flexibility, you'll pursue brittle strategies and tactics long after they've ceased to work.

From Ken's desk

Your Dreams

I want to help you understand that every question has an answer, every problem has a solution, and every answer and solution is right at your fingertips if you will just BE solution oriented and answer oriented rather than focusing on the problem. If you are solution oriented, everything that is not working right in your life would begin coming into alignment.

You have this long list of problems or a long list of what you want to be different, and I want you to understand that the universe is all lined up orchestrating and standing by, ready to do anything and everything you want PROVIDED you are a vibrational match to it.

But you have to clean up your vibration—which means simply that you have to focus on what you desire and where you are going, your dreams. You have to tell the story of your life the way you want it to be and not the way it is. Forget about "WHAT IS." Stop looking for sympathy and for people to agree with you. When you turn your list of desires over to other people and want them to become the vortex by which your desires come to you, that's when the trouble begins. Do not give your power over to other people in an effort to bring you what you desire. Give your list to the universe because it will get it for you EVERY SINGLE TIME.

You get to decide how far you want to reach beyond "WHAT IS." You have so much power because you come with the nonphysical energy that is moving downstream in such a powerful way. The problem is most of the time you are trying to go way downstream with a net and gather up all the good stuff and bring it all into your life right now with the following attitude: "If I don't go get it all now, it will get away from me." But the truth is, it won't get away from you. It will keep reappearing and reappearing because it is a never-ending stream. Your ship won't come in and have you miss it, or you won't take one ship and miss another one. You can take any ride you want, and in the middle of that ride, you can keep asking for more. There is nothing you cannot have if you flow WITH the stream and don't try to dam it up out of fear. There is no need to build a dam because the *flow* never stops.

Look, the truth is, you will live a dream. The problem is, it might not be your dream if you let others influence you with their dream. Get your dreams together and let no one else stop you. Fight for your life, your vision, and your dreams . . . and then others will follow you.

Wishing you all life has to offer.

From Ken's desk

Index

KEN GRIFFITH

137, 142–43, 160, 172–73, 183, 185, 196, 201, 211–12, 215–19, 235, 241–42, 253, 275, 279, 295, 302, 306, 323

F

Facebook, 12–13, 332
factory, 112
failure, 1, 18, 41, 59, 80, 84–85, 109–11, 113, 115, 128, 139–41, 152–53, 171, 182–83, 188–89, 235, 250, 257, 285, 295, 301, 313–14, 329, 334, 336, 340
faith, 16, 36, 42, 46, 54, 60, 78, 108, 134, 157–58, 165, 168, 193, 229, 231, 285, 289–90, 316, 325
family, 2, 6, 19, 43, 56, 62, 69, 74, 85, 89, 109, 112, 118–19, 139, 149, 191, 204, 225, 240, 285, 328, 335
fantasy, 29–30, 41, 77–78
fear, 9, 15–16, 25, 27, 32, 38, 43, 46, 59–60, 70, 75, 77, 79–83, 85–86, 88–89, 98–99, 102, 105, 108, 111, 121–22, 128, 142, 150–51, 155, 165, 180–81, 187, 189–90, 193, 195, 198–99, 221, 229, 239, 243, 249–50, 262, 290, 295, 302, 316, 325, 327, 329–31, 335, 341
Ferrari, 144, 230–31, 338
field, v, 17, 23, 96, 176, 183, 216–17, 249, 275, 279, 298, 302, 309
filters, 23, 160–61, 165
finances, 39–40, 109, 222, 312, 315
forecasts, 262, 281, 329
freedom, xiii, 53, 92–93, 114, 172, 188, 200, 226
frequencies, 38, 142, 158, 211
friend, 19, 56, 79, 81, 114, 131, 139, 144, 168, 182–84
frustration, 59–60, 63, 117–18, 135, 141, 150, 245, 330, 339

G

game, 17–18, 24, 106–7, 115, 175, 223, 225, 227, 229, 257, 279, 286, 295, 309, 313, 337

gatekeeper, 195, 304
gifts, 7, 180, 219, 232–33, 240, 244, 328
goals, 1–4, 8, 11–12, 15, 17, 19, 34, 46, 55, 60, 67–68, 70, 73, 78, 85–86, 95–102, 112, 116, 122–23, 127, 133, 145, 149, 152–53, 163, 166–67, 186, 190–91, 208–10, 212, 214, 239, 245, 249, 253, 266, 274–77, 285–89, 301, 311, 328
gratitude, 3, 40, 94, 96, 160, 184, 204, 229, 249
growth, personal, 99, 124, 133, 208

H

habits, 50, 59, 86, 95, 128, 131, 146, 152, 195, 208–10, 215, 241, 249, 291
happiness, 26, 31, 98, 104, 142, 145, 163–64, 170–71, 173, 180, 182–84, 196, 244, 302, 316
heart, 1, 15, 32, 58, 83, 111–12, 139, 156, 172, 236, 249, 252
home, xiii, 69, 71, 95, 97, 99, 104, 131, 139, 148–49, 182, 191, 214, 260, 287, 305
honesty, 103, 331, 340
humility, 14, 176

I

ideas, 4, 30, 39, 44, 55, 67, 76–77, 80–81, 127, 130, 134, 137, 141, 143–44, 148, 150, 158, 160, 162–63, 185, 192, 215, 241, 244, 253, 259–60, 275, 281, 325, 330, 335, 339
instinct, 36, 121–22, 203
intentions, 47, 50, 58, 67, 109, 137, 168, 185, 219

J

job, 7, 16, 20, 34, 43, 47, 49, 56, 60, 62, 64, 83, 85, 99, 105–6, 108, 113, 115, 124, 130, 135, 139, 144, 147, 159, 170, 172, 175, 178, 189, 191, 203, 206, 214–15, 240–41, 252, 255–56, 258, 260, 293, 302, 307, 314, 317, 329, 339